Greek and Roman Art
3000 B.C. to A.D. 550

Greek and Roman Art
3000 B.C. to A.D. 550

ERNST KJELLBERG & GÖSTA SÄFLUND

THOMAS Y. CROWELL COMPANY

New York · Established 1834

L.C. Card 68–20758

1 2 3 4 5 6 7 8 9 10

Preface

In 1957 the publishing house Albert Bonniers Förlag asked me to revise the part of *Bonnier's History of Art* (Stockholm, 1932) that dealt with antiquity. It was originally written by Ernst Kjellberg who died in 1938. He had been on the staff of the National Museum in Stockholm for many years, and also a lecturer at Stockholm University. This revised edition was published in 1958; a second and further revised edition appeared in 1964. The present English edition has again been substantially revised.

It may seem a hopeless task to try and describe in one volume the history of three and a half thousand years of unremitting artistic activity in the lands where western art began. I nevertheless thought the attempt worth making. I hope it will provide interested laymen and students with an easily accessible survey of Greek and Roman sculpture and architecture, and at the same time perhaps supply a cicerone which will not add unduly to the weight of personal luggage on a holiday in classical lands.

G.S.

Contents

Contents

Contents

List of Illustrations

List of Illustrations

Hagia Triada, ca. 1500 B.C., ht. 0·465m. (*Heraklion Museum*)

13 Early Minoan jug from Vasiliki in East Crete, end of second millennium B.C., ht. 0·355m. (*Heraklion Museum*)

14 Stirrup-jar decorated with octopuses and other fish, Mycenae 1200–1125 B.C. (*The Metropolitan Museum of Art, Kontonlakes, Louisa Eldridge McBurney Gift Fund, 1953*)

15 Jug of Kamares style from the earlier palace of Phaistos, Middle Minoan II, ht. 0·27m. (*Heraklion Museum*)

16 Vases of Kamares style from the earlier palace of Knossos, Middle Minoan II. (*Heraklion Museum*)

17 Matt-painted pithos

18 Vase with representation of a chariot, from Cyprus (period Mycenaean IIIB) (*British Museum, London*).

19 Mycenaean dagger with hunting scene (*National Museum, Athens*).

20 Statue dedicated by Keramyes to Hera at Samos, mid-sixth century, ht. 1·92m. (*Louvre, Paris*)

21 Limestone statuette, 'Daedalic' in style, from Auxerre, second half of seventh century. (*Louvre, Paris*)

22 The votive-offering of Mantiklos to Apollo in Thebes, in bronze, first half of seventh century, ht. 0·2m. (*Museum of Fine Arts, Boston, Francis Bartlett Collection*)
The inscription on the thigh forms a distich: 'Mantiklos has offered me as a tithe to the God of the silver bow. | Mayest thou, Phoebus, now bestow the wished-for gift in thanks.'

23 Male statue from the Sacred Way leading to the shrine of the Branchidae, Miletus. (*British Museum, London*)

24 Head of a goddess in stucco, from Mycenae, ca. 1200 B.C., ht. 0·168m. (*National Museum, Athens*)

25 Limestone head, probably from the archaic cult-statue in the temple of Hera in Olympia, ht. 0·52m. (*Olympia Museum*)

List of Illustrations

List of Illustrations

List of Illustrations

List of Illustrations

List of Illustrations

List of Illustrations

List of Illustrations

List of Illustrations

List of Illustrations

List of Illustrations

List of Illustrations

Greek and Roman Art
3000 B.C. to A.D. 550

CReTe, Cyclades,
mainland

I · The Art of the Aegean World

1. CRETAN ART

DURING the Bronze Age, Crete and Hellas formed an independent
and distinct artistic region as did Egypt and the plains around the
Euphrates and the Tigris. There were indeed external impulses, and
direct imitations of the products of older cultures are not uncommon,
but in matters of decoration, architecture and representation of the
human form the Cretans of the Minoan period and the Hellenes of
the Mycenaean epoch gave their work their own stamp, which
entitles them to be considered alongside the people of the great
river-valleys as a separate cultural area with a high level of achievement.

It is scarcely more than sixty years since, as a result of the discoveries of Evans and others, the world became aware of the great
flowering of culture and art in Crete in the prehistoric period;
previously knowledge of it had survived only in myths such as the
story of Minos and Pasiphae, Ariadne and the Minotaur. These
myths were the divining-rod that led archaeologists to devote special
attention to the ancient monuments of Crete. As a result of the intensive research of the last decades both in Crete and in areas in
contact with it, it is now possible to set the various cultures of the
lands around the Aegean Sea with some precision in their historical
context. Further, since these areas were intermittently in frequent
communication with Egypt and other historically better-known lands
in the Near East, we are able to fix the chronological limits of the
most important epochs still more closely.

In the Stone Age and the earlier Bronze Age, in the fourth and third
millennia before Christ, Crete, along with the western part of Asia
Minor, the Cyclades and the Greek mainland formed in broad terms
a single cultural area. The Bronze Age in Crete, the Minoan age, as it
25

is called, is divided into three main periods, Early Minoan, Middle Minoan and Late Minoan, which are subdivided in their turn into periods traditionally expressed by Roman figures. The earliest period of Early Minoan is contemporary with the climax of the Old Kingdom in Egypt. Impulses from the brilliant culture of Egypt reached as far as Crete, whose links with Egypt became continually closer, especially during the second stage of Early Minoan (Early Minoan II). By that time the Bronze Age culture of Early Minoan I had spread to the Cyclades and to certain parts of the Peloponnese; and, for example, the Swedish excavations at Asine in the Argolid have thrown light on the relations between mainland Hellas and Crete in this period. The terms 'Cycladic' and 'Helladic' are employed to describe the Bronze Age cultures of the Cyclades and the mainland, with subdivisions corresponding to those used for the Minoan periods.

Although the boundaries and styles of the various cultural regions remained the same, Crete made great advances in artistic and cultural spheres in the second Early Minoan period. The cities of eastern and southern Crete reached their highest point at this period: Gournia, Pseira (Psira), Mochlos. To this period belong a number of dome-shaped tombs (tholos tombs) in the Mesara plain, near the south coast, which forms the largest and richest area of plainland on the island.

At the beginning of the Middle Minoan period, shortly after 1800 B.C. the greatest palaces in the central portion of the island were built, notably Knossos and Mallia in the north and Phaistos in the Mesara plain in the south, and these now overshadow all the other centres. After some centuries the palaces were destroyed by a mighty earthquake. They were rebuilt at the close of the Middle Minoan period, and there then followed the most brilliant period in the palace-culture of Crete.

About 1500 B.C. a new catastrophe occurred. The palaces of the north coast were laid in ruins, and its flourishing small cities like, for example, Palaikastro and Gournia were destroyed and abandoned. This catastrophe has been associated with the mighty volcanic eruption which caused much of the island of Thera (Santorin) to sink beneath the sea.

In the middle of the fifteenth century B.C., after the destruction of most of the important sites throughout Crete, power was centred on Knossos, and the palace at Knossos seems at that time to have

The Art of the Aegean World

been the seat of a dynasty from the mainland. As we now know, it used Greek as its chancery language.

The palace at Knossos was destroyed by a great fire, which marks the end of the supremacy of the dynasty of Knossos. In the two following centuries Crete passed under the shadow of the Mycenaean power of the Peloponnese, although the island long retained its cultural individuality.

i Pottery

The neolithic period is characterized by a coarse hand-made ware, which is mostly dark grey. The shapes of the vessels are simple and undifferentiated, and their decoration consists of scratched linear ornament, squares and triangles. In a certain number of cases the incised lines are filled with white chalk.

In the following period, the Early Minoan, Crete's relations with neighbouring cultural areas became closer, and prosperity correspondingly increased. The quality of the pottery improves too, and the forms of the vessels are differentiated. Alongside the grey ware there now appears a ware made of finely-washed, pale fawn clay with linear decoration in dark lustre against the light surface of the pot. That preference for 'torsion', characteristic of the decoration of Minoan vases of all periods, is already apparent.

An unusual ceramic effect is produced in the 'Vasilike-Ware' by the application of the paint in patches, which are then burnt to different shades of yellow, red and dark brown (known as 'mottled ware'). The forms of the vases of this type—for example a teapot shape with a long horizontal spout — show the unmistakable influence of Asiatic forms. Jugs and bowls of similar shapes were also made in a handsome veined stone by a technique which the Cretans seem to have learnt in Egypt: see Figure 1 and Plate 13.

At the end of the Early Minoan period a new method of decorating pottery, by the application of a light colour against a dark background, makes its appearance. At the same time new designs, including the spiral, appear. The colour-range is thus gradually extended to include chrome-yellow, orange and red. In the Middle Minoan period the Cretans also learnt the use of the potter's wheel and, by this means, made vases whose elegant profiles can stand comparison with the finest oriental porcelain. The forms are at times borrowed from metal originals.

The polychrome style of vase is called the 'Kamares-style', from

27

FIG. 1 Neolithic and Early
Minoan ware with incised decoration from Crete
Below, stone vessels from Mochlos

Kamares *and potters wheel, polychrome* [handwritten annotations]

the site where a large number of these vases was first encountered. Kamares is the modern name of a sacred cave high up on Mt Ida, where these splendid vases were found in abundance, along with other votive gifts; the cave is visible from the palace in Phaistos.

The decoration in winding curves now develops further, and is enriched by numerous natural motifs, especially from the vegetable

FIG. 2 Kamares vase from Knossos (Middle Minoan II), and a vase with a pattern of lilies, also from Knossos (Middle Minoan III), ht. 0·27m

world. The painters knew how to emphasize the volume and shape of the vase by intricate patterns of leaves, spiral runners and flowers, the latter frequently in the form of rosettes.

The Kamares vases show very clearly the sensitive and responsive character of the Cretans: see Figure 2. The style, however, is not naturalistic. The objects taken from nature are subordinated to the free rhythm of the decoration which does not aim at realistic representations. The lines are drawn with remarkable speed and energy; there is movement and life in these complexes of curves and spirals, of rosettes and trailing leaves. The ornamentation has a dynamic character, which is utterly different from the static decoration of the Egyptians. The Cretan attitude to symmetry is characteristic. Very often it is wholly absent, but at times they seem almost to play with a symmetrical design; this is, however, never completed: the balance is disturbed so that the decoration is full of movement instead of a static energy (see Plates 15–16). This artistic, at times artificial, pottery is a product of the manufactories of the older palaces in Knossos, Mallia and Phaistos.

The Middle Minoan technique of decoration survives in the early period of the newly built palaces. But in this 'Palace-Style' of the Middle Minoan period it is clearly influenced by the naturalistic fresco-painting of the palace. Groups of palms and lily-stalks are among the most characteristic motifs as in Figure 2.

From the later period of the new palaces (Late Minoan I) the most frequent pottery is that decorated with dark brown glaze on a light, lustrous surface. The principle of the decoration, the syntax, as it were, remains very largely that which dominated Minoan art from its earliest period: the pattern encircles the body of the vase as a unit, and emphasizes the volume of the vessel. The dynamic character of the decoration is often stressed by means of 'torsion'.

Side by side with the abstract patterns, among which the spiral is increasingly dominant, there now appears a widely varied repertory of motives drawn from the world of nature and principally from the deep sea (the 'marine' style). Molluscs and mussels, algae and the rugged spurs of the shore are now represented in loose arrangement over the surface of the vase, and cuttlefish embrace the vessel with imprisoning arms: see Figure 3. We now encounter for the first time among the shapes of vases the 'stirrup-jar', which subsequently becomes the most popular type of Cretan-Mycenaean pottery.

In the fifteenth century B.C. there appears alongside the naturalistic style another ornamental style with a more tectonic character. The naturalistic patterns are stylized and arranged vertically, so that the dynamic torsional character disappears or is greatly reduced.

The most representative vases of this style were manufactured in the pottery workshops in the palace at Knossos, and the style has therefore come to be known as the 'Palace-Style'. It was previously thought to represent a particular chronological stage (Late Minoan

II), but recent investigations have shown that it is a mistake to draw a sharp chronological distinction between the styles of decoration designated as 'Late Minoan IA', 'II' and 'IIIA'.

After the collapse of the Cretan palace-culture about, or soon after 1400 B.C. (Late Minoan IIIA2) pottery continued to be manufactured and decorated in the Late Minoan IIIB period according to

FIG. 3 Above left, 'The Marseilles' vase (Late Minoan IB). Above right, vase of 'Palace Style' (Late Minoan II). Below, 'Stirrup-jar' with decoration of marine style, (Late Minoan IB)

the earlier traditions, but it now lacks the elegance and richness of the previous period. The most characteristic forms are bag-shaped alabastra with patterns of water-fowl and fishes in a close net of geometric and vegetable motifs used to fill the space, and also tray or bath-shaped sarcophagi with similar decoration. It is a style of decoration which corresponds closely to the late Mycenaean 'Close style'.

ii Sculpture

We already encounter in the Stone Age simple figures of stone or clay, usually placed in graves. The slender pieces of marble were so moulded that the artist's intention to represent a human figure can be made out. This primitive art of sculpture is particularly frequent in the Cyclades. The materials used were clay, bronze and, above all, marble: see Plate 9.

Cyclades

marble

In the Middle Minoan period these figures take on typical Cretan forms. In spite of the lively intercourse with Egypt the monumental sculpture of the land of the Nile was not adopted: no instances have been found of statues of human or larger size. This is part and parcel of profound differences in religious conceptions and political systems, and especially of the Cretan repugnance for the static and heavy. The Cretans attempted above all to represent the body as a dynamically operative whole. Movement, the momentary position, is often better represented than the functional construction of the body. The absence of a smooth finish gives the bronzes an impressionistic air. We also find significant departures from frontality, which the Cretans mastered either because of their interest in movement or because of their insufficient sense of the static.

pic ✱

The ivory statue of a young man who is clearly turning a somersault is one of the most outstanding works of Cretan sculpture in the round (Plate 6). Other representations, both paintings and engraved seals, show persons in the same stance as this young man. He has seized an onrushing bull by the horns and thrown himself up in a high curve so as to land behind the beast in a somersault. The athlete's supple body, and the swift movement are captured with unsurpassed elegance.

pic ✱

Relief sculpture is illustrated by a number of beakers from Hagia Triada made of steatite, a very soft black stone which can be cut with the knife like soapstone. A vase, of which only the upper part survives, portrays some sort of procession, probably on the occasion of a harvest-festival (Plate 5). The participants are carrying staves for knocking down the olives from the trees. A section of the procession is singing to the accompaniment of an Egyptian-type rattle. Another large funnel-shaped beaker portrays athletic scenes, wrestling, boxing, and leaping over wild beasts: see Plate 12.

The important role played by the bull in the religious conceptions of the Cretans is also evident from the myths of Europa and Pasiphae, of the Minotaur, and of the Cretan bull captured by Heracles. Bullheads and bull-horns appear frequently in Minoan Crete as religious symbols and as decoration.

Among the finest products of Cretan art are some pieces of gold-work found on the Greek mainland: two beakers from Vapho near Sparta (see Plates 10 and 11), daggers from Mycenae the handles of which are inlaid in silver and enamel, and the beaker decorated with cuttlefish from Dendra. They all attest a freshness of observation and a love of nature which have rarely been surpassed.

Clay vases apart, the largest single group of Cretan and Mycenaean discoveries consists of seals of stone or of gold. The seals of the Early Minoan period were first carved in some soft material, especially ivory; later in semi-precious stones, such as rock-crystal,

FIG. 4 Goddess sitting beneath a tree. Gold ring from Mycenae

amethyst, etc. In addition to abstract patterns such as spirals or meanders they also bear representations of animals and humans. The arrangement of the patterns is accommodated to the round surface of the seal, with a strong emphasis on the movement revolving round the centre.

Religious motifs from monumental painting are found on large gold rings discovered in princely graves on the mainland.

iii Architecture

Stone Age man originally sheltered from the cold, the rain and the wind in caves in the rock or in simple huts, which were usually round, with walls of plaited branches packed with mud. As a protection against damp the structure was set on a low stone foundation. This type of building survived to a later date, and has counterparts in the shepherds' huts of the Balkan peninsula today. From the outset the distinction holds that the Cretan dwellings do not have permanent hearths, while these occur in mainland houses. In addition to round huts, oval and half-oval types occur. The round huts were also sometimes united into larger entities, in a circle round a courtyard or inside a common round enclosure. One large oval building (49 ft. × 72 ft.) on Crete consists of twelve rooms grouped round a yard, which is itself so small that it might more properly be called a light-shaft.

These early primitive forms of houses survived in the tholos tombs on the Mesara plain in southern Crete.

Thus Cretan architecture clearly advanced gradually in pace with the developing cultural needs of the inhabitants of the island. Houses of unbaked tiles (mud tiles dried in the open) on stone bases were already constructed in the earlier Bronze Age. They were erected close together in urban-like conglomerations, in a huddle of cube-shaped houses, and narrow lanes consisting of steps, much like mountain villages in Crete, the Cyclades and elsewhere in Greece today. The latest American excavations on Keos give us an idea of what such a Bronze Age community was like. At an earlier date American archaeologists uncovered an entire small city, Gournia, in north-eastern Crete; this in fact dates from the beginning of the Late Minoan period, but it has certainly preserved some characteristic features from earlier constructions. The later date is apparent from the presence of a palace which, together with a public court, forms a monumental centre in the highest part of the settlement. The private houses are grouped together in separate quarters, and an attempt has been made to construct so far as possible a rectangular ground plan.

The typical and most monumental products of Cretan architecture are the royal palaces in Knossos, Phaistos, Hagia Triada, Mallia, Kato Zakro and elsewhere. At Knossos, Evans' excavations in depth have enabled us to follow step by step the development of the settlement from the beginning of the Middle Minoan period. Similar discoveries have been made for instance at Phaistos and Mallia.

The earliest palace at Knossos (Middle Minoan I) consisted of a number of independent units grouped round a central courtyard. The sloping terrain east of the central courtyard was constructed into terraces. In the following period (Middle Minoan II) the different buildings were unified, and the line of store-rooms in the western part of the palace was constructed, while the royal pottery-workshops were built in the north-eastern section. The earlier terraces along the east side of the central courtyard were replaced by a royal residential block. This early palace, particularly in its eastern part, was subsequently severely damaged by an earthquake.

The new palace belonging to the transition to the Late Minoan period is in essentials that of which we see the ruins today. Its architecture embodies several technical innovations; inter alia the old wall-construction of irregular stones set in mud was replaced by regular ashlar walls. The bases of the columns, previously high and of veined stone, are now low and made of gypsum or limestone.

The residential quarter on the east of the central court was entirely reconstructed, and elaborated with a remarkable system of light-shafts and view-holes. A grand staircase led up to the central courtyard. The colonnade-motif with the characteristic vertically diminishing columns was employed with artistic refinement in the residential block, and with great monumental effect in the ceremonial quarter of the palace. The columns themselves were smooth, but traces have been found of columns with concave and convex and also spiral channelling. The walls were painted al fresco, partly in low relief on plaster.

Immediately before the great catastrophe which destroyed the palace about or soon after 1400 B.C. the famous throne-room complex, with its griffin-fresco, was built in the north-west part of the palace, with entry from the central courtyard (See figure 5).

During the last period of the palace a small shrine was installed in the south-eastern part of the palace, the shrine of the Double Axes (see Figure 5). The worship of the Great Goddess to whom the shrine was dedicated continued there until it was suddenly and permanently interrupted by the final invasion.

The plan of the palace at Knossos shows a clear differentiation according to the function of its parts: the southern part of the eastern side contains the real residential section, while the northern part is occupied by the royal workshops where, among other things, the splendid 'Palace-style' vases were made. The area west of the central courtyard possesses a sacral and ceremonial character. The row of store-rooms to the west of the long corridor is not an obstacle to this interpretation, since such repositories form an important element in most oriental temple-complexes.

The different parts of the palace centre round the great central courtyard, though without any rigid orientation. However, only the western, sacral section has the façade of its ground floor facing on to

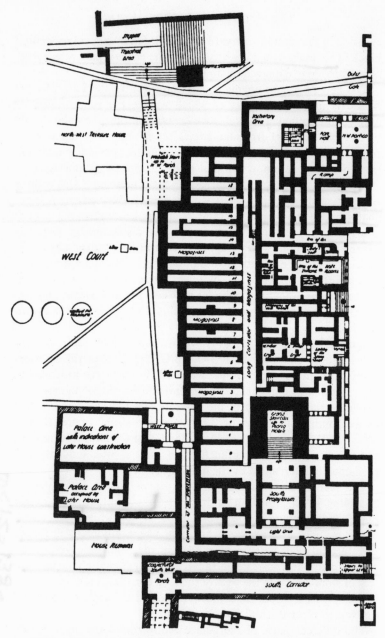

FIG. 5 Plan of the Palace of Knossos. The plan shows mainly the ground floor which consisted largely of storage-rooms and supported the main residential floor. Some parts of the latter however lie within the ground-floor area

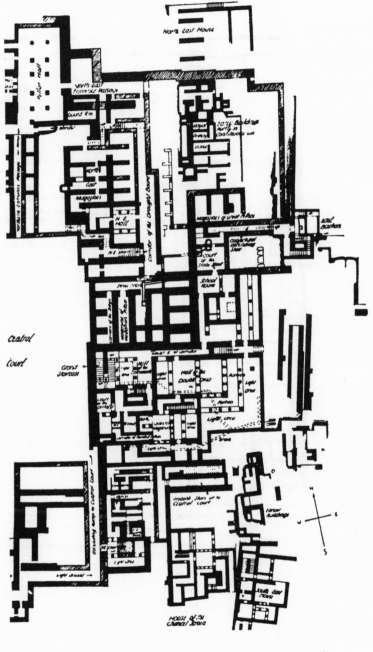

North East House

Other Hall

North East Insula or Maison

Guard Rm

North East Magazines

N. E. Hall

Corridor of the Draught Board

N. E. Entrance

House partly in restoration use

SOTK Buildings partly in restoration use

Magazines of Great Palace

Copper-ingot catching Slab

Court of the Stone Spout

School Room

East Bastion

Royal Villa

Magazines with Pithos

Central Court

Grand Staircase

Hall of the Colonnades

Hall of the Double Axes

Light Area

Court of the Distaffs

Portico

Light Area

Light Area

Light Area

Modern Stairs to Central Court

Upper Level

Stepped Ramp to Central Court

Latter Buildings

South East House

House of the Chancel Screen

N · W · S · E

50 M.

the courtyard; the residential quarter itself faces away from the courtyard, and opens on to the gardens constructed on the east slope.

The formation of the 'piano nobile' of the sacral region of the palace as an architectural climax along a single axis is certainly due

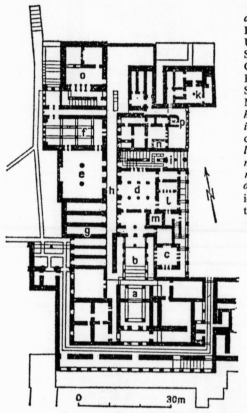

a. South Propylaea, *b.* Steps and Upper Propylaea, *c.* South-east loggia, *d.* Central Tri-Columnar Hall, *e.* Great Hall, *f.* Sanctuary-Hall, *g.* Upper Magazines (S.W. Hall), *h.* Upper Long Corridor, *i.* Stepped Porch, *k.* Area of Miniature-Fresco, *l.* Reception Room, *m.* Treasure Chamber, *n.* Probable Clerestory, *o.* Reception Room (unidentified), *p.* Staircase to Throne-Room system

FIG. 6 The 'Piano Nobile' of the Palace of Knossos, religious and ceremonial sections. Reconstruction.

to the absolute political authority of the rulers of Knossos over the rest of the island during the final golden age of the palace. The decoration of the long labyrinthine processional corridor leading to the monumental propylaea indicates that the princes of this period were invested with a divine kingship.

FIG. 7 The Palace of Knossos: south propylaea with the Fresco of the Procession.
Reconstruction

The frescoes in the long corridor in the south-west of the palace at Knossos also show that processions played an important part in the sacral court-ceremonial of the Minoan kings. The staircase in the north-western part of the palace with its 'Royal Box', the purpose of which has been much discussed, probably served as a spectators' stand for the arrival of the festal processions (see Figure 5). A similar, still larger free-standing staircase existed at Phaistos outside the monumental main entrance of the palace.

Analogies and, in part, probably, prototypes of the Cretan palace-architecture are to be found in oriental palaces of the first half of the second millennium B.C., as they are known from recent excavations at Mari in northern Mesopotamia and in Beyçesultan in south-western Asia Minor. But the stamp of natural enjoyment in the observation of nature and of aesthetic and hygienic refinement, which is characteristic of the way of life of the Cretan aristocracy during the golden age of the palaces, seems to be a gift of the natural world of the Aegean and of the gods of Crete.

iv Painting
The homes of the Cretan princes were richly decorated with fresco paintings on limestone and plaster and with painted reliefs in stucco.

Although most of this decoration has been destroyed in the course of time, sufficient large fragments have survived to give us a good idea of the characteristics of the paintings.

The rooms in the older palaces were already given a higher aesthetic quality by painting the walls red and decorating the lower parts with geometrical ornament. In the later palaces there suddenly appears a style of fresco-painting which, in spite of predecessors in oriental palace-culture, nevertheless carries an original and unmistakably Cretan stamp.

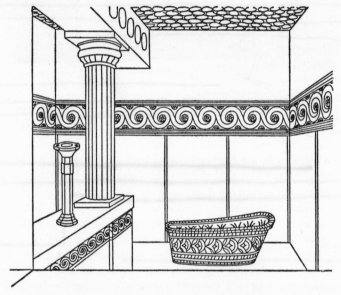

FIG. 8 Bath-house of the Queen in the Palace of Knossos. Reconstruction

In so far as the functions and motives of the wall-paintings are concerned it is possible to detect a ceremonial-monumental art and an intimate, naturalistic, partly miniaturistic art. The latter style belongs to the earlier period of the later palaces, while the former is typical of the last period of the palace at Knossos. It is characterized by the concentration of power at Knossos; the sacral role of the ruler is stressed.

While on the one hand the later palace at Phaistos has so far yielded no sign of the naturalistic style of fresco-painting, the nearby villa-palace at Hagia Triada has provided the most exquisite examples. Even today the surroundings of the palace are a source of delight with their air of benign plenty and the sound of running water, a rarity in the summer heat of modern Crete. The prince of this Cretan *Generalife* wished to surround himself with such a landscape, formed like an oriental 'paradise', and the painters whom he employed achieved a room-decoration which foreshadows the garden-views of Roman palace-villas and the great mosaics in the Imperial palace in Constantinople: see Plate 1.

The paintings covered the walls without interruption at the corners and for the most part without vertical divisions, from which Cretan art normally kept aloof. A horizontal framework is provided in the form of decoration of lintel and cornice.

One group of fragments portrays a cat creeping forward through a copse to surprise a pheasant (Plate 1); on another fragment we see a girl picking crocuses. The representation of space is very characteristic and far from naturalistic: the level of the earth is indicated even in the upper part of the painting, and flowers grow down from this towards the centre of the picture. By this means the Cretan artist concentrated his composition round a central point, and the attempt to achieve this is already noticeable in the composition of the early Minoan seals.

A similar park-landscape formed the subject of the paintings in 'The House of Frescoes', in the city-area of Knossos, outside the palace. On one fragment we see an ape in a rocky landscape, surrounded by papyrus, crocuses, irises and ivy (Plate 2). The colouring is not restricted to naturalistic shades: the ape is blue, the background red, the rocks veined in different shades of yellow, blue, green, white and grey. The same colour-range appears in the flowers, with the addition of pale red, pale green and violet.

A room in the sacral area of the palace at Knossos has yielded some fragments of the so-called 'miniature-style': see Plate 3. It shows a crowd of people of both sexes in front of a tripartite sacral building, the central section of which is raised above the ground. The crowd is portrayed in an abbreviated manner, the men as dark contours against a reddish brown background, the women against a white one, according to the Egyptian and Archaic Greek way of representing sex by different coloured skin.

The 'Priest-King' or 'Prince with the crown of feathers' (whom one, with equally little certainty, might call the 'Cretan Dionysus') belongs to the earlier period of the sacral-monumental group. It is a painted low-relief in stucco, slightly more than 2 ft. high, and was found in a hall in the southern part of the palace at Knossos. Other painted stucco-reliefs of colossal size, some with magnificent representations of bulls, were found by the northern entrance.

A stiff, hieratic movement is to be seen in the representations of processions which decorate the 'Procession-Corridor' in the south-western part of the palace at Knossos. Here it is life-size young men and women who bear offerings to the divinity and ruler of the palace. Similar scenes adorned the Mycenaean palaces in Thebes and Tiryns.

A remarkable and hitherto unique example of Cretan painting in the service of the cult of the dead is provided by a limestone sarco-phagus from Hagia Triada (about 1400 B.C.). The two long sides carry sacrificial scenes. On one of the sides a drink-offering is being poured on the left by two women and a harp-player, while on the right three male sacrificial attendants are bringing forward sacrificial calves and a little boat towards an armless cult-image standing in front of a shrine or tomb-façade (could he be the deified dead man?). On either pediment two women are driving a two-wheeled chariot, drawn in one case by a pair of horses against a white background, in the other by winged griffins against a red background—a distinction of colour which is hardly accidental: see Plate 4. We encounter similar representations much later on Etruscan grave-monuments, the subject of which is the journey to the kingdom of the dead.

2. ART ON THE GREEK MAINLAND
i Pottery
A technically distinguished pottery with painted decoration was already being produced on the Greek mainland in the late Neolithic period. The patterns are abstract and their arrangement corresponds in general with that we have already encountered in the oldest Cretan painted pottery. In the later style, customarily named after its place of discovery, Dimini in Thessaly (west of Volos), spirals and meanders play an important part.

In the Early Helladic period, which is contemporary with Early Minoan, the Argolid already assumes the cultural leadership which it retains until the late Mycenaean period. In the earlier phases of the Early Helladic period painted decoration on pottery plays a subordinate role. The vase-shapes are analogous to those of Asia

Minor: for example, the principal ceramic shape of the older Early Helladic period, an elegant bowl with a spout, known as the sauce-boat (see Figure 9), has been found in gold in the second city of Troy.

sauce boat

The latest phase of the period (Early Helladic III) is characterized by new styles in shape and decoration. We now find a ware with linear decoration in a dark, half-lustrous colour painted on the buff surface of the vase. The most characteristic form of this period is

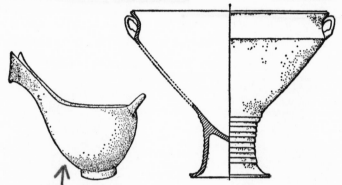

FIG. 9 *Left*, 'Sauce-Boat', the most popular shape of early Helladic pottery. *Right*, grey Minyan bowl with high foot (Middle Helladic)

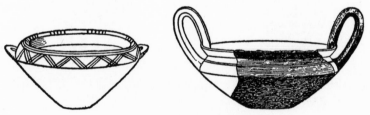

FIG. 10 *Left*, matt-painted bowl. *Right*, grey Minyan bowl

the tankard-shaped vase with a semi-spherical lower part and high tapering upper part, provided with two vertical handles.

Entirely new types of pottery appear on the mainland and in the Cyclades at the beginning of the Middle Helladic period. They consist in part of the so-called 'grey Minyan ware' (which already had antecedents in matters of technique in the earlier period), and in part of the matt-painted ware. The shapes of the vessels are characterized by a sharp profile which strongly emphasizes the structural

43

division of the vase into foot, body and mouth-section: see Figure 10. The decoration is geometric; in the 'grey Minyan ware' it is incised in the still unfired clay; in the 'matt-painted' ware it is applied in a flat, thin, dark colour on the pale slip on the exterior of the vase.

Towards the end of the Middle Helladic period the 'grey Minyan ware' is superseded by a pale buff ware, which, like the grey Minyan has a burnished surface which feels smooth to the touch. This 'Yellow Minyan ware', as it is called, is often decorated with geometrical patterns in a matt brown colour. The 'matt-painted' pottery is supplanted by a style with polychrome geometrical decoration on a dark ground, the product of influence from Crete or the Cyclades.

FIG. 11 Vase from Shaft-grave I, Mycenae (Late Mycenaean I-II), and a magnificent vase from a Beehive Tomb in Berbati (Late Helladic II)

Late Helladic or Mycenaean pottery preserves certain technical and decorative features, and certain vessel-shapes, from the Middle Helladic period. But its particular feature derives from its strong and lasting indebtedness to contemporary Minoan pottery, both in respect of decorative patterns and styles and also in vase-shapes: see Figure 11. The pottery of the mainland thus gradually achieves greater independence, and during the Late Helladic III period (1300–1200 B.C.) the workshops of the Peloponnese, and especially of the Argolid, produce pottery with specific mainland characteristics. These include a tendency to a tectonic arrangement of decoration and a gradual geometrizing, and so conventionalization, of motifs which were originally naturalistic.

Certain larger types of vases from the Late Helladic period have figure motifs and compositions which clearly reflect contemporary large-scale painting, such as the chariot processions and magnificent representations of bulls: see Plate 18.

In the fourteenth and thirteenth centuries B.C., the Late Helladic IIIA and B periods, Mycenaean vases were very widely distributed. They have been discovered not only in the lands around the eastern Mediterranean, to which area the factories of the Argolid seem

FIG. 12 Stirrup-jar from Assarlik in Caria (sub-Mycenaean-proto-geometric), now in the British Museum

FIG. 13 Mycenaean Stirrup-jar from Asine, and a bowl from Mycenae (period IIIC), 'Close Style'

to have had a monopoly of export, but even as far west as Sicily and the Apennine peninsula as far as Etruria, as we know from the Swedish excavations at Luni. In Egypt Mycenaean pottery is especially frequent in Akhnaton's palace at Tell el Amarna, which was abandoned in about 1350 B.C.

The style of ceramic decoration changes at the end of the thirteenth century after the collapse of the Mycenaean palace-culture. In this period (IIIC) two styles predominate: the 'Granary style', as it is called from the grain-store inside the 'Lion Gate' at Mycenae, which is of great importance for the chronology of Mycenaean pottery, and the 'Close style'. In the first, decoration has been reduced to a few wavy lines and festoons in the wide zone on the belly and

45

shoulder of the vase. In the 'Close style'—which is particularly typical of stirrup-jars—the decoration is spread in zones over the whole body of the vase with close rows of concentric half-circles, angles, triangles, etc. At times figure motifs such as birds and fishes are included in the decoration. One group of stirrup-jars is characterized by a magnificent stylized decoration of octopuses.

The 'Granary style' passes naturally into the protogeometric style, as seen in Figure 14. The figure-designs of the 'Close style', on the other hand, did not survive the last phase of late Mycenaean culture.

FIG. 14 Protogeometric amphora from Assarlik in Caria, and protogeometric urn from Ialysus (Rhodes), now in the British Museum

ii Architecture

In the palace-architecture of the later Bronze Age there is a clear distinction between Crete and the mainland. In the former, open princely dwellings, notable for an attempt at comfort and for an art which aimed at reproducing and preserving on the walls of the palaces the noble element in nature and life; in the latter, strong castles, in which considerations of defence predominate. On the mainland, halls, megara, open on one side with a circular hearth in the middle, which both kept the cold at bay and also formed the assembly-point and ceremonial centre of family-life, corresponded to the open Cretan halls which allowed the light to enter from different angles and had no permanent hearths.

In its simplest form a megaron consisted of a rectangular room

46

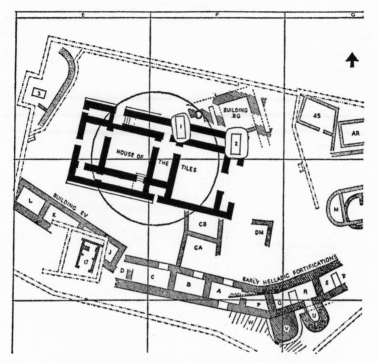

FIG. 15 'House of the Tiles' at Lerna (Early Helladic II)

with its entrance and external porch on one side. The porch was constructed by means of the extension of the walls of the long sides and the roof. In the larger houses a pair of poles in the front corners of the porch helped to support the roof. At times a room which extended across the entire width of the building was built between the main room and the porch. Complete symmetry was preserved between the two long sides of the megaron.

In the Peloponnese, as we know from the Swedish excavations at Berbati in the Argolid, the megaron with a permanent round hearth occurs already in the Early Helladic period (II). However, a royal dwelling of an entirely different plan is also found at the same time: this is the 'House of Tiles', excavated by the Americans at Lerna, south of Argos; see Figure 15. It is of rectangular plan, but lacks the strong emphasis on the central axis found in the megaron-house, as also its asymmetrical orientation towards the entrance-gable. The prototypes of the Lerna palace are probably to be sought

47

in the southern and south-western regions of Asia Minor. This region has only been systematically investigated in recent years, but discoveries so far point to important cultural and perhaps even racial links between the Aegean and this region in the earlier Bronze Age.

The 'House of Tiles' at Lerna, orientated east-west, is 13 ft. wide and 32 ft. long. The walls, 3 ft. thick, consist of raw tiles on a stone bedding, the usual form of construction in the Aegean world at all periods. The roof, which like the roofs of the earlier megaron-houses

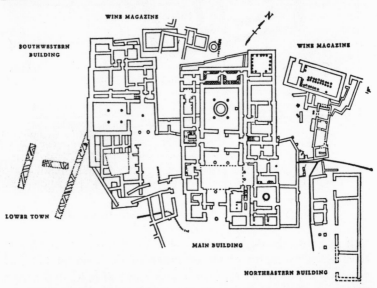

FIG. 16 Plan of the palace at Pylos, end of fourteenth century B.C., period IIIB

was probably a flat saddle-roof, was covered with rectangular tiles and pieces of slate.

A monumental Early Helladic building on the hill at Tiryns exhibits an entirely different plan, which has its roots in the architecture of the Mediterranean Stone Age: it is circular, with a diameter of 92 ft.; here too remains of a tiled roof were discovered.

At the end of the Early Helladic period and in the following Middle Helladic Age we find houses with absidal ends side by side with rectangular houses. Houses of a monumental size do not however reappear until the Late Helladic, Mycenaean period. Mycenaean palace architecture finds its classic, most brilliant

1. Fresco from the palace-villa
in Hagia Triada, ht. 0·8m.

2. Ape in park landscape: fresco
from Knossos, ht. 0·8m.
Restored.

3. Fresco in miniature-style from Knossos.

4. Limestone sarcophagus from Hagia Triada. Yoke of griffins, ca. 1400 B.C.

5. Vase of steatite with harvest-scenes in relief from the palace in Hagia Triada, ca. 1500 B.C.

Bull-acrobat, ivory statuette from the palace 7. Two goddesses with a child. Ivory group from
of Knossos, ht. 0·299m., ca. 1550 B.C. citadel of Mycenae, ca. 1500 B.C.

8. The 'Royal Seal-stone', an agate from the tholos-tomb of Dendra (Midea) in the
Argolid. Enlarged twice.

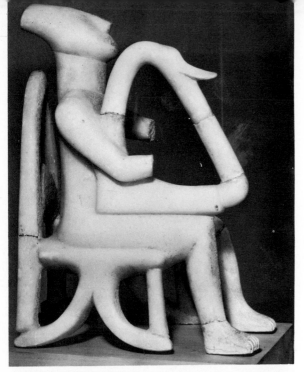

9. Lyre-playing idol from the Cyclades.

10 & 11. Scenes on two gold beakers from a Mycenaean beehive-tomb at Vaphio in Laconia.

12. Detail of steatite cult-vessel with athletic scenes, from
Hagia Triada, ca. 1500 B.C., ht. 0.465m.

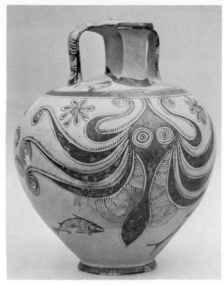

13 (*left*). Early Minoan jug from Vasiliki in East Crete, end of second millennium B.C., ht. 0·355m.

14 (*above*). Stirrup-jar decorated with octopuses and other fish, Mycenae, 1200–1125 B.C.

15 (*left*). Jug of Kamares style from the earlier palace of Phaistos, Middle Minoan II, ht. 0·27m.

16. Vase of Kamares style from the earlier palace of Knossos, Middle Minoan II.

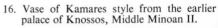

16A (*above*). Another vase of Kamares style from the earlier palace of Knossos, Middle Minoan II.

17 (*above, right*). Matt-painted pithos.

18 (*below*). Vase with representation of a chariot, from Cyprus (period Mycenaean IIIB).

19 (*right*). Mycenaean dagger with hunting scene.

20. Statue dedicated by Keramyes to Hera at Samos, mid-sixth century, ht. 1·92m.

21. Limestone statuette, 'Daedalic' in style, from Auxerre, second half of the seventh century.

23. Male statue from the Sacred Way leading to the shrine of the Branchidae, Miletus.

22. The votive-offering of Mantiklos to Apollo in Thebes, in bronze, first half of seventh century, ht. 0·2m. The inscription on the thigh forms a distich: 'Mantiklos has offered me as a tithe to the God of the silver bow. Mayest thou, Phoebus, now bestow the wished-for gift in thanks.'

24. Head of a goddess in stucco, from Mycenae, ca. 1200 B.C., ht. 0·168m.

25 (*above*, *right*). Limestone head, probably from the archaic cult-statue in the temple of Hera in Olympia, ht. 0·52m.

26. Head of colossal kouros statue from Dipylon, Athens, ca. 620 B.C., ht. 0·44m.

27. Goddess (kore) with pomegranate, from Keratea in Athens, beginning of the sixth century B.C., ht. (with base) 1·93m.

28. Ionic kouros in bronze, ca. 550 B.C., ht. 0·164m.

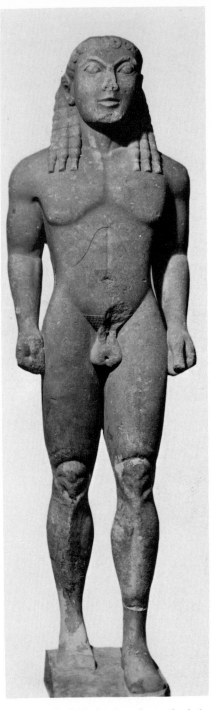

29. The 'Cleobis' of Polymedes, early sixth
century B.C., ht. 2·16m.

30. The 'Peplos Kore', ca. 530 B.C., ht. 1·21m.

31. Column from Artemision at Ephesus, with reliefs, given by Croesus.

32. Detail of frieze of the Treasury of the Siphnians at Delphi, end of the sixth century B.C.

33. Metope from the Treasury of the Sicyonians at Delphi, mid-sixth century B.C., limestone.

34. Fleeing women. Metope-relief of sandstone from the temple of Hera at the mouth of the Silaros, late sixth century B.C.

35. Detail of relief on statue-base found in the wall of Themistocles in Athens, ca. 500 B.C.

36. Temple of Zeus at Olympia, east side.

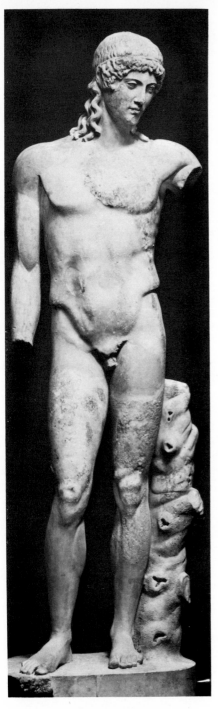

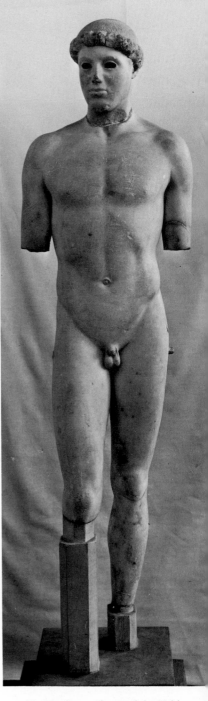

37. The 'Tiber Apollo', marble copy.

38. The figure of a youth by Kritios, ht. 0·86m.

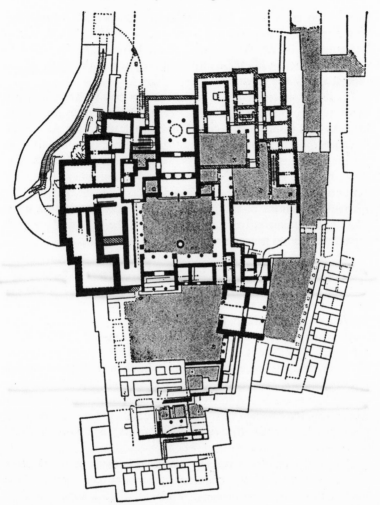

FIG. 17 The fortress of Tiryns, first half of the thirteenth century B.C., period IIIB

expression in the royal dwellings of Pylos, Tiryns and Mycenae at the end of the fourteenth century B.C. (Late Helladic IIIB), after the large-scale destruction of the older palaces, perhaps as a partial result of political changes. The best preserved are the palace-constructions in Pylos and Tiryns: see Figures 16 and 17. The palace at Tiryns has the more developed plan of the two.

In front of the megaron lay a courtyard surrounded with colonnades. The entrance to the court was monumentally constructed with a propylaea opposite the megaron, but slightly to one side of its central axis. At Tiryns there was a round altar dedicated to chthonic deities inside the courtyard-propylaea to the right, on the central axis of the megaron.

The megaron itself consists of an entrance-hall with two columns between the projecting antae. At Tiryns three entrances lead to the entrance-hall from which a central entrance leads to the main room in which the round hearth is situated. The ruler's throne stood on the long right-hand wall, facing the hearth. Round the hearth were four columns which probably supported a clerestory. From the entrance-hall side-passages provided access to the surrounding residential portions of the palace, on two storeys, and to a store-room and administrative offices situated on the bottom floor or in separate buildings near the main dwelling.

The walls in the throne-room and in the other ceremonial rooms were coated with stucco and decorated with frescoes. The floor was also stuccoed, and was painted with ornamental patterns in squares. The round hearth was also covered with stucco, and its surround painted with geometric patterns.

In technique, motives and spatial conceptions the wall-paintings are largely an offshoot of Cretan painting of the last Palace period. In Tiryns and Mycenae, however, certain characteristic features in the choice of subjects correspond to the patron's heroic conception of life: battle-scenes and hunting-scenes predominate (see Plate 19). Apart from this the men wear a dress of mainland type very different from the Cretan male attire as it appears in art, i.e. a short coat with sleeves.

The most original and striking contribution made by the Mycenaean rulers in the field of architecture consists of their fortresses and their tombs, the 'tholos-tombs'. Pride of place among the latter belongs to the grave which Pausanias calls 'The Treasury of Atreus': see Figure 18. This grave consists of a round vaulted chamber with a diameter of 46 ft. and a height of 44 ft. Beside it is a smaller, vaulted rectangular room. The vault is constructed by a corbelling-out of each course of stone blocks over the one immediately below it, with the result that the diameter of the room diminishes regularly. At the summit the remaining opening was closed with a large block. The sides of the different layers of stone which face the inner room were subsequently smoothed to a continuous surface.

This primitive system of vaulting is very much less solid than the true vault. But even though in the course of time the other tholos-tombs fell in, the tomb of Atreus still stands as one of the finest and best-balanced rooms in the history of European art. It already possesses that harmony which radiates from the later vaultings from the Pantheon and Hagia Sophia.

An entrance 118 ft. long and 19½ ft. wide, between high walls, led to the tholos-tomb. It creates the impression of a ceremonial entrance or entrance-hall to a royal residence inside the hill.

At about the same time as 'The Treasury of Atreus' was built, Mycenae's older 'Cyclopic' fortress-wall was constructed, in such a way that it also embraced the slope where the early Mycenaean

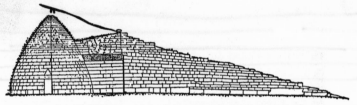

FIG. 18, 'The Treasury of Atreus', longitudinal section

shaft-graves excavated by Schliemann were situated. The slope was terraced and the graves were surrounded by a low enclosure of stone plaques set on end. The entrance to the fortress, which at a still later date was protected by a projecting bastion, was by means of a monumental gate, the famous 'Lion Gate'. This consists of four massive monoliths hewn in conglomerate, the stone characteristic of constructions of this period at Mycenae, and also employed in the monumental entrance-passage to 'The Treasury of Atreus'. The stone above the door measures 14½ × 7 × 3 ft., and is estimated to weigh 20 tons. The relieving triangular gap above the door is disguised by a stone-plaque 12 ft. wide at the base and 9½ ft. high. On the plaque is carved the relief which has given the gate its name: two lions stand *en face* on either side of a column which supports a beam. Their front paws are resting on the stylobate of the column, which in turn stands on altar-shaped plinths. The heads have been separately worked, perhaps in bronze, and were probably turned towards the viewer.

This arrangement of two symmetrically standing animals on either

51

FIG. 19 Gold ring from Prosymna (Heraion)

side of a column is familiar from a number of representations on seals; sometimes the column is replaced by the figure of a goddess. The lion-relief is the ruler's seal or escutcheon, enlarged to a monumental size, a symbol of the strength and power of the master of the fortress and of the god under whose protection the palace stood. This ruler-symbolism has antecedents in oriental art, but no parallels are known from Greek architecture.

The art of Crete and Mycenae became a closed chapter in the history of the world's art. Its particular character died in the storms of the migration of peoples which troubled the Mediterranean lands and the Orient from about 1200 B.C. and brought with it a general decline of culture.

The millennial Bronze Age artistic achievement was only able to fructify subsequent Greek art to a very limited extent. We have already referred to the megaron-house. In the handicrafts technical proficiency with regard to shaping and firing clay-vessels, and also the vital knowledge of the use of dark brown lustrous colour as decoration were preserved. Most important of all, however, was the fact that the priceless treasury of myths and sagas was not entirely lost to the Aegean world. It became the main source of inspiration for the Greek literature and art of the future.

II · Art in Greece

1. THE PERIOD OF GEOMETRIC ART

THE period between the end of the Mycenaean age and the beginning of the Classic age is frequently called 'The Greek Middle Ages'. The similarities with the period of European history which bears this name are many and great.

A period of high cultural achievement and a rich and varied artistic life with lively communications between peoples, characterized by mighty states with wide territories, is followed by an epoch whose artistic activity is marked by extremely limited material resources and means of expression; the links between states and peoples are substantially reduced. In the place of great empires we find a number of isolated and independent small states.

Egypt had declined into political weakness after the heights of the eighteenth and nineteenth dynasties. Philistines, Israelites, Phoenicians and Aramaeans established small independent kingdoms in the region of Asia which had previously obeyed the great Pharaohs. Darkness hung over Babylonia and Assyria, and the Hittite kingdom had been destroyed by the migrations of about 1200 B.C. Agamemnon's Mycenaean kingdom had succumbed to the storm of the Dorian migration, and the royal palace lay in ruins.

Whilst intercourse with the people of the Orient was maintained, particularly through the mediation of the Phoenicians, and a sort of mixed Egyptian-Oriental culture was evolved, the links between the lands around the Aegean Sea and the Orient were restricted for several centuries. The Greek world became isolated, and this in itself certainly contributed to the development of the Greeks as a race with a lively consciousness of their nationality.

Within Greek society itself tribal hereditary royal power was increasingly overshadowed by a land-owning aristocracy. Just as in the Middle Ages the Christian Church and the Papacy formed a unifying link, so in Greece the worship of particular gods in certain sacred spots succeeded in uniting Greeks of different tribes and cities through common sacrifices and common competitive games to the glory of the Olympian Gods.

ANCIENT GREECE

0   50   100 MILES

Gradually the epic poems, which passed from city to city on the lips of the rhapsodes, came to play the same role as religious legends played in the development of mediaeval art. The rich merchant in Miletus and the Athenian land-owner listened to the epic stories no less willingly than the Spartan warrior.

In the latest Mycenaean period the naturalistic ornamentation had been increasingly stylized, creating a certain resemblance to geometric figures, but without giving rise to a strictly geometric style. This saw the light of day in Attica, a region whose population, according to tradition, had remained uncontaminated by the Dorian invaders. On the other hand descendants of the princely families of the Pylian kingdom had taken refuge in Attica on the occasion of the 'Heraclid' Dorian invasion of the Peloponnese.

54

The excavation of the cemetery in the Kerameikos quarter of Athens has enabled us to follow the growth and development of the earliest Geometric style of decoration, the protogeometric, from the last 'sub-Mycenaean' descendants of Mycenaean date to Attic pottery of the historic period.

Vase-shapes and decorative motifs such as semicircles, wavy lines and zigzags are borrowed from the sub-Mycenaean repertoire, but *attica* they are all adapted to a strictly architectural style with a rhythmic balance of ornament and undecorated surface.

The semicircles are painted with the aid of compasses and a 'multiple-brush', which were not used on vases in the immediately

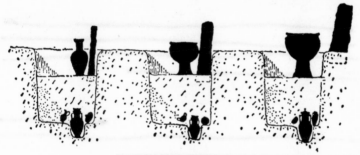

FIG. 20 Graves at the Dipylon of the Geometric period

preceding period. The craftsmen had inherited a knowledge of the methods employed in the Bronze Age to clean and prepare the clay, to turn the vases on the potter's wheel and to prepare the lustrous colour, which now in general acquired a darker hue and closer consistency than was customary in the Mycenaean period.

The Geometric style reached its fullest development shortly after about 800 B.C. The largest and most characteristic vases come from the Kerameikos burial area by the Dipylon Gate, and the whole category of vases was formerly called 'Dipylon Vases'. The Argolid, Boeotia, and islands such as Melos and Thera, Rhodes and Crete, all have clearly defined local varieties of the Geometric style.

The largest Dipylon Vases served both as sacrificial vessels and as tomb-monuments. Sometimes a hole was pierced in the bottom to allow the liquid offerings, wine, oil or honey, which the living brought to the dead man, to run down into the earth, where he dwelt. We can only admire the technical skill which created vases of more than human height in such a carefully calculated form, and fired them in a single piece, even if foot, belly and throat were each formed separately.

The architecture of the vases makes a much stronger visual impression than that of the vases of the Bronze Age. They appear rather to have been built than to have grown organically. There is regularly a clear division into foot, belly and mouth. The upper part of the belly is defined as the shoulder by means of its contour. The clear construction is emphasized by the decoration. The widest part of the belly is normally decorated with a particularly richly articulated band, to which there usually corresponds a slightly smaller band round the neck: this often reproduces the motive of the belly-pattern on a slightly smaller scale: see Plate 56.

In addition to square patterns, rhomboids, triangles and zigzags, we encounter meander-ornamentation, often in a richly varied form such as the double meander, and the simple or double indented meander; the swastika design was frequent, particularly on Attic and Boeotian vases. The Mycenaean spirals are succeeded by simple or concentrically arranged circles linked by tangents. Especially in the East Greek area, the islands and Asia Minor, the friezes round the vases are often partitioned into square fields, metopes, in which swastikas, rings and other items are placed. It thus seems as if the painter was dominated by a fear of a vacuum, *horror vacui*; every little field or corner had to have its decoration, and all together they encircle the vase like a variegated textile or plaited basket-work.

That aspect of the Greek genius which stands in strongest contrast to the Cretan finds expression in this style. This is the feeling for analytical clarity and order, for rhythmic regularity, for 'kosmos'. Kosmos means, in Greek, (good) order, and the Greeks used the word themselves to describe the Universe, the whole of nature. The Greek spirit never wearied, so long as its vital energy was not impaired, in the search for a pattern and laws in the world of matter.

Representations of figures occur on later Geometric vases, especially Attic ones. But the humans and animals have had to submit to the tyranny of the two-dimensional, analytical style. Each part of the body is portrayed from the side which most clearly shows its two-dimensional character: thus heads are portrayed in profile, while the torso is shown frontally with both arms visible, and the legs are wholly separated but drawn from the side, as also the hips. The human torso appears as a triangle with the apex pointing

56

downwards. Objects lying horizontally, like the chequered bier-cover
in the representation in Plate 55, are, as it were, folded up vertically.
Overlapping of objects is avoided by the objects in the rear plane,
for example one wheel of a two-wheeled chariot, either not being
represented or being represented by the side of the front one.

No branch of art gives us clearer information regarding this early
phase of Greek art than pottery. The same style is found on bronze
vessels and ornaments—fibulae—and weapons of the same metal.
Their ornamentation and representation of objects corresponds

FIG. 21 Temple-model from the Heraion in the Argolid, sub-geometric period

exactly with that familiar from the vases. Bronze statues reproduce
the same analytical representations of the human form which we
find in the Geometric pottery: see Plate 22.

It was towards the close of the Geometric period, so far as we can
judge from archaeological discovery, that the first temples were built
in Greece. The megaron-form was a bequest from the Bronze Age, but
models were found in a simpler form of this than that represented by
the palaces of Tiryns and Mycenae. The entrance-hall between the
porch and the main room was omitted. Further, the flat roof seems to
have been abandoned, and, to judge from a little model of a temple

from the Argolid, a very high and steep saddle-roof seems to have been built over the flat roof. The foundation of a temple of the Geometric period at Thermos in Aetolia indicates that the structure was surrounded by a colonnade, the rear part of which encircled the temple in a curve, while the side with the entrance was straight.

The late Geometric vases show us how the new motifs from the Orient begin to make themselves apparent. One of the finest vases of this transitional period is the big amphora in Stockholm, reproduced in Plate 62. A new epoch with its own new and strong impulses was on the way. The Greek Geometric style stands as the finest representative of European art of the first stage of the Iron Age. It stands like an elder sister beside the Hallstatt culture of Central Europe and the Iron Age cultures of Italy, and inspires them. In particular the geometric ornamentation on weapons and fibulae of bronze seems to have inspired the related cultures of Italy and Central Europe from the second half of the eighth century B.C.

After about 700 B.C., and throughout the seventh century oriental influences are very marked in Greek art. Homer portrays a Greece in which all precious works of art are brought from Syria and Cyprus in Phoenician bottoms. The humble Greek colonial graves of the earliest period on Ischia, which date from the beginning of the seventh century contained, in addition to pottery of various late Geometric and early Protocorinthian types, simple Syro-Phoenician seal-stones. The rich Etruscan graves of Etruria and Latium from the later seventh century have yielded luxury vessels of silver, the decoration of which indicates that they were Phoenician imports.

There can be no doubt that the intensified connections with the Near East and Egypt were of great significance for the growth and the earlier development of the Greek temple and of the monumental cult-statue. Both these events, which are fundamental to Greek art, begin to take shape towards the close of the Geometric period. The late Geometric cult-statues were often of wood; the primitive cult-statues survived long in cult-practice. On vases of the fifth century statues of Dionysus are often represented as a pole provided with a face-mask and sometimes with clothing. From this primitive representation an artistic form such as the herm derives: this is a rectangular pole, with a human head, neck and shoulders.

Art in Greece

2. THE ARCHAIC PERIOD
THE EARLY ARCHAIC PERIOD (ca. 700–550)

In the late ninth century the Assyrians had extended their sway over Syria. As a result the trade-routes from Phoenicia to the Tigris and the Euphrates had fallen under the control of a single power. In 709 Cyprus, with its partially Greek population, had also had to submit to the authority of Assyria, whose suzerainty over Western Asia persisted until towards the close of the seventh century. Egypt came under the Assyrian yoke too, though for a briefer period. In the various changing residences of the new world-power artists were busily engaged in the construction and decoration of the palaces of the autocrats.

In these circumstances the world trade in the Mediterranean received a new impetus. At the same time Greece was suffering from overpopulation, and many Greeks began to seek their livelihood on the sea. Greek mariners competed with the Phoenicians and succeeded in mastering the sea-trade of the Aegean, the Black Sea and the Ionian and Adriatic Seas. Contemporaneously many Greeks settled at various points round these seas, partly as merchants and partly as agricultural settlers.

These communications with foreign lands gradually led to profound changes in the internal life of the cities. The old agrarian society with its aristocratic structure began to dissolve. A natural economy was replaced by a monetary economy; floating capital came to have an ever-increasing importance. In Hesiod's *Works and Days* we see the distress under which the smaller farmers laboured. The opposition between rich and poor led to violent strife. The old aristocracy of birth saw the advent of a new class: rich merchants and industrialists, who demanded their share in the determination of the fate of the cities, in the administration of justice and in government.

The outcome of the strife differed from place to place. In some cities the complete dissolution of society was only obviated by the establishment of a sort of dictatorship. Legislators were appointed with full power to reform the life of the community. In many places powerful men of action took advantage of the strife to hoist themselves up to sole rule: these are the so-called tyrants. Many of them were statesmen and patrons of culture on a grand scale, under whom

59

their cities rose to great brilliance: such were Cypselus and Periander in Corinth.

However, not only social traditions were broken. Faith in the gods of their fathers and obedience to hereditary morality were also shaken. Men had the courage to give expression to their individuality in life and in poetry. Archilochus' hymns of hate and uninhibited confessions, and Sappho's love-poetry were the children of this age.

Trade brought prosperity, especially to the Ionian cities, such as Ephesus and Miletus, to Rhodes and to industrial cities such as Corinth and Chalcis. The import of eastern wares, Phoenician and Babylonian textiles, and metal-work from Assyria and elsewhere increased rapidly. And very soon the Greeks began to imitate the foreign models in different spheres.

The new, 'orientalizing' style developed first in Cyprus, the artistic products of which give an impression of Phoenician rather than Greek work. Rhodes, Miletus and Crete also soon absorbed the new impulses, and created new styles from them. In Corinth and the neighbouring cities a flourishing industry arose, best known to us from their painted vases. Motifs drawn from the vegetable world now began to predominate: rosettes, palmettes, the lotus flower and

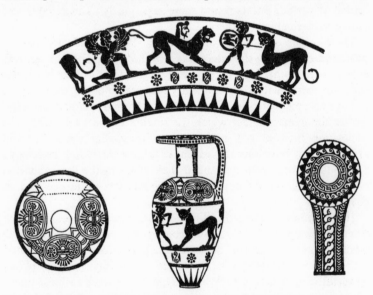

FIG. 22 Corinthian aryballos, 0·68m. high; end of the seventh century B.C., Boston

bud now began their long and important career within the development of European decoration. We further find wreathed patterns of various kinds such as the guilloche, and at the base upward-pointing 'rays'. Eastern creatures, real and imaginary, also appear: the lion, panther, chamois, antelope, sphinx and griffin. At one time it looked as if Greece would become entirely submerged in the oriental and semitic cultural worlds. The Greeks now approximated to the East in their customs, dress, and even religion and outlook. Thales of Miletus sat at the feet of the Chaldaean priests and studied the movements of the stars, but, instead of becoming an astrologer, he became the founder of free scientific inquiry in the West, combining philosophy and natural observation. In the same way Greek artists knew how to transmute the foreign material and give it a Greek stamp.

FIG. 23 Hephaestus is brought back to Olympus; Corinthian vase-painting of the sixth century

There can be no doubt that this current of foreign contacts was of outstanding importance in the development of the Greek people. It gave them an enormous stimulus. This is most tangible in the representational arts.

The sculpture which flourished in the kingdom of Assyria portrayed the deeds of their kings and armies, hunting-scenes and battles, the capture of cities and triumphs in lengthy friezes. The Greeks took from the Assyrians their portrayal of the human form, their style and technique, as they learned them through the mediation of the Syrians, the Phoenicians and the peoples of Asia Minor. But they chose themes from what they regarded as their own history, from the heroic sagas, the songs about the Trojan War and the wanderings of Odysseus, about Heracles' mighty Labours against monsters and giants. Fabulous Greek creatures such as Centaurs rush forward

61

Art in Greece

swinging huge trees, and the Calydonian boar succumbs to Atalanta's arrow and the heroes' shafts.

Art on a large scale, architecture, sculpture and we may add, though little of it has been preserved, painting, did not become primarily, as it was in the East, a means of glorifying rulers; it was on the contrary entirely at the service of the gods. Art had a role in society. The votive-offerings of individuals were all crowded together in the shrines with the monuments of the kings, the tyrants and of the free societies. By means of art, all, strong and weak, expressed their worship, their prayers and their thanks to the real lords of heaven and earth, the everlasting gods, the carefree inhabitants of Olympus. The finest architectural works were the temples of the gods, and in them or beside them were erected the noblest works of art, so that the god of the place might have them ever before his eyes and retain benevolent memories of the donors.

The Greek artist was not, however, bound by any religious restrictions in the practice of his art, as the Egyptian sculptors had long been, although these were pre-eminently the teachers of the Greeks in the field of monumental sculpture. Obviously the form must to some extent be determined by the theme of the representation or by the place where the finished work was to stand, but this did not restrict the artist determined to give of his best, and did not hinder the development of the art.

In certain shrines the numerous small votive gifts of clay, lead or bronze preserved a tenaciously uniform character, but the industrial mass-production to which this gave rise has very little connection with art. For example no less than thirty-eight thousand small lead figures of largely uniform style came to light in the excavations of the shrine of Artemis Orthia at Sparta. As the circumstances of the discovery show, this production extended over six centuries from the Geometric period until far into the Hellenistic age. Similar discoveries have been made in many temples.

From the point of view of Greek art the two most important sanctuaries are those of Delphi and Olympia, which although or because they were situated in politically insignificant places, had risen to become meeting-places for Greeks of all regions and tribes. Delphi owed its importance and its wealth to its oracle, Olympia to athletic competitions. Even foreign cities, and their potentates honoured these shrines with rich gifts, and treasure-houses for the preservation of the gifts grew up around the temples.

These shrines provided abundant opportunities for artistic inter-change between different regions, just as the regulations for inter-course between cities first developed under their protection.

The artistic character of the age can be described as that of a period of searching. The feeling for clarity and order in the con-struction of the work, which the Geometric age had established, was not lost with the disappearance of the Geometric style. Indeed, liberation from its schematization through the use of oriental models had opened the door for individual, direct observation of nature. It is interesting to observe the differences between the study of nature at this time and among the Minoan Cretans. The Cretan observation of nature was directed to the whole, to the whole figure of the plant, the animal or the human, as it presents itself in daily life, in move-ment. The new study of nature concentrates rather on details. The Cretans had openly aimed at producing an illusionistic total por-trayal, while the Greeks began by inserting naturalistic details in a rigidly constrained totality, and only gradually, step by step, advanced to the creation of a fully executed study of living bodies. But this patient work of construction had its reward in the fact that the achievement of the Greeks remained of lasting value for the whole art of Europe, while the impressions of the Minoans were forgotten after a few centuries.

i Architecture

Architecture is the field in which the Greeks appear as most independent of oriental influences. The example of the East probably contributed to the enthusiasm with which temples were built to the gods, but the Doric style is essentially built on native foundations, the age-old megaron-house.

Attempts have long been made to discover the origins of the most important element in the Doric style, the fluted column, in the 'proto-Doric' Egyptian columns of the Middle Kingdom and the beginning of the New Kingdom. But one element is absent from these columns, which from the artistic point of view is of even greater importance than the fluted column, and that is the capital with round echinus. The Egyptian proto-Doric columns are crowned simply by a rectangular plaque, which also occurs, as the abacus, on Doric columns. The round, swelling echinus of the Doric column has its nearest counterpart in the upper element of the Mycenaean column, whose torus was now adapted so that it provided a

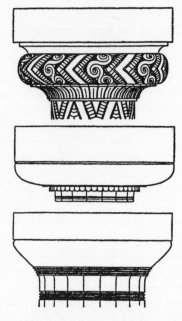

FIG. 24 The development of the Doric capital: Above, capital from 'The Treasury of Atreus', Mycenae: Centre, Archaic capital from Corfu: Below, capital from the Parthenon (from the drawings of E. Lundberg)

transitional element between the round column-shaft and the rectangular abacus, and at the same time expressed in visible terms the function of the column to support.

At this time the Doric style was still in the experimental stage. The ground plans of the temples differ substantially from one to another. Structures with very long and narrow cellas, such as the temple of Apollo at Thermos appear beside those with short wide ones. All the later main types already occur: see Figure 25.

Various experiments were made with the shapes of the columns. The number of flutings varies from sixteen to twenty-four, the abacus is sometimes higher and seems heavier than the echinus, and at other times the opposite occurs. As a rule the echinus is very broad in relation to the column-shaft.

The oldest Doric temples make a light impression by comparison with the heavy and rigid structures of the Later Archaic period, and attest thereby their origin in wooden constructions set on mud walls.

There are signs that wooden poles were employed in the place of columns. In the temple of Hera at Olympia the wooden columns were gradually replaced by stone ones, and there are other examples of this. The entablatures above the antae or columns were also of

wood, and the roof was covered with tiles with runnels of the same
material. Projecting baulkheads were provided with a protective
covering of terracotta. More valuable material was also used:
Athena Chalkioikos at Sparta derived her title from the copper
covering on the temple.

The Doric temple seems to have developed particularly at Corinth.
It was here that, probably on the basis of oriental models, stone was

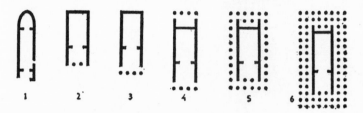

FIG. 25 Forms of temples: 1: Absidal house. 2: Temple *in antis* 3: Prostyle
4: Amphiprostyle. 5: Peripteral. 6: Dipteral.

FIG. 26 Archaic Ionic capital from the Acropolis, Acropolis Museum

used in place of wood on the outer parts of the building. The proportions now inevitably became heavier. The temple of Apollo at
Corinth, which was built towards the end of this period, illustrates
the powerful impression of gathered strength which was the aim of
art at this time. It had six columns on the short sides and fifteen on
the long ones. It is significant that the central structure, the cella,
was not geometrically co-ordinated with the colonnade; its corners
were placed independently of the neighbouring columns.

The Ionic style derives its name from the section of the Greek

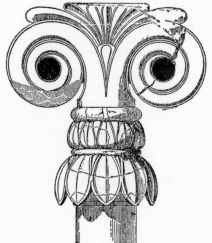

FIG. 27 'Aeolic' capital from Neandria

people that ruled the majority of the Cyclades and large parts of the west coast of Asia Minor, with cities such as Miletus and Ephesus. Of the islands, Chios and Samos were both of importance as artistic centres.

The Ionic temple is also stylistically a development of the megaron-house, but the architrave resembles other early constructions with criss-cross beams. Stone imitations of similar style of construction are found on graves in Lycia in Asia Minor.

The column, with its capital of leaves and spiral volutes, has its own particular history. In Phoenicia and Cyprus forms were developed from the Egyptian lotus-capital, in which large spiral volutes grow from the column-shaft on two sides. A direct descendant of this type is the so-called 'Aeolic' capital: see Figure 27. The Ionian architects abandoned the direct link between the column-shaft and the volutes and linked the volutes directly with each other. The result was that emphasis was laid on the horizontal instead of the vertical line. Transverse head-pieces above pole and column-supports occur in the architecture both of Asia Minor and of Persia. Thus, while the Doric column has a similar appearance from all four sides, the Ionic column has two long and two short sides.

The same two main regional divisions, the western and the eastern, can also be observed in general terms within other branches of artistic production. To the western belongs the Greek mainland, the home of the Doric style, and the boundary followed in general the east coast of Greece. Aegina belonged to the western area, while Euboea and the Cyclades belonged to the eastern, whose most productive centres were the Ionian cities in Asia Minor and the areas nearest the Asiatic mainland, especially Samos.

ii Painting

Painting is mainly known to us from the vases of fired clay. The silhouettes of the Geometric period are replaced by a method of representation in which the pure contour-outlines played an important part, in particular for the parts such as the faces for which a more detailed treatment was deemed desirable. The background of the figures was left light; in the East Greek area the vase was normally covered with a white or buff slip before the ornament and figures were added; in the mainland area the ground was normally yellow, frequently bordering on red, according to the shade of the clay.

The proto-Corinthian vases occupy a pre-eminent position in the manufacture of pottery. They were produced in Corinth, and are conspicuous for their extraordinarily high technical level. The clay was of the most refined quality and the walls of the vases are often extremely thin. The painting is usually executed with very great care, and the firing is even. This class of vase was already being manufactured before the close of the Geometric period, and continued into the sixth century. The commonest types were the little oil-flasks known as aryballoi, and open beakers, the skyphoi or kyathoi. The shapes vary at different stages. Thus the aryballoi are originally bellied, subsequently ovoid and pear-shaped and finally spheroid. The so-called 'Macmillan lekythos' belongs to the ovoid group (after the middle of the seventh century); it is a veritable miniature masterpiece. The decoration of the body is arranged in bands of diminishing width: the main band (just over ½ in. wide) contains warriors fighting, the second a horse-race, the third a hunting scene. Below this frieze is a band of alternate purple and black vertical rays. Purple is used also for the crests of the helmets, for the greaves, details of the shield, and the blood of the wounded warriors. Similar representations in still more colourful execution are to be seen on the Chigi Vase in the Villa Giulia in Rome: see Plates 58–60.

The styles of the eastern area are less rigid; animal-friezes indeed play a large part in them as at Corinth, but it appears that the change to representations of figures from mythology came earlier. For example, a well-known plate from Rhodes portrays a scene from the Trojan War, the single combat between Hector and Menelaus for the fallen body of Euphorbus, who lies on the ground between the combatants. The figures are mainly portrayed by painted contour-lines, but for the naked parts of the body the contours are filled out with the same colour; they are thus drawn silhouettes.

A group of vases customarily assigned to Rhodes (though it is likely that it was made in many places of the East Greek region) is conspicuous for its fondness for chamois, goats and other animals, which peacefully graze their way round the vases in long friezes (the so-called 'Wild-goat style'). This group consists especially of oino-choai with round, and later clover-leaf, mouths: see Plate 61. The forms are elegant and clearly copy metal-ware. The 'Wild-goat style' flourished in the second and third quarters of the seventh century B.C., but lasts into the first quarter of the sixth, now imitating Corinthian black-figure.

East Greek, or, as we may call it after the main body of Greeks in the area, Ionian art is characterized by lively fantasy and a striving after effective expression, but it lacks the rigid discipline of mainland art.

Pausanias, the topographer, in his description of the temple of Hera at Olympia, describes a remarkable chest, which was given to the sanctuary by the tyrant Cypselus of Corinth (first half of sixth century) or by his son Periander. The chest was of cedar-wood, and decorated with representations, in relief or intaglio, of wood, ivory and gold. Some of the figures are said to have been black: these must have been made of ebony. There were thirty-seven scenes, arranged in five rows of panels like metopes, with compositions complete in themselves, alternating with friezes in which the different scenes were arranged side by side, without any division between them except what could be understood from the composition of the figures. Thus there stood side by side: (1) the race between Pelops and Oinomaus, which was regarded as the origin of the Olympic Games; (2) the Corinthian seer Amphiaraus setting out for the war in which he was to meet his death; (3) the games held at the burial of Pelias; (4) Heracles' struggle with the Lernaean hydra; and (5) the blind Phineus whose food the Harpies stole, and the sons of Boreas, who come to his aid. It is a varied collection of stories drawn from different cycles of myth. The popularity of Heracles is shown by the fact that he appears five times, while many scenes are taken from the Trojan War. The stories of the Argonauts and of the war of the Seven against Thebes are also represented. The whole work illustrates how the sagas found reception among the various Greek racial elements. The sagas, like the shrine at Olympia with its athletic competitions and common worship of Zeus, formed a strong link between all Greeks. And art, which spoke a language all could understand without distinction of dialect, contributed much to strengthen this bond.

The description of this work of art gives us an idea of the style of the models which inspired the vase-painters. We can determine certain overall motifs in the different rows of scenes, but we are still far from the great compositions of the Classic period, executed according to a uniform plan. Compare in this respect the sculptures on the temple of Zeus at Olympia or on the Parthenon.

iii Sculpture

In the great cities of the Orient and in Egypt there were temples with huge images of the gods made of wood, metal or stone, which the Greeks now attempted to copy. Since the art of casting hollow bronze figures was not yet known, and huge statues would have demanded an excessive amount of this precious material, statues were constructed of chased sheet-metal over a wooden core. The Egyptians, for example, had already employed this technique during the Middle Kingdom. It was, however, still easier to employ stone, for Greece was plentifully supplied with different sorts of limestone which could be easily cut and sawn.

In the Near East a style had been elaborated which sought to convey to its figures a strong and concentrated impression of volume. The limbs were represented in one piece with the body so as to create a single block. The Greeks became acquainted with offshoots of this style of sculpture in Cyprus and in Syria, and it made a great impression on them. But the Egyptians were the teachers of the Greek sculptor in the execution of the standing naked male figure, which was to play so important a role in Greek sculpture. The static unchanging element in the Egyptian portrayal of the male, which is the direct result of the special conditions of Egyptian art, did not suit the Greek character. In Greece, too, sculpture served a religious purpose, but its ideal foundation was the athletically perfect male body. In Egyptian sculpture the human figure had lost all trace of the unrest which is part and parcel of life on this side of the grave—the Greek 'Kouroi' from the very beginning are full of restrained dynamic force and embody the brilliant possibilities of human existence.

The nature of the encounter between the oriental-cubist and the Greek architectural tendencies appears in standing figures such as a small limestone statue from Crete now in the Louvre (Plate 21). The left arm is stretched straight down the side, the right arm is bent, and the hand lies on the breast in an attitude of supplication. The brow is low and broad, while the face diminishes in small curves towards the chin. The nose projects in a straight line. The eyes protrude. The hair falls in regular tresses down to the side and forward over the shoulders. The torso is small in relation to the lower part of the body. The hip is emphasized by the contraction of the contour and by an edge of the overhanging part of the dress, the peplos. The whole figure gives the impression of an architectural construction rather than of a living organism. The lower part of the body resembles a post on which the upper part rests. In the former the carrying, vertical lines are stressed, in the latter the quiescent, horizontal ones: the lower right arm, the lower ends of the tresses on the shoulders, the wide strong chin and the frontal tresses. It is difficult to imagine a sharper contrast with the figures of Minoan art, composed in freely flowing rhythms.

It cannot, however, be said that the artist did not have nature before his eyes. He has conscientiously included everything of importance. His aim was to create a complete work, and not a conglomeration of loosely assimilated parts; his imagination has been fertilized by the constructive idea, the tension between the parts which seem to carry and those which are carried. The statuette reveals the same play of forces as that between the columns and the architrave of a Doric temple. Works such as this from Crete and other stylistically similar works from the Peloponnese are customarily grouped together under the name 'Daedalic'.

Greek sculpture found its monumental form towards the end of the seventh century. The magnificent head of grey limestone discovered in the German excavations at Olympia near the temple of Hera is a rare survival of a cult-image of colossal size (Plate 25). It probably belonged to the group of an enthroned Hera and a standing helmeted Zeus, described by Pausanias. The large triangular eyes give the face a demonic appearance, which is somewhat lessened by a

70

suggestion of a smile on the goddess's mouth. The hair is gathered over the brow by a diadem; the head is surmounted by a crown of leaves from which flowering twigs hang down over both eyes. At the time of excavation there were still traces of a reddish yellow colour in the hair and of dark red on the diadem.

The oldest example of the monumental Attic Kouros-style is a large marble head found near the Dipylon, the chief city-gate of Athens. The statue to which the head belonged must have been about 10 ft. high. The firm semi-circular form of the skull bestows a unity and strength on the whole work. The eyes are wide open, and their upper limit especially makes a high curve, while the lower eyelids are sculptured as a slightly curved line (Plate 26).

A statue of a goddess discovered in Attica, and now in Berlin, is also of marble (Plate 27). The forms of the rectangular block reveal themselves in the finished statue, although the architectural structure is not emphasized as strongly as in the Cretan statuette. The goddess has a polos on her head, and she holds a pomegranate in her hand, the attribute of Kore (as also of the Argive Hera). The original colours are still in part preserved: the chiton and pomegranate are red, the mantle and hair yellow. The great wide-open eyes and the smiling lips give the marble face a divine sublimity and brilliance.

If we place the statue which Keramyes of Samos dedicated to Hera beside the Cretan statuette we see a different artistic structure (Plate 20). The figure, instead of being rectangular, is cylindrical. The delicate parallel vertical folds emphasize its height. The edge of the outer garment does not have the same dividing effect, since it runs in a curved line, and the descending sides of the curve link the upper and lower parts of the body. A contemporary bronze figure in the National Museum in Stockholm is of the same character (Plate 28). This has been assigned on stylistic grounds to Samos, the rich and powerful island off the coast of Asia Minor. It too is primitive, but round figures form the foundation of its form, not rectangular ones. We notice in particular that the statuette is executed as a unit; the division of the parts is secondary by comparison with the unified rhythm which stamps the figure.

The same artistic conception also marks the row of sitting statues which were erected along the 'Sacred Way' from Miletus to the temple of Apollo at Didyma. To judge by the treatment of the dress, which wholly lacks all tendency to folds, the earliest of these statues belongs to this period (cf. Plate 23).

FIG. 28 West pediment of Temple of Artemis on Corfu. Reconstruction

Among the ruins of a temple on Corfu dated about 600 B.C. were discovered the fragments of a large relief which filled one pediment of the temple: see Figure 28. In the centre is an immense Gorgon moving towards the right. The head is represented *en face*, surrounded by the snakes which constituted the Gorgon's hair; her face is round, her tongue is stuck out from the open maw with its huge teeth. The upper part of the body is represented frontally, while the lower half is presented in profile. The left knee is bent upwards, while the right is close to the ground. This method of representation indicates the act of springing or fleeing. A pair of curved wings of the type borrowed from the East project from the Gorgon's back. Her head gives the appearance of a mask. Similar masks of terracotta sometimes occur as terminal features in the central rafter of older architecture in wood. Medusa's children, Pegasus and Chrysaor, are portrayed beneath the arms of the Gorgon. The Gorgon herself is flanked by two fantastic leopards also represented *en face*. The furthest angles of the pediment are occupied by groups of two figures in combat.

As a result of particularly fortunate circumstances we know more of the oldest sculpture of Athens than of any other Greek city, though it must not be supposed on that account that Athens was already at that time a leading centre of art. In the sixth century it happened that, on the occasion of the reconstruction and extension of the temples on the Acropolis, the oldest sculptures were taken down and buried in the earth as filling for a terrace. They were rediscovered in the 1880's, and we have thus acquired sculptures which decorated two larger and several smaller temples on the Acropolis. One of these lay between the present Parthenon and the Erechtheion. From the outset the building lacked a colonnade and opened east and west with antae. To the left of one pediment Heracles appeared in a half recumbent position wrestling with Triton, the mighty spirals of whose serpentine body filled the corner of the pediment. The reconstruction of the centre of the pediment is uncertain. To the right another fabulous creature contemplated the struggle. Three snake-bodies, entwined in each other, each terminate in a man's torso and head. Two of the heads are turned in wonder towards the struggle on the left, while the third faces outward towards the spectator. Two wings belong in common to the three unified bodies. One hand holds a bird, another the representation of a stream of water. He is the representative of the sea, who watches Heracles' struggle against the grim Triton. The soft, porous limestone did not itself possess a pleasing surface; instead the figures were painted in bright colours: red, blue, green and black. The beard of the face turned outward was blue. The painting did not aim at illusionary results, but was simply decorative. Rich painting of this sort was a feature of stone sculpture throughout antiquity.

Among the other groups of limestone sculpture we may note a group showing a bull succumbing to the claws of a lioness. The head of the bull and its throat with its tight fold of skin are sculpted with unparalleled strength and expression. These Attic limestone groups were worked as free-standing sculptures, but their position in the pediment of the temple made them appear as reliefs.

The liberating influence which the East exercised on Greek art was of decisive importance, and bore rich fruit already in the period immediately following. During this period Greek art had extended its circle of activity far outside the area of the Aegean Sea. In the Greek colonies on the Black Sea, on the coasts of South Italy, Sicily and Gaul, new art-centres arose, and in Etruria the Greeks conquered the oriental influence which had existed earlier. The Etruscan graves with their furniture of Greek imports have made a particularly important contribution to our knowledge of the art of the period.

Art in Greece

THE LATER ARCHAIC PERIOD (ca. 550–480)

The cultural development of the Greek people probably continued in this period at an even faster pace than hitherto; the links with the old cultures of the East continued and indeed increased, but at the same time the Greeks began with ever-increasing independence to develop the foreign impulses according to their own disposition; so gradually there arose a reaction against the oriental influence. The Egyptian Pharaohs established friendships with Greek princes such as Polycrates of Samos and gave an unfailing welcome to Greek merchants in Naucratis in the Nile Delta. The great powers of the East, first Lydia, and, after 546, Persia, pushed westwards and subdued the Greek cities on the mainland of Asia Minor and the adjacent islands, along with Cyprus. The Persians even pushed across the Bosphorus and Dardanelles and brought under their yoke the people, cities and princes of the north-east Balkan area. But Persian hegemony evoked a general reaction among the Greeks settled in Asia Minor. Many sought to extricate themselves from it by emigration; such were the Phocaeans who now journeyed westwards and strengthened their earlier colony Massalia (Marseilles). The Greek colonies in South Italy, Magna Graecia as it is called, thus received many immigrants from Asia Minor and the islands. Many fled to the main cities of the Greek mainland, among which Athens increasingly emerged as the cultural centre after Solon had replaced the old aristocratic constitution with a timocratic system, that gave scope and political freedom of action to the leaders of trade and industry as well. During a supremacy of over thirty years the great statesman Pisistratus, whom his fellow-countrymen called a tyrant, raised the state to a political and economic power of outstanding performance, beside which the eminence of Corinth, Megara and Aegina began to pale.

In the Peloponnese Sparta achieved its final political form, and associated most of the cities of the peninsula in a confederacy which became of decisive importance in the struggle against Persia; but Argos succeeded in preserving its independence, and the attempt of the Spartan king Cleomenes to extend the authority of the great Dorian state as far as central Greece had to be abandoned because of the internal situation at home. The same factors, the ruling class's military upbringing and organization, that gave Sparta its

74

pre-eminent position over its neighbours in the Peloponnese, resulted in it playing no part in the general cultural and artistic progress.

In the Greek areas west of the Ionian Sea, Syracuse, Acragas (Agrigentum), Selinus and Taras (Tarentum) emerged as important political and cultural centres, in competition with the semitic Carthaginians in present-day Tunis, who attempted to subdue Sicily from the west, and the Etruscans in the north, who made themselves suzerains of Campania and, for a time, also of Latium, thus threatening the Greek trade-routes.

In the east the loss of political freedom led to economic and cultural stagnation among the Greeks, though in the field of art some compensation was to be found for this in the fact that oriental princes such as Croesus in Lydia, Carian dynasts and Sidonian kings employed Greek artists. Even in Persepolis itself Greek artists were active. The important cultural links with Egypt were broken by the subjection of Egypt to Persia in 525.

Within the Greek cities themselves a great ferment was taking place. The old aristocracy had been shaken by the economic development which introduced trade and industrial activity—important levers for the growth and prosperity of society. The warrior-charioteers of the aristocracy, who fought with spears in single combat, had to give place to the citizen hoplite army which advanced in tightly-closed lines. Only Sparta succeeded in preserving its aristocracy, but it did so only at the price of the subjection of the individual to the discipline of the state in every aspect of life.

The struggles between the classes often took particularly bitter forms, of which an echo survives in the poems of Theognis. In many places a consequence of this internal strife was that power fell into the hands of an individual for a longer or shorter period. These autocrats were called tyrants, to distinguish them from the old hereditary kings. As has been mentioned, the concentration of power in the hands of an individual raised some cities to great brilliance; such a city was Athens under Pisistratus and his son Hippias.

In spite of the material prosperity of the rule of the tyrants the desire of the citizen-body for freedom continually increased; it was no longer a distinguishing characteristic of the aristocracy alone, but of the large mass of the people also. In this milieu the intellectual currents of the time could expand without barriers of class, and the new ideas be understood by all whose education enabled them to do so.

On the one hand social adversity had created a fruitful ground for religious ideas which sought the best for humanity in surrender to a higher spiritual world, for example in the ecstatic side of the Dionysiac religion which derived its name from Orpheus. The mysteries, particularly those of Eleusis, found many adherents, and those in need of help streamed in ever-increasing numbers to the old cult-centres such as the shrine of Apollo at Delphi.

At the same time the first philosophers in Ionia attempted to organize all the new information which was the product of expanded knowledge of foreign lands and of familiarity with oriental learning into a rational concept of the universe, and thus became the pioneers of science in the West. The spirit of inquiry spread from Miletus, where Thales (about 585 B.C.) and Anaximander worked, to Ephesus (Heraclitus), and travelled west to the Greeks of Italy with Pythagoras and Xenophanes. The Greek people, their youthful period of ferment over, began to strive forward to a clearer and more reasonable conception of their environment. The spirit of organization, which dominated the Geometric style, now reappeared in art, but far from shackling artistic development it refined it.

While science advanced along its own road in the hands of individuals, philosophy, literature and the imitative arts enjoyed the support of society. Pisistratus and his sons assembled poets and artists in their court, and under their protection the civic authorities organized festivals in honour of Dionysus, where the first dramas were performed.

We can clearly follow this developing self-consciousness of the Greeks within the sphere of painting and sculpture; the foreign influences are always received, but they are winnowed more carefully now. The artist creates his work with closer attention to nature, and this rational observation of nature contributed to the rupture of the bonds of one style after another. Imagination was chastened. The fabulous beasts, the sphinxes, the griffins and others are assigned to subordinate places in decoration. The main preoccupation is with the themes treated by the Homeric poets and their successors, and works of art enable us to follow the triumphant march of the epic poems through the Greek world.

The sources for the history of ancient art flow very thinly. According to one tradition Dipoinos and Skyllis, pupils of the Cretan sculptor Daidalos, moved to the mainland and founded a school of sculptors in Sicyon near Corinth. This little city was subsequently for three centuries one of the leading artistic centres of Greece. Some of their statues were of wood, others of marble. Gitiades decorated the temple of Athena in Sparta with chased reliefs of copper, which gave the temple its name, Chalkioikos (the Bronze House). Smilis worked on Aegina; statues have been found in Delphi signed by Polymedes of Argos, representing the twins Cleobis and Biton. We also hear of the Ionian Bathycles from Magnesia, who constructed the splendid throne of Apollo for the Spartans at Amyclae. Otherwise the Peloponnese is a complete contrast to Ionia in artistic matters. Rhoecus and Theodorus, the discoverers of the art of casting statues in bronze, worked on Samos. Apart from the information from literary sources we also have artists' signatures and dedicatory inscriptions on a number of works.

During the Archaic and Classic periods all artistic work of any importance possessed a religious significance. By the gift of a statue to the gods the individual placed himself under their protection, and their wrath was turned to benevolence. Male deities were normally given statues of men, female deities statues of women, even when the dedicant was a man. Some of the figures of women erected on the Acropolis in Athens, the so-called 'Korai', were dedicated by men to the goddess of the rock. The gods thus looked with pleasure on their own statues in their temples. These representations were in the first instance cult-statues, and had their place in the cella of the temple. Often, however, the cult-statue of the god consisted of some object which had been worshipped from primitive times, a tree-stump, a stone, or some similar object. Votive statues representing the god might then be erected by the side of the object, which was regarded by the faithful as the seat of the godhead.

The close association with religion had an elevating effect on art. The subjects possessed an importance which forbade carelessness in execution, and prevented frivolous trifling with the forms. Artists did not thoughtlessly abandon the lessons of their predecessors, and tradition acquired a solidity absent in modern art.

On the other hand the strength of Greek art lay in the fact that the religious authorities did not shackle the artists with fixed written prescriptions. Religion provided the norm for the choice of themes, and for their material representation, but in respect of form the artist was free of all compulsion; only quality and dignity of style were required. Thus the great masters had freedom to work for the development of art according to the ideals which inspired them.

During this period athletics also came to exercise a real influence on art. The Olympic Games had indeed begun earlier, but it was now that Olympia first won its importance as a meeting-place for citizens from all Greek cities. The Pythian Games at Delphi were inaugurated in 576; in Athens Pisistratus followed the current fashion by establishing the Panathenaic Games in 564. The custom of competing naked gave artists and their public the opportunity to study anatomy in motion and made the representation of naked figures in art wholly natural.

The public to whom the artists turned consisted of men. Women played no significant part in social life; the priestess of Demeter was the only woman entitled to watch the Olympic Games. The artists who treated male nakedness with such natural freedom did not feel the same freedom in regard to women. Although male gods were early portrayed wholly nude, nakedness was avoided for goddesses, except for some types of primitive idols, where special cult-regulations demanded nakedness.

Each artistic region continued to preserve its own special features, and within these regions we can distinguish smaller centres. In Ionia Miletus and Samos are pre-eminent, and on the coast of Asia Minor the art of Aeolis seems to have stood out by its fresh and alert power of observation. Chalcis also belonged to the eastern region, and from time to time Ionian influence was dominant in Athens. Many attempts have been made to distinguish schools of sculpture on the mainland at Argos, Corinth, Cleonae, Sicyon and Sparta, but the particularities of these schools, and their role in the development of Greek art, are far from clear.

Our sources tell us that artists worked sometimes for one city and sometimes for another. As we have already seen, Bathycles from Magnesia in Asia Minor worked in Sparta, and we must in general assume that artists, like the rhapsodes who performed the Homeric songs, wandered from city to city. As a result influences often crossed. In the great shrines such as Olympia, Delphi and Delos, works of different style and origins stood side by side.

Within the eastern area we can observe an effort at synthetic form. The sitting figures from the Sacred Way to the shrine of the Branchidae south of Miletus are so formed that the unity of the mass stands out. They are encompassed within a single firm contour with rounded corners. The different parts fuse into a unity. The Ionian 'Kouros'-figures from the Cyclades have the same characteristics. Alongside this tendency to synthesis, detail is treated with great affection, but it is regarded as a decorative rather than a constructive element of the whole work. Among the Ionians a sharp eye for the essential, for the momentary impression, is associated with a remarkable elegance in the elaboration of detail and an extraordinary technical skill in the treatment of the material, particularly of marble.

It was in this period that ancient sculptors first made full use of marble as a means of artistic expression. Other types of stone, which had previously been widely used, were regarded from the middle of the sixth century as inferior substitutes, when for geographical or economic reasons marble was not available.

Work in marble was perfected, and the ability of Parian, Attic and other sculptors to extract from the material all its aesthetic value has never been surpassed. It also became customary to select the most suitable marble; while at first artists had been content to use the stone offered by the region in which they worked, it later became the practice to employ marble quarried on Paros as the most beautiful. Statues of Parian marble are to be seen both in Delphi and Athens and elsewhere.

That a fragment of a genuine Archaic work, a hand or a foot, can radiate more life and make a stronger impression than a whole statue from later times, is not simply the result of the character of the stone itself; it depends also on the technique of the Greek sculptors, which enabled them, with simple tools, to bestow intense life on their creations.

There is a profound difference between the artistic productions of a Greek sculptor, and of his modern contemporary, and it is consequently of importance to understand the conditions under which Greek work in marble came into being. It is a general rule in this period that artist and craftsman were one and the same. This was certainly disadvantageous for the social standing of the former, but his work undoubtedly profited thereby. In more modern work in marble the actual artistic creation occurs with the formation of the clay model, and the work in marble is simply directed at reproducing this as faithfully as possible. This has been achieved by means of the 'pointing' process by which an exact reproduction is executed with the help of mathematically fixed points; this task is frequently left to someone other than the sculptor himself. In the Archaic period the act of artistic creation was effected directly in marble. The sculptor had to be present from first to last—though this does not exclude the possibility that he may have been assisted in the initial rough blocking-out. Even if (as seems likely), models in clay or plaster were used, the work on the marble itself was not intended as a mechanical reproduction of the model; if the whole was not to be a failure it had to be guided throughout by the feeling for the emerging form. The sculptor indicated on the block itself how much had to be cut away on each side. From the outset the work was considered from a rectangular point of view, and the sculptor was thus closely tied in the beginning. From the first probe till the finer chisellings the sculptor worked his way into the depth, where the surface of the work under creation was to be found. Throughout the entire work he must keep the final form clear in his mind, to ensure that too much was not removed. The quadrilateral form, itself a product of the method of work, is clearly visible even in the finished sculpture, although artists aimed at levelling out the transitions at the corners of the original block.

It was also of fundamental importance that the main work was done with the pointed chisel. As the final surface was approached the sculptor tapped his way forward with this, employing a particularly sensitive and delicate technique, instead of peeling off the surface with the wide, flat or rounded chisel such as was commonly used in the studios of Roman copyists. Particular care was bestowed on the naked parts of the statues. The folds in the drapery were sometimes worked with a type of saw or rasp, which would produce long and deep furrows. Drill-bores were also employed from the Classic period onwards (Parthenon), though only very occasionally in the immediately following centuries. Work with these tools was not left to subordinate assistants; the same artist whose imagination had first been fired normally continued his work with his own hands to its ultimate completion.

This direct method of work explains how it was that the Greeks remained true to their traditional types for so long. The artist stood firm on well-tested ground, and when he moved forward he felt his way carefully. The pursuit of originality was foreign to the artist of the Archaic period.

In addition to marble, bronze now began to be employed for monumental sculpture. Chased work in bronze had long been known, and the art of casting small figures in the same material was also

39. Central figure of the west pediment of the Temple of Zeus at Olympia, ca. 460 B.C., ht. of pediment 3·3m.

40. Bronze statue found in the sea off Piombino, ca. 480 B.C., ht. 1·5m.

41. The 'Blond Ephebe', ca. 480 B.C.

Athena, Heracles and Atlas: :tope-relief from Temple of us at Olympia, ca. 460 B.C., ht. 1·6m.

The 'Basilica', the oldest temple of Hera at Paestum.

44. Zeus (or Poseidon), bronze statue found in the sea near Cape Artemision, ht. 2·09m.

45. 'The Charioteer', bronze statue; eyes are inlaid with glass flux, and the lips were originally coated with silver lead, ca. 460 B.C., ht. 1·8m.

46. The 'Boston Throne'.

47. The 'Ludovisi Throne': the birth of Aphrodite, ca. 460 B.C., ht. ca. 1m.

48. The 'Ludovisi Throne': woman performing a sacrifice.

49. The 'Ludovisi Throne': hetaera.

50. The 'Diadoumenos' of Myron. Roman copy in marble of the head.

51. Myron's 'Discobolus'. Roman copy in marble.

52. The 'Doryphorus' of Polyclitus. Roman copy in marble.

53. Geometric krater from Dipylon cemetery, mid-eighth century B.C., ht. 1·23m.

54. (*above, right*). Early Geometric amphora, first half of the ninth century B.C., ht. 0·695m.

55. Scene of lamentation around a bier, on a Geometric vase. Second half of the eighth century B.C.

56 (*left*). Geometric jug, ninth–eighth century B.C.

57. Late Geometric kantharos, ca. 700 B.C., ht. 0·17m.

58. Late proto-Corinthian olpe, known as the 'Chigi Vase'.

59 (*above*, *right*). The blinding of Polyphemus, neck-decoration of a proto-Attic amphora, ca. 650 B.C., ht. of amphora 1·42m.

60. The 'Macmillan lekythos', late proto-Corinthian, ca. 600 B.C., ht. 0·068m.

61. Oinochoe from Rhodes, seventh century B.C.

62. 'Cycladic' style amphora, with representation of grazing fallow deer, seventh century B.C., ht. 0·59m.

63. Corinthian krater from Cerveteri, ca. 560 B.C., ht. 0·425m.

◀ 64. The 'François Vase', Attic krater from Vulci, signed by Clitias and Ergotimos, ca. 560 B.C., ht. 0·66m.

◀ 65. Caeretan Hydria, ca. 525 B.C., ht. 0·41m.

66 (*above*). Ajax and Achilles playing backgammon, amphora by Exekias, from Vulci, ca. 540 B.C., ht. 0·61m.

67. Kyalix-krater with representation of Heracles and Antaeus, by Euphronios, from Cerveteri, ca. 510 B.C.

68. Eos laments Memnon. Attic amphora, ca. 540 B.C.

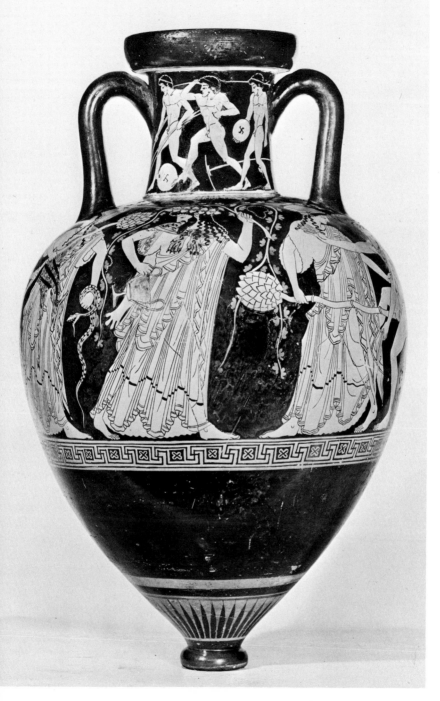

69. Dionysus-procession and scene in palaestra. Pointed amphora by the
Cleophrades-painter, from Vulci, shortly after 500 B.C., ht. 0·56m.

70. Silenus and Hermes, amphora by the Berlin-painter, ca. 590 B.C., ht. 0·69m.

known. During this period Rhoecus and Theodorus from Samos introduced the art of hollow-casting large statues. This discovery, however, only acquired general artistic importance in the following period, that of the Persian Wars; discussion of the Greek bronze-casting technique is therefore reserved for a subsequent chapter. The works executed by Bathycles of Magnesia for the Spartans in about 550, the throne and statue of Apollo at Amyclae, and Gitiades' temple of Athena Chalkioikos were still of chased copper.

Architecture is best treated in connection with the classic form of the temple, which was first achieved in the fifth century with the temple of Zeus at Olympia and that of Poseidon at Paestum.

i Sculpture

In the long row of naked male statues, 'Kouroi', which go back even as far as the small angular figures of the Geometric period, the Twins executed by the Argive Polymedes at Delphi occupy a prominent position (see Plate 29). Herodotus tells us that Solon praised the happiness of the brothers Cleobis and Biton to King Croesus of Lydia. They were the sons of an Argive priestess of Hera, and had themselves drawn their mother's chariot to a sacrifice in the remote temple, when the pair of oxen had failed to appear. Their mother had then prayed to the Goddess to bestow on them the greatest favour which a god can give a mortal, and when she left the temple after the sacrifice, she found her two sons in the sleep of death. Cleobis and Biton were worshipped by the Argives as heroes for the particular grace shown them by the gods, and their statues were set up at Delphi, where they were rediscovered in the French excavations. The inscription on the base tells us the name of the sculptor, along with their own: 'Polymedes of Argos made me'. As so often in dedicatory inscriptions of an early date, the sculpture itself is made to speak.

The stance is the same in all Archaic male standing figures. The left foot is set forward (as on Egyptian statues), the trunk upright, usually without inflection to left or right, the head held straight to the front, the eyes open, the mouth shut. Cleobis' brow is wide and low, his cheeks fleshy with projecting cheek-bones, his chin wide. The large eyes and fleshy lips give him the air of a country lad with a healthy appetite for life. The wide shoulders and powerful loins point to athletic training. But the fashion of cutting the hair short has not yet won the day among athletes. The brow is framed above and on the sides by small spiral locks, the hair falls in thick masses on the back and shoulders, where it is elaborately divided vertically into tresses—as seen from the front there are three on either side—which are also divided horizontally so as to give a chequer-pattern. The skull is low, and the head which is almost rectangular, rests in its turn on the quadrilateral formed by the shoulders, trunk and down-stretched arms. These heavy parts are supported by the strong legs, the contours of which, with their elegant curves, suggest the elasticity of a steel spring. The Peloponnesian artist's feeling for tectonic construction does not desert him. But beside that his eyes were also alert to the natural structure, and he has elaborated the knee-caps with great care so that their function is immediately apparent. He has also shown particular interest in the muscles of the arms and legs, but he has succeeded less well with the trunk. The great chest muscles are the only ones actually sculptured. Their lower edges form an angle with each other, which serves as a connecting-link between the obtuse angle formed by the lines of the shoulders and the line of demarcation of the thorax, which is engraved like a sharply curved bow on the trunk.

The intense interest in joints and limbs forms one of the new departures by which the Greek sculptor is differentiated from his Egyptian colleague. A wide field was opened for fresh observation of human nature, for which Greek athletic life provided artists with invaluable material. Human beings were now studied more scientifically, almost like a machine with power to move, and artists began to aim at revealing the whole mechanism. The new discoveries were not however made all at once, and four generations were needed before Polyclitus provided the classic solution of the representation of a body in repose.

Ionic sculpture keeps pace with the Peloponnesian masters. Its main interest lay in the delicate interplay of lines and elegant curves, which expressed a sensual reality. The development of the Kouros-type can be followed in a large number of exemplars from different parts of the Greek world.

The areas of the human body which became subject to naturalistic treatment were extended from generation to generation. Each decade shows an increase in the complement of correct anatomical observation. An observation once made is held firmly by subsequent generations. Examples of this sequence of development are provided by the long-famous statue of Apollo from Tenea near Corinth (ca. 550 B.C.), and the Kouros from Anavysos (ca. 540 B.C.) which portrays a youth named Kroisos—the first in the long series of Greek heroic portraits. The Kouros No. 692 from the Acropolis forms a terminal point in the chain of representation which was broken when the different movements of the limbs were allowed to affect the musculature of the trunk. Then the law of frontality, which had hitherto dominated the representation of the human form in Egypt, the East and Greece, was abandoned.

Draped figures were now developed with an ever-increasing wealth of detail. In particular some Ionian sculptors on the Aegean islands seem to have been conspicuous in this field; Chios is especially mentioned in antiquity in this connection. Other sculptors on marble-producing islands, Paros and Naxos, certainly contributed to this progress.

The fashions of dress in Ionia were in keeping with these tendencies. Women wore thin, soft fabrics in the rich industrial cities. Linen and cotton of finer quality were imported from the East and from Egypt, and the artist learned to reproduce these too. Material dyed in purple became extremely popular, and also expensive. The typical under-garment, the chiton, acquired a new form suitable to the softer materials, and was gathered together over the shoulders and upper-arms so that a sort of sleeve was formed; variations in the form of dress were achieved by folding over a part of the material and by using a girdle. In addition the mantle was draped asymmetrically over the shoulders, and thus achieved further variation.

Sculptors aimed at indicating the different materials by varying surface-treatment, as by closer or looser folds. They also experimented with deep indentations in the block, and detached some parts from the bed of the stone by undercutting. From this there followed a richer play of light and shade, which thus acquired great importance in artistic representation. The artist's attempt to infuse life and expression into his subject was not limited to the drapery; by raising the corners of the mouth a friendly smile, the 'Archaic smile', was bestowed on the features. The expression is strengthened at times by setting the eyes aslant. The figures were painted in polychrome. The hair was painted yellow-ochre or red, and occasionally carried ornaments of yellow or black; the eyebrows and the eyes were painted a dark colour; the eyes were also often inset in a more precious material. The drapery was resplendent with red, green or blue; on the mantle was a border, the decoration of which stood out in clear colours against the marble. The natural colour of the marble was also exploited, and the naked parts of the body were left unpainted.

The refined skill in the use of marble, the graceful Ionian treatment of folds and the happy smile are all found on the female figures, the Korai, which were found in excavations on the Acropolis. Alongside a heavier Doric style we find works which are quite certainly the product of the Ionian sculptors who settled in Athens in large numbers in the times of Pisistratus and his sons. The gulf, and the rivalry, between the two tendencies can be followed till the next generation, when masters such as Antenor (who carved the first group of the 'Tyrannicides') discover a synthesis which unites Ionic skill in the treatment of material with Doric gravity. We then stand on the threshold of an age whose spirit was wholly opposed to the brilliant and friendly *ancien régime* which flourished under the sceptre of the tyrants.

After the Athenian Acropolis, Delphi is the most important place of discovery of Archaic art. As a result of the Sacred War of about 590, in which a number of Greek cities such as Athens and Sparta, the tyrant Cleisthenes of Sicyon and others took part, the shrine was liberated from the sway of its immediate neighbours and was internationalized under the administration of the Amphictyony. The religious festivals, the Pythia, which were celebrated there every fifth year, achieved Panhellenic importance. In addition to the usual athletic competitions musical events were also held: lyric poems and musical compositions were performed. The increasing reputation of the oracle made it a spiritual centre of importance, whose religious and cultural significance in the period before the Persian Wars outshone that of Olympia. The various Greek peoples and tribes, from Massalia and Syracuse in the West to Phocaea in the East, sent their gifts of honour thither, and built treasuries to house them in safety and exhibit them worthily within the sanctuary. The wide-open, almost triangular eyes, of a splendid marble sphinx, the gift of the island of Naxos, set on a tall Ionic column, reveals a primitive form which cannot be much later than the Sacred War. The beast's lion-body has an elasticity which shows that artists found it easier to create a correct animal body than a human one.

To about the middle of the sixth century belong some metope-reliefs which were found built into the foundations of the Sicyonian Treasury. On one of them (Plate 33) three armed men are portrayed, with spears in their hands, leading a herd of cattle. The men march

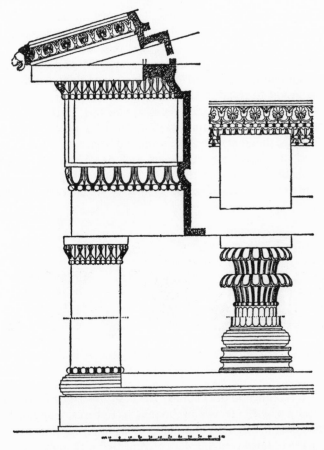

FIG. 29 Archaic Ionic order. The Treasury of the Massaliotes at Delphi

forward with long strides, all very much alike, and the oxen move in
the background in a military column; those immediately behind the
men turn their heads outward and look at the spectators. Inscriptions
tell us that the sculptures represent the Dioscuri leading home their
booty. Another metope carries a representation of two riders, the
Dioscuri, *en face*, in front of the ship Argo. The sculptor has daringly
attacked the problem of creating figures in depth in a surface-
representation. The difficulty has been overcome in a very simple
way: in the first relief the legs of the inside oxen are sketched,
rather than modelled, in front of the outermost ones, so that a sort

85

of perspective results. In the second, later relief the back parts of the horses represented *en face* simply disappear in the background. On contemporary 'black-figure' vases we very often see a chariot portrayed straight from the front; it remains a projection on the surface without any perspective, and one has to think before saying what is meant to stand in the forefront of the picture and what is conceived as further back. Another metope portrays Europa anxiously trying to maintain herself on the back of the bull. On all the reliefs the different planes are separated from each other by sharp contours, and softer transitions are lacking. A pair of Caryatids also probably belonged to the same Treasury. They are the oldest representatives of this class of sculpture, which carried out the

FIG. 30 The Treasuries of the Cnidians, the Massaliotes and the Siphnians at Delphi. Reconstruction by Dinsmoor

architectural function of columns. The best preserved are associated stylistically with the temple of Artemis in Ephesus, many of whose columns bear dedications of King Croesus of Lydia (560–546). The lower parts of these columns were ornamented with sculpture in high relief, fragments of which are preserved in the British Museum. Their value resides especially in the fact that they can be dated with relative certainty: see Plate 31.

The sculptures from the Siphnian Treasury can be dated on historical grounds with some certainty to 530–525. Here too the architrave of the entrance hall was borne by Caryatids. Their faces have the Archaic smile which we know from the Ionian Korai in Athens. The pedimental relief portrays the duel of Heracles and Apollo over the Delphian tripod. A frieze ran round the upper part of the Treasury, the eastern section of which portrays the assembled gods watching a battle between Greeks and Trojans. Both as a composition and in regard to the treatment of detail the frieze on the north side is the finest; this portrays the War of the Gods and the Giants (Plate 32). Cybele hurries forward in a chariot drawn by a lion, the brother and sister Apollo and Artemis destroy their enemies with the bow, a giant whose helmet is decorated with a kantharos rushes away in flight. Athena fights alone against two foes, and Hephaestus is working his bellows. The figures are firm and muscular, the movements varied. The groups are closely welded together, and the figures overlap. The sculptors have learnt from contemporary painting which, as vases show us, made great advances at this time in the representation of movement and the perspective of individual figures.

In the following decades a new temple was also built to Apollo at Delphi in the Dorian order, the old one having been destroyed by fire in 548. One pediment was ornamented with marble sculpture, the other with work in limestone, the material of which the building as a whole was made. The composition of the pedimental sculptures reminds one of the old relief from Corfu, with two large animal-groups on either side of a central figure. Two massive lions each rend a deer in pieces; one of them leans his head backwards towards the head of the lion, which has hurled itself on to its back and rends it with its claws. This pediment can be dated to the end of the sixth century.

A series of metopes which were the fruit of an outstanding archaeological discovery by two Italian archaeologists, Paola Zancani Montuoro and U. Zanotti-Bianco, and were discovered along with the remains of the temple of the Argive Hera at the mouth of the river Silaros (Sele), north-west of Paestum, are approximately contemporary with the Siphnian Treasury: see Plate 34. The temple is Doric, but it has strong Ionian elements, which can also be observed elsewhere in the architecture of the great temples of the sixth century.

The metope-reliefs from the Athenian Treasury at Delphi, with representations of the adventures of Heracles and Theseus, belong to the transition to the next stylistic epoch. Heracles had for a long time been recognizably the most popular of Greek heroes in art. Theseus had now become the symbol of the re-won Athenian self-government, and the Athenians were urged by their growing self-confidence and also by political motives to extol him as their representative.

From Solon to the outbreak of the Persian War Athens had grown persistently stronger. No city on the mainland could compete with it for external brilliance. But Sparta's tough warriors were the best in Greece, and had given their state the hegemony of the Peloponnese. From the east the danger grew gradually nearer; the Persian War cast its shadows before it. The Archaic smile died away, to survive only here and there in frozen form, as a memory of the good old days when men had worn their hair richly curled in tresses as on the famous 'Rampin head' in Paris. The reliefs on the Athenian Treasury at Delphi testify to a straining of all forces. The warrior, the fighter, is the ideal of the day, and the type of person of whom Greece then had need.

ii Vase-Painting

Already towards the end of the previous period figures of myth and saga and scenes from the Homeric poems had made their entry into vase representations and begun to supplant the oriental animal-friezes. Pride of place in decoration was now given to representations of human figures, even if they were gods. We are able to follow the contemporary advances in painting on the vases.

In the manufacture of vases Corinth now had to yield the first place to Athens, beside which the 'Chalcidian' workshops preserved their independence till shortly after the middle of the sixth century.

The chronology of vases can now be built, among other things, on the Panathenaic amphorae, which are sometimes dated exactly by inscriptions. These were distributed with their contents—olive oil —as prizes at the games which were held every four years. Inscriptions now become frequent on other vases, and their alphabet and dialect point to Athens as their place of origin, whether they be found in Etruria, Asia Minor or Attica.

Variety in the use of colour, previously so frequent, is gradually much reduced. The flesh of women indeed continues to be represented in white, and wine-red panels are a frequent feature of drapery, but the main item is now the brilliant black figures which are outlined against the red clay. No other vase-style has achieved such decorative effects.

The first masterpiece in this style is the large crater in Florence signed by Clitias and Ergotimos, which is usually named after its discoverer, François (Plate 64). The lavish wealth of scenes makes the vase a mythological picture-book, a Greek 'biblia pauperum'. The style is characterized by precision in details. The artist has achieved a certain rhythm in the portrayal of the procession of the gods to the wedding of Thetis by means of a division of groups.

The vase-painting of Eos and Memnon (Plate 68) demonstrates the ability of the 'black-figure' style to achieve a sense of space and an impression of landscape. The placing of the figures in a reserved picture-panel emphasizes the central portion of the whole vase, and compels a more conscious composition.

Towards the middle of the sixth century the style becomes increasingly austere. The figures are frequently isolated from each other, and their effect as silhouettes thereby increased. The climax of the 'black-figure' style is represented by such masters as Exekias and the painters of Amasis and Andokides, who were active in Athens from ca. 550 for a generation or so. The sure stance of the figures is combined with minute work in detail. In the picture (Plate 66) in which Achilles and Ajax are playing a form of draughts, all details are incised with a sharp instrument. A clear love of story-telling radiates from this masterpiece, where the tension inherent in vase-painting between its narrative and decorative functions has achieved a perfect balance.

This artistic tension led rapidly to the decline of 'black-figure' painting as an artistic form of expression. The silhouette-style had contributed to the isolation of the individual figures. A new wave of naturalism penetrated the age. The black silhouettes were too austere for the current taste, and the incision of the details too cumbrous.

The colour-scale was now reversed, and figures were reserved in the surface, the rest of which was painted black. The delineation of the details of the figures was now executed with the brush, and with a special instrument, with which it was possible to achieve the hair-thin relief-lines in the black glaze. The transition to this 'red-figure' style seems to have taken place in the 'thirties of the sixth century.

On some vases from the transitional period we find both techniques side by side, and we can sometimes compare how the same theme was presented in the rival methods of painting. The two techniques were used simultaneously with particular frequency in the atelier of Andokides. Among the various anonymous painters active there is an unknown man called, after the owner of the atelier, 'the Andokides-painter'. His style is delicate and elegant even in the new style, and a breath of *ancien régime* and court-culture lies over his creations. One of the best known and most prolific painters from the period immediately following was Epiktetos, whose preference

Art in Greece

was the decoration of drinking-cups, kylikes. This type of vase now became fashionable, and many of the best artists devoted themselves wholly or almost entirely to decorating these vases. On the inside of the vase at the bottom there was a circular field, which was usually decorated with a single figure. The disposition of the figure within the available space was a favourite artistic problem, which produced a number of solutions. On the outside apotropaic eyes are sometimes represented, borrowed from Ionian studios, or else palmette-tendrils originating at the handles, are used to frame the figures.

The Archaic period created the first monumental forms and types in Greek art. Its striving after fidelity to nature is combined with a firm sense of style; both these qualities helped the Greeks to artistic independence. From this date until the very end of antiquity this naturalistic art, created by the Greeks and continued by the Romans, prevails.

THE TRANSITIONAL PERIOD (ca. 480–460)

There is no period in the history of the world which manifests such a concentrated spiritual stress and development as the time of the Persian Wars, the period when Pindar was at the height of his powers and Aeschylus in early manhood. The ideas and impulses which the Greek people had or received during their previous growth now developed so powerfully that they became decisive for their future evolution. The slightly superficial elegance and formal discipline of the courts of the tyrants disappeared. The directly human factor became more prominent, stamped with the strict gravity of the age. At the same time religious questions began to take a central place; people sought to find contact with the powers which determine the destiny of man.

Political conditions prompted seriousness and concentration. The prosperity of the Ionian cities had been devastated by the Persians, and Greece the motherland had to exert all her strength to withstand the great Asiatic power, which at one time controlled the northern part of the Balkan peninsula. The outcome of the struggle brought with it a readjustment of power in Greece, where Athens became the leading political force and a pre-eminent centre of culture which brought under its patronage all the progressive forces of Greece. Athens led the Greek counter-attack against Persia, succeeded in

Art in Greece

liberating her fellow-countrymen on the west coast of Asia Minor from the yoke of the foreigner and thus created an empire round the shores of the Aegean.

The external danger had swept away the Ionian elegance which had flourished at the courts of the tyrants. Heavy woollen clothes of Dorian cut became the fashion for both men and women. The political struggle against Persia awoke and strengthened the feeling of contrast with orientals in all walks of life. Free citizen-government was contrasted with despotism, equality before the law with the slavery of the subjects of the king and his officials, freedom and responsibility against weak submission to the orders of an individual, natural dignity in public appearance with servility, simplicity with love of luxury. The creative spirit of the age is embodied in literature by Pindar's poetry, with its strong emphasis on religion, and by Aeschylus' strict moral gravity.

i Sculpture

In sculpture the art of casting large statues in bronze now developed. The fundamental discovery had already been made in the earlier period, but it now wholly won the day. From this period bronze became the chief material for the art of statuary, and it was in the world of the bronze-casters that the decisive step in the natural expression of the human figure was made. Marble statuary became less valued than masterpieces in bronze, and was for more than a century restricted to less important and decorative purposes.

The art of casting in bronze as practised by the Greeks marks a great step forward from the achievements of their predecessors. The Egyptians had for long produced bronze work by means of the 'cire-perdue' technique. They were, however, unable to cast on a large scale, and made only small figures or else divided large figures into smaller sections which they then riveted together. It seems that the Egyptians smelted their metals in crucibles over open fires and consequently were unable to handle large masses of the heavy material at one time. Technical studies of ancient bronze statues show clearly that the Greeks had already in the Archaic period a more perfected form of smelting-oven, the shaft-furnace, which enabled much larger quantities of metal to be smelted at once. For small bronze figures the 'cire-perdue' technique had long been used in Greece as well. But the large Archaic bronzes were constructed on models of something other than wax, and most probably wood.

91

There is a head in Athens on which one can see signs of work in wood at a point which was hidden from the onlooker, and therefore was not wholly chased after casting. The Archaic figures as a rule have very thick bronze walls. Projecting and cut away parts are worked independently and held with a hard solder. On the Delphic Charioteer, for example (Plate 46), the skull from the diadem upwards, the rest of the head with the trunk, the arms, and the whole lower part of the body as far as the hips, were made individually. The locks at the temples and the knot of the diadem on the neck have been soldered on. As far as can be determined from the scanty information we have regarding the few surviving bronze-works, the 'cire-perdue' technique had already replaced the use of wooden models in the fifth century.

The Greek artists did not use bronze to secure for all time the appearance of the viscous surface of clay; nor did they conceal the bronze under a layer of dull patina. On the contrary the brilliant surface provided by the shining metal was the cause of its popularity for monumental sculpture. In some cases indeed the artists went further, and gilded the bronze. The eyes were customarily represented with the aid of inlay in enamel, glass-paste, rock-crystal, and other substances, the eyebrows and nipples were picked out with fine applications of silver.

The chasing was of fundamental importance for the artistic impression created by bronze. The expert sculptors of this period had complete mastery of this technique, and were skilful enough to select those metal alloys which facilitated its execution. The art of chasing was of such importance for the Greeks that they gave the name 'toreutike', or chasing, to this whole category of sculpture, and its practitioners were 'toreutai'. Chasing brought out the metallic character of the bronze, nor was this obscured by subsequent treatment with acids or other means, the purpose of which was to create a flat surface.

The use of models of less valuable material gave artists greater freedom in experimenting and was certainly one of the most important factors leading to liberation from the old law of frontality.

In his *Natural History* Pliny the Elder has assembled a great deal of information regarding the first generation of bronze-casters. The discovery of the Samians, Rhoecus and Theodorus, soon won a foothold in Greece proper, and the flourishing commercial city of Aegina, along with Sicyon, near Corinth, became the centre of the leading schools. The bronze-caster Kanachos worked in Sicyon. His most famous work was the statue of Apollo Philesios at Didyma, outside Miletus. This shrine was devastated by the Persians in 494 B.C., and the statue was carried away to Persia to be returned to its original home some two hundred years later by Seleucus I.

We are here faced with one of the difficulties of method in the study of classical art. The ancient literary tradition provides us with a whole list of names and statements regarding different connections between schools, but the original works of the masters they mention are lost; the few statues which have been securely identified as copies of the works of the great masters are often of a mean and uninformative character. We cannot however omit them from any account of ancient art and concentrate solely on the preserved originals, for that would mean that we exclude precisely those artists of most importance for the development of art. Fortunately a number of original works survive, though their creators usually cannot be determined. The quality of their technical execution must, however, be the yardstick with which the lost work of the masters must be judged. Sculpture in marble and the minor arts, in metal and terracotta also provide us with additional means of enriching our picture.

In Kritios' Figure of a Youth from the Acropolis (Plate 38) which belongs to the period immediately before the Persian destruction of the Acropolis in 480, we see for the first time that the weight of the body does not rest equally on both legs. It is carried by the left leg, while the right is advanced and takes only a part of the burden. The left half of the body is taut, while the muscles of the right are slightly loose, and the right hip has dropped. The head is slightly turned to the right. The feet are missing in fact, but we can be certain that the soles of the feet rested firmly on the ground. The external, formal scheme has been replaced by an internal cohesion. The stance is no longer imposed; it has been deliberately chosen, and henceforth becomes the main medium of the characterization of the subject.

After the fall of the tyrants in Athens, Harmodios and Aristogeiton, who had a few years previously murdered one of Pisistratus' two sons, were given the extraordinary honour of statues on the acropolis of Athens, by which they were raised to the stature of heroes These statues, which were the work of Antenor, were carried away by Xerxes to Susa. When the Persians departed new statues were hastily made. Kritios and Nesiotes were commissioned, and their work was dedicated as early as 476. The two youths are portrayed in action, rushing forward with long strides. Harmodios has lifted his arm to strike, while Aristogeiton stretches out his left arm to protect his brother. The torsos do not fully participate in the movement; they are vertical, the stomach muscles drawn in, the torsos stretched. The features are given in simple, large lines. The short-cut hair covers the head like a thick skull-cap, and the lay-out of the brow and the cheeks is large and simple. Individualization goes only so far as to portray Aristogeiton with a full beard, while Harmodios is clean-shaven.

Among the draped figures from the first part of the transitional period some of the Korai from the Acropolis are noteworthy; they are contemporary with the Youth of Kritios. Particularly to be noted is one dedicated by Euthydikos. The drapery is rendered with a greater attempt at simplicity than in her sisters' figures, her mouth has a serious expression, and her gaze is turned inward. A figure of a boy with long fair hair is one of the most attractive objects from the Acropolis (Plate 41). His features are stamped with a still and expressive melancholy.

It was in single statues of individuals, in which no action was represented, that this introspective attitude found expression. Figures portraying action, such as the Tyrant-Slayers or the numerous representations of adventures from sagas, are more extrovert. This is true of the most important group-compositions that survive from the first third of the fifth century, the pedimental groups from Aegina, most of which are in Munich. These portray battle-scenes. In the centre stands the goddess Athena, watching over the struggle. The earlier, western pediment from shortly before 490 portrays the old theme of two warriors fighting over the corpse of a third, which is repeated twice beside the central figure. The corners of the pediment are occupied by fallen figures, while the space as far as the corners is filled by kneeling spearmen and bowmen. The artist has thus succeeded formally in solving the difficult problem set by the triangular form of the field; but the solution has been effected at the cost of the unity of the action. The whole has had to be divided into smaller groups, and the fighters of each party are held together only by the direction in which they fight. The sculptor of the later eastern pediment has matched up to his difficulties better than his predecessor at the western end. A fallen warrior from the west side is drawing a spear out of his wound without losing his Archaic smile. In the eastern pediment we see a bearded warrior, trying vainly to raise his trunk with the support of his shield; his features express a quiet controlled pain. The art of the period could and would go no further in the portrayal of feeling. A loud cry of pain or a triumphant cry of joy would have broken the style.

The Homeric heroes shrieked and laughed, and rarely controlled their feelings; but in Archaic Greece a new discipline of life had grown up: the civic spirit had acquired civic discipline, and it was in this soil that Pindar's deep religiosity and Aeschylus' mighty tragedies grew up. The restraint in the representation of the fallen and wounded in the east pediment increases the impression of youthfully conquering force and tension in the figure of Heracles shooting his bow.

We have already noted how the new spirit is reflected in two sculptures from the Acropolis (Plates 38 and 41). A further consequence of its triumph was that the Ionic dress with its numerous artificial pleats and folds was increasingly abandoned in draped sculpture in favour of the Doric peplos with its larger forms and heavier fall of drapery. As an under-garment under the woollen mantle the Ionic chiton of a finer material, knotted over the shoulder to form sleeves, retained its popularity. A noticeable effort is made by the sculptors to distinguish the various materials.

The Delphi Charioteer (Plate 46), is one of the most splendid discoveries of the French excavations in the sanctuary of Apollo. The statue was discovered near its original position not far from the entrance to the temple. It stood, together with another statue, on a chariot with an associated team of four horses. An inscription tells us that the whole group was a gift of a prince of Syracuse in about 470, when that city was in the hands of the family of the great Gelon. The exaggerated length of the lower part of the figure is due to the fact that they were represented on a chariot, the bar of which concealed the lower part from the viewers below. The Ionic chiton, which formed part of the charioteer's traditional dress, is gathered in by a girdle which forms a division between the almost columnar lower part of the body, and the upper part in which the representation of the folds is freer. This is fundamentally the same contrast between the supporting and the supported element as in the female figure from Auxerre (Plate 21), but what life and richness the figure has acquired! The young man has no other thought than to drive; his whole being is concentrated on his one task. The dome-shaped head assembles the whole work to a unity which the spiral locks at the temples are not enough to disrupt. The naturalism of some details, the sinews and veins of the arms, and the thin angular feet form a contrast to the firmness of the whole figure, and thus enables its completeness to stand out with absolute clarity.

A later discovery yielded a bronze original which is superior even to the Charioteer. In 1928 fishermen off Cape Artemision chanced upon various fragments of sculpture including the statue of a bearded god, with his left arm stretched out in front of him and the right stretched behind him, as if he was hurling some object (Plate 44). This may have been a trident or a thunderbolt: the statue thus represents Zeus or Poseidon. It is not only the strength of this muscular giant that is so wonderful. His strength has been subordinated to a unifying and curbing law, which lies within his own will. The mighty figure is surmounted by a head the simple, large form of which unifies the whole work to an expression of controlled virility. The extraordinarily complete chasing contributes very greatly to the impression created by the work.

The Sculptures on the Temple of Zeus at Olympia

The greatest sculptural work of the early Classic, 'severe' style is that from the temple of Zeus at Olympia. The eastern and western pediments of this temple were filled with groups of sculpture like the temple at Aphaia on Aegina. In addition, the six metope-fields on each short side of the cella were filled with high reliefs portraying Heracles' Twelve Labours. With the exception of a few fragments of metopes all these sculptures are in the Museum at Olympia. Their style is simple, but a development towards greater freedom in composition is discernible from the east to the west metopes, and thence through the east pediment to the western, with its magnificent figure of Apollo and daringly assembled groups (see Plates 36, 39 and 42).

As compared with the Aeginetan sculptures the forms of the bodies are softer and more rounded. The weight and completeness of the figures are due to the unified and collective treatment of the surface. The composition is rhythmically balanced. On the metope which portrays Atlas three figures stand upright side by side; they form a parallel to the vertical triglyphs which frame them. In others of these reliefs, particularly those on the west side, this harmony with the surroundings has been replaced by an attempt to achieve a contrast with the frame; the main lines cross the panel diagonally, first of all uncertainly and cautiously as in the 'Augeas Metope' on the east side, and then with complete mastery in the portrayal of Heracles' struggle with the bull, in which the powerful figure of the hero crosses diagonally over that of the rearing bull. In the 'older' metopes the play of lines, along with the weight of the figures, has a decisive effect on the impression; the contours shift gently and without sudden breaks, and the folds of the drapery emphasize their direction; in the 'later' metopes the figures are more mobile.

The execution of the groups in the pediments is in many respects simple and summary, and the complaint has often been made that they are raw and lacking in care. This is, however, an unjustified accusation. The forms are simple but grandiose, and they are well-suited to their situation high up in the pediment, 53 ft. above the ground.

The choice of theme is significant. In the east pediment we see the race between Pelops and Oinomaus, which, according to the myth, was the origin of the Olympic Games. Oinomaus promised to wed his daughter to whomever defeated him in chariot-racing, but the stake was the life of the vanquished man. Oinomaus was defeated in this competition, and killed, and Pelops won his daughter and the kingdom. According to the usual version Oinomaus' death was due to the fact that his charioteer, bribed by Pelops, removed the pin which held the axle of one of the chariot-wheels.

The artist chose to portray the moment immediately before the competition, and not the excitement of the competition itself. The atmosphere is tense; the coming disaster already casts its shadow. The future victor, Pelops, is bending his head listening, while Oinomaus, with his head high and his mouth open, announces the cruel conditions of the contest. But his old seer, who alone knows the tragic outcome of the race, sits in a mournful posture with his head inclined and his hand supporting his chin.

Zeus, in whose honour the Olympic Games were held, stands in the centre, an extremely powerful figure. He is understood as being invisible to all the other figures in the pediment. According to the most satisfactory view of the grouping of the figures in the pedimental field, Zeus has on his right side Oinomaus, whose wife stands beside him and is balanced, on the other side of Pelops, by his daughter Hippodameia, for whose sake the contest is being held.

These five standing central figures, with their vertical lines, lend this pediment an undeniable elevation and grandeur.

Apart from the main figures, there are on either side their four-horse chariots with serving-men, seers and other secondary figures. Furthest in the corners lie a pair of powerful figures of youths, as representatives of the river-gods of the site of the competition.

In contrast to the east pediment, which portrays a concentrated, dramatic excitement, the west pediment is full of life and movement. Its theme is as follows. The Centaurs had too much to drink at the wedding of the hero Peirithoos, and attempted to rape the women present. The bridegroom and his friend, the Athenian Theseus, at the head of Peirithoos' fellow-countrymen, the Lapiths, race to their assistance. A wild struggle followed. In the centre of the pediment stands a youthful God (Apollo) making an imperious gesture; he is here the god of order and culture, and looks with grief on the violence of the monsters. By his side the struggle rages, the Centaurs claw with their hands and hooves at the women's clothes and bodies, while the women use every means to defend themselves, and their male kin try to help them. Blow and counterblow, kicks and bites are exchanged. Far in the corners some recumbent women are anxiously watching the outcome, which can, however, no longer be in doubt: the presence of the god assures the onlooker that the forces of barbarism will be hurled back.

The idealism in the conception of the theme and the powerful ethos of the groups in no way exclude, as already noted, a very considerable realism in the details.

It has long been debated to what school the master of the Olympian sculptures belonged. The marble is Parian, and it has therefore been suggested that the work is the product of Ionian art. Others, having regard to the heroic character and simplicity of form, have thought of the Peloponnesian school. According to the statement of Pausanias, which is usually discredited, Alcamenes was the sculptor of the western pediment and Paionios of the eastern. Some Attic vase-paintings very closely resemble some of the groups of Centaurs on the western pediment. We know of another large monumental representation of the strife of the Lapiths with the Centaurs from the same period, namely Micon's painting in the temple of Theseus in Athens. The new spirit embodied in the work of the Olympian masters was especially at home in the new cultural centre of

Greece, Athens, where the painter Polygnotos executed most of his works.

Work in relief during this period closely followed painting. We see in it the same attempt to render figures in movement and at rest; the same progress in respect of the perspective of the body and in foreshortening, which is noticeable on vase-paintings. Most of these works are gravestones, in which the spiritual concentration, the calm air of melancholy resignation, characteristic of the art of this period, finds a new and important means of expression. The previous period, with its extrovert character, had been unable to produce gravestones portraying the same moving calm. In those days the figures had looked outward, whereas now they look inward or are occupied with an object which represents their daily life: a man plays peacefully with a grasshopper as he supports himself on his staff, a youth with a dog, a hare or a cock, a girl with a bird, a young married woman with the jewel-box she received on her wedding-day or will receive beyond the grave. Representations of this type are not found in Attica for several decades to come. The preserved examples appear mainly to have been executed on the Cycladic isles, rich in marble and inhabited by Ionians, especially Paros, and also Thasos. The formal traditions of the Archaic period lingered here in many places. The finesse and grace of execution make us forget that it was craftsmen and not epoch-making artists who made these works. Certainly, as already pointed out, the gulf between artists and craftsmen was less in antiquity than in the history of modern art; but nevertheless both in aristocratic Sparta and in democratic Athens the proud nobles would not recognize as their equal the man who lived by the work of his hands. With the development of monumental work in bronze, which presupposes a fairly comprehensive organization with numerous assistants, a sort of distinction arises between those whose imagination is engaged in discovering ever new and better forms of representation, and those who aim at keeping to traditional paths. Two classes may be distinguished among the grave-monuments. Within the Greek region, properly so-called, the stones were tall and narrow. In addition they were often crowned by a palmette, which was sometimes fashioned on its own, but was more frequently a direct continuation of the stone. This type is commonly called by the Greek name 'stele'. Among the finest examples of this class we may note two relief-portraits of women, now in Rome, in which the Ionian chiton is still preserved, a portrait of a young girl with a dove now in the Metropolitan Museum of Art, New York, and a woman with a little box in Berlin; both the latter are wearing the Doric peplos.

In Asia Minor Greek art penetrated triumphantly even among peoples of different nationality. Great men employed Greek artists to execute and decorate tombs of native type. In Phrygia, which lay in the inland part of Asia Minor, the graves were cut in the rock, in imitation either of houses or of sarcophagi, with the cover in the form of a roof. In Lycia, in the south-western part of Asia Minor, the graves were tall and cut out of the rock, and the upper part resembled a temple. The most striking example is the 'Monument of the Nereids' from the city of Xanthos, the reliefs of which are in the British Museum. The works commissioned were beyond the means of private persons in Greece, but one has the impression that the artists employed were not the most distinguished; their work is marked by a certain haste in execution.

The most distinguished works in low-relief in the 'severe' style are the 'Throne-Reliefs' in the Ludovisi Collection and in Boston. They were both found in Rome; some Roman connoisseur and collector, possibly the historian Sallust who once owned the region where they were found, had them brought from their original place in a Greek city, probably Locri in South Italy, and decorated his park with them. Their original use has been the subject of much discussion, and no certain solution has been reached. In the centre of the Ludovisi Throne a goddess (Aphrodite) is rising from the sea (Plate 47). On the right side-piece a woman is portrayed in mantle and veil performing a sacrifice; on the left a naked woman is sitting and playing the flute.

The body of the goddess on the Ludovisi Throne emerges with admirably fine modelling under the fine Ionian chiton. Her head is turned wholly in profile, and she gazes upwards with shining face at one of the Horai, who help her to rise from the water. Her body is presented frontally; her breasts are directed slightly sideways, an Archaic error in draughtsmanship which is also to be seen in some contemporary painting. The whole group breathes a fresh and chaste sensuality, which reminds one of the best work of the Italian Quattrocento. On the Boston Throne the main figure is Eros, who is weighing two male figures on a balance the arms of which were added in metal. He stands between two sitting women, one of whom manifests joy, the other sorrow, at the result of the weighing (Plate

45). On the side-reliefs were the ages of life, represented by a young man and an old woman.

That great importance must also be attached to the work of Greek artists in the colonies on the shores of Sicily and Italy is shown by various works, particularly by the magnificent Archaic reliefs from the Heraion at the mouth of the Seler, and by such a significant work as the statue of a sitting goddess, in the Berlin Museum, and usually assigned to a west Greek master; it is slightly older than the Ludovisi Throne. The sculptures on some of the Sicilian temples, in particular that of Selinus, are also noteworthy examples of a west Greek art which had its own particular character.

ii Vase-Painting

In the absence of paintings on walls and canvases we must follow the development of painting mainly on vases. Here, too, the main interest was bestowed on the representation of individual figures. The artist concentrated attention round the problems which the body in movement and at rest created. The emergence of painters such as Euphronios at the end of the sixth century marks a new stage. His earlier work actually belongs chronologically to the Archaic period, but since his activity continued for several decades in the fifth century he and his contemporaries are considered here. From the formal aspect, the decades around 510 were a decisive period for painting, though the spirit of the Archaic period survived longer among vase-painters than among statuarists.

The artists attempt to reproduce twists of the body, and to portray different parts of the body in foreshortening; individual objects are sometimes shown in oblique perspective. Study of detail is pushed still further. In the face, however, which is portrayed from the side, the eye is first placed as if seen from the front; artists then gradually learnt to set the iris nearer the bridge of the nose and to distinguish the upper and lower contour-lines in the inner corner of the eye so that the eye is portrayed wholly in profile. The best artists had reached this stage by about 470.

Lively battle-scenes alternate with peaceful scenes. The adventures of the heroes take turns with scenes from everyday life. Feasts and drinking-parties with hetaerae play a leading part. Dionysus and his following of drunken satyrs and playing and dancing maenads constituted one of the most popular motifs on these vases.

Although ancient literature is entirely silent about vase-painting no branch of Greek art is so well known as Attic vase-painting from the emergence of the 'red-figure' style until the middle of the fifth century. Many tens of thousands of vases are preserved, many of them of the highest artistic value. Through the signatures on the vases we know the names of hundreds of people who were involved in this craft. The signatures are of different types: 'X painted me' (in Greek, 'egrapsen'), 'X made' (epoiesen), 'X made and painted', and 'X made and Y painted'. The signature with *epoiesen* describes the fabricant, in whose workshop different artists worked, but it is natural that the head of the workshop also sometimes participated. It also happens that the same artist worked for different workshops.

Another important group of inscriptions on the vases is that of the names of public favourites. They normally have no direct connection with the subject of the painting. We encounter, for example, 'Miltiades (is) fair', *kalos*, 'Leagros fair', or simply, 'Leagros', 'Glaukon', 'Panaitios' and others. They are presumably the names of popular young Athenians. Sometimes we find women's names, but these cannot be the names of the daughters of patricians, who passed their days in the seclusion of their homes, but of hetaerae who were familiar within the circles in which people enjoyed themselves. Some of these members of the *jeunesse dorée*, to whom homage is paid on the vases, played a leading role in society in their maturity, and on this basis attempts have been made to determine their age and the period at which they can have been the object of homage from the creators of drinking-vessels. For example, the name Hipparchos probably refers to the tyrant who was murdered in 514. Consequently the vases which carry his name were painted at the latest in that year. Others of these public favourites have also been identified, and a chronology of the vases has thus been constructed.

Apart from Euphronios, to whom reference has already been made, Epiktetos the second, the Cleophrades-painter (Plate 69) and Euthymides, who worked in the studio of Euphronios and is perhaps identical with him, are conspicuous at this time. Euphronios' painting of Heracles' duel with Antaeus on a crater, in Paris (Plate 67) represents the high-water mark of vase-painting in regard to penetrating detail and characterization of the contrasts between the two opponents. The master has here achieved shading and colour effects by means of attenuation of the glaze. In the decorative sureness of his slender and finely drawn figures the Berlin-painter (Plate 70) beats all rivals, of whom Douris is the best known, though in boldness of temperament he is inferior to the Brygos-painter, who is pre-eminent in Dionysiac scenes (Plate 71).

By the end of this period the painters are masters of the representation of the human exterior. Oblique stances and foreshortening no longer present insuperable difficulties. The artists had prepared the way for a new sphere of activity: the portrayal of man's inner world.

Polygnotos

Ancient authorities tell us that Polygnotos of Thasos created a new epoch by his art. He is indeed regarded simply as the father of painting in general. Aristotle refers to his work when he wishes to express the concept 'ethos', elevated temper of mind, which he denies to Polygnotos' successors. He discovers in the Thasian painter's work the same temper which he finds in the tragedies of Aeschylus and Sophocles. The great impression made by Polygnotos' work can be read in the long descriptions given by Pausanias of his works at Delphi, which are only paralleled by the same author's accounts of Phidias' two greatest statues. Pliny gives a brief characterization of him in which he informs us that Polygnotos was the first to paint womens' clothes in transparent style, to give them head-dresses of changing colours and to introduce other novelties (such as portraying his characters with their mouths open, and revealing their teeth), and to substitute greater mobility for the rigidity of an aged face. These details cannot be correct. Most of these characteristics were familiar to vase-painters a generation before Polygnotos. He is also said to have represented the ground with curving lines and so arranged the figures that it was evident which stood in front and which further away. This is clearly the first step towards a perspective of space; it was evidently effected by means which, so far as we can judge from contemporary monuments, were insufficient to create a genuine illusion. Above all, however, Polygnotos is eminent as the painter of character. He chooses not the moment of action, but of deliberation and reflection: in the assembly-hall (lesche) of the Cnidians at Delphi a magnificent painting of his showed the Greeks and the Trojans the day after the conquest and destruction of the city. Another painting in the same room portrayed the visit of Odysseus to the Underworld. In Plataea there was a painting by him of Odysseus after his victory over the Suitors. We do not know what this looked like, but the subject shows us that it did not reproduce the scene of strife, but rather the calm that came after it. In Athens he collaborated with Micon in the ornamentation of the Theseum and of the Stoa Poikile, a promenade-hall in the Market-place, for which a brother-in-law of the general Cimon paid. In the latter building Phidias' brother, Panainos, also collaborated. While Polygnotos portrayed the Greeks after the destruction of Troy, Micon painted the victory of the Athenians over the Amazons, and Panainos the battle of Marathon. In the shrine of the Dioscuri Polygnotos portrayed their espousal with the daughters of Leucippus, that is, the event which followed on the kidnapping of the women, not the rape itself. Micon for his part preferred to portray battle-scenes; apart from the battle with the Amazons we hear also of a scene of Theseus' struggle with the Centaurs, painted in his Athenian temple which was founded in 475.

Polygnotos was certainly the most important of these artists. His colour-range was archaically simple: black, red, white and yellow-ochre, but by mixing these he achieved a number of intermediate tones; he also painted bodies gleaming from the water, and shining through clothes. His attempt to give a sort of space-perspective led him also to develop the background as a concrete reality. A number of vase-paintings show figures grouped on curved ground-lines, one above the other. On others we observe a new attempt to characterize materials; this is particularly evident on some Amazon-Vases, probably inspired by Micon's painting.

Polygnotos was a native of the Ionian island of Thasos, and it is recorded that his father Aglaophon was also a painter, and his son's teacher. But Polygnotos' art was wholly impressed with the spirit of his age. It was he who made painting a part of culture. Previously painting had consisted of coloured drawing and exterior decoration. He was the first to discover some of the especial potentialities of this branch of art. Athens became the centre of his activity and he there founded the mainland school of painting. His activity there can be followed for three decades, from the '70s to the '40s of the fifth century.

The style of composition of the school of Polygnotos is illustrated by a large crater from Orvieto, now in Paris (Plate 72), in which a number of standing, sitting and reclining figures are represented in different planes.

The representation of space in individual items in small compositions is best illustrated by Sotades' vase-paintings, which are painted
in various opaque colours on a white field, and portray bushes,
trees and flowers alongside the figures.

3. THE CLASSIC AGE
THE PERIOD OF ATHENIAN SUPREMACY (460–430)

The Persian War had ended advantageously for the Greeks,
thanks to Athenian sea-power, and it was now Athens that not only
thrust forward into the leading position among the Greek states, but
also built up an empire in the islands and on the shores of the
Aegean Sea. She even won a foothold in Egypt and on Cyprus off
the coast of Syria, but in about 460 she was checked by an attack
from Sparta and other cities of the mainland which felt Athenian
supremacy to be a threat against their own independence. Shortly
after 450 the political situation was stabilized by agreements both
with Persia and with neighbouring Greek states. Athens, led by
Pericles, had the opportunity to consolidate her own position, but
refrained from expansion further east.

Athens now became the cultural and economic centre of the whole
of Greece. The old centres of culture in Ionia had suffered greatly
under the Persian yoke, and only slowly recovered their strength.
The Athenians completely supplanted the old commercial cities and
operated a deliberate commercial and customs policy which drew all
trade to the Piraeus. It was of some significance that the tribute which
Athens's subjects paid as a contribution to the common fight against
the Persians, was used for the beautification of the new capital.

Artists from all parts of the Greek world were now drawn to
Athens. Poets and story-tellers here found their most appreciative
audiences; here the possibilities of cultural enlightenment were
greater than elsewhere.

Along with the development of external power there had come a
democratization of the constitution, so that the old distinctions
between class and rank disappeared from political life. Isonomia—
the equality of all before the law—was one of the Athenian ideals.
Their victories had awoken in the people as a whole and in the
individual citizen a self-consciousness which soon yielded to nothing.
The philosophical critic who directed his attacks against all that was

old-fashioned and out of date, against gods and society, and set the individual critical intelligence as judge over right and morality, found willing hearers in Athens, though this development acquired a more general importance in the later part of this period.

Those who had experienced Xerxes' attack were full of gratitude to the gods for their miraculous aid. The religious mood of this generation is best represented by Sophocles, who portrays the supremacy of the gods and the transitoriness of human happiness in a gripping and magnificent manner. The critical attitude of the following generation found prime expression in Euripides' dramas, in which doubt about accepted ideas is associated with profound psychological analysis. The historians exhibit the same contrast between the two generations. Herodotus depicts the Persian War as a background for Athenian greatness; for him events are determined by the dispensation of the gods and of fate, but he is by no means lacking in a critical sense regarding individual historical details. Thucydides, on the other hand, describes the heroic story of Athens in the last struggle for supremacy. He depicts how Athenian superiority in the spiritual sphere was so great that only when an Athenian—Alcibiades —wrought great harm to his fatherland, and thus showed its enemies how best they might harm it, did that city succumb to superior force.

The sources for our knowledge of art are also more plentiful now. In particular Pliny in his *Natural History* discusses the classic masters of bronze-casting, marble sculpture and painting, using as his sources writers on the history of art who gave expression to notions emanating from the school of Aristotle. We also have topographical descriptions, of which that of Pausanias, written between A.D. 160 and 180, is the most important. Further, since so much artistic production commemorated victories at the Olympic Games, the lists of the winners at the games are very important for the determination of chronology. Among the inscriptions found in excavations there are, in addition to dedications and signatures, more detailed texts. In Athens in particular it became customary to inscribe the more important popular decrees and the audits of financial officials, together with a summary of accounts, on stone stelai which were erected in a consecrated place. The Acropolis has been a rewarding site for such epigraphical discoveries. As fixed chronological points we have the temple of Zeus at Olympia, which was consecrated in 456, and the Parthenon, which we know from the preserved frag-

Art in Greece

ments of accounts to have been constructed during the period 448–432. We possess decrees of the Athenian people from 448 and 420 regarding the building of the Temple of Nike. The Caryatids of the Erechtheion were erected in 410, and the balustrade round the Temple of Nike in 405–404. We also possess further chronological indications in some dated reliefs of the three last decades of the fifth century.

The spiritual content of the art of the High Classic period is a direct continuation of that of the immediately preceding period. The artist learns how to portray expressive figures and associates with them a rich and flourishing style in drapery with strong ornamental effects.

i Classic Architecture

After the collapse of the Mycenaean princes the remains of their castles still stood as the objects of wonder to subsequent, poorer generations, but it was many centuries before the Greeks reached a level of economic and social prosperity at which they could afford to create architectural works of a monumental character. The ultimate impulses still come from the east, and it was during the period of oriental influence that Greek architecture began to develop. But in its formation the Greeks held fast to their own traditions.

The typical architectural creation of the Greeks is the temple. It was only the dwelling of the gods which was in the first place deemed worthy of this form. When later on it was desired to bestow a beautiful form on other types of buildings, the architecture of the temple provided the necessary repertoire of forms.

Two different styles (or orders) developed within the Greek world: the Ionic and the Doric. These derive from different constructional pre-suppositions, and each develops its own particular repertory of forms. The Corinthian style forms a variation of the Ionic, and will be discussed in a later context.

The Doric Order

The forms of the Doric temple achieved their distinct and fully considered form only after many generations of common labour. The different types of cella can be seen in Figure 25. The temple '*in antis*' is quite simply the primitive megaron-type in its simplest

107

In Antis

form. In the temple of Apollo at Thermos and that of Hera at Olympia, and also in the earlier temple of Hera at Samos, the cella is very long and narrow. When it was found necessary in larger temples to employ supports for the inner roof, they were first set in the central axis of the building. Subsequently this arrangement is matched by an odd number of columns on the short sides of the peristyle, as at Thermos and in the 'Basilica' at Paestum, which has nine columns in the front. It later became customary to construct double inner colonnades, which did not conceal the statue of the god at the back of the cella.

The relation between the peristyle and the cella-building was thus particularly varied in early times. The cella might be set more or less far back within the surround of columns, and the distance between its long walls and the columns was not a matter of rule.

The Classic Doric peripteros-temple is a finely thought-out creation, of which from the outset the essential elements were conceived as executed in stone, although there doubtless are reminiscences of earlier stages in wood. At an earlier period, however, the outer edge of the roof was protected with a coloured terracotta covering, and the acroterion was also of this material. The temple of Hera at Olympia had an acroterion in the form of a segment of a circle, the diameter of which was $6\frac{1}{2}$ ft. This temple originally had wooden columns which were gradually replaced with stone ones. In about A.D. 160 Pausanias tells us that one wooden column still survived at that date.

As long as the upper structure was of wood and terracotta, a few standing wooden columns were sufficient. But when architects began to build temples of stone—the terracotta roof-tiles were already replaced by stone plates in the sixth century—they first set the columns very close together and made them of unexampled thickness.

The stability of the individual columns was assured by making them taper upwards, and the capitals were made wide to enable them to support the weight of the architrave. The capital itself was of such a form that it, as it were, concentrated the weight from above on the neck of the column. In old temples like that of Apollo at Corinth and that of Hera at Olympia the echinos is shaped like a squashed cushion, but its profile becomes increasingly sharp, and its curve increasingly taut until it achieves its finest form in the so-called 'Temple of Poseidon' at Paestum and the Temple of Zeus at Olympia, which represent the climax of the severe Doric style.

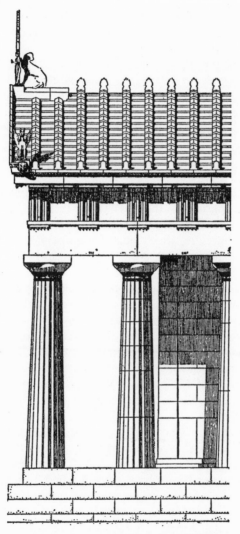

FIG. 31 'Corner-Contraction'. Because of the 'conflict of Triglyphs' the distance between the columns nearest the corners is necessarily less than that between the others. The result is that the corner column is not placed centrally beneath its triglyph. From the Temple of Aphaia on Aegina, around 490 B.C

Most of the older Doric temples have been destroyed in earthquakes or by human hands. In Athens, apart from the Parthenon, there survives only the temple of Hephaestus, previously called the Theseun. In the western Greek world, in Sicily and south Italy, large-scale ruins survive at Paestum, Selinus and Acragas, which give an immediate impression of the harsh grandeur of the Archaic and Classic Doric style.

On the summit of the Athenian Acropolis stands the most perfect of all Doric temples, the Parthenon. Here all the possibilities of the style have been exploited to achieve a masterpiece, which is at one and the same time rich and harmonious. The architects Iktinos and Kallikrates certainly also employed means which properly belong to the Ionic style to consummate their creation, but its Doric character is nevertheless clearly expressed in all parts which are significant for the overall impression.

The Parthenon (see Plate 77) draws attention to itself from whichever side one approaches. It seems as if the temple had grown out of the living rock, so naturally does it stand in its place. This is typical of Greek architecture, which smoothly accommodates itself to its natural surroundings, so that a happy balance is achieved between the work of art and its environment.

The best general impression of the Parthenon as an architectural whole is to be gained from immediately in front of the main entrance to the Acropolis, the Propylaea, whence one can see both the west pediment, which is better preserved than the eastern, and the north side. Thanks to intelligent restoration the latter now presents a whole and unbroken contour. The columns which were overturned by the explosion of 1687, when a Venetian army besieged the city, have now been re-erected. Some fragments of the roofing survive at the west pediment.

The Parthenon is a peripteros, i.e. surrounded by a colonnade on all sides. On the short sides there are eight columns, on the long seventeen. The temple is 193 ft. long and 102 ft. wide.

The building stands on a base which is raised from the ground by three steps, which stand in a precise relationship to the size of the temple, and disregard the span of the normal human step. On the Parthenon the step is over 1½ ft. high and of the same width. Outside the entrances steps of normal size were inset in the larger variety. By means of these three steps the temple is set off and raised from the ground. The base in its turn rests on a foundation of limestone, the stereobate, which extends down to the living rock and was concealed below the ground. All parts of the building above ground-level are of Pentelic marble, the warm golden tone of which contributes very markedly to the beauty of the temple.

The base with its steps not only raises the building above the surroundings; it also gives it an air of firmness and calm. The highest course, the stylobate, carries the columns, which have no bases of their own, and reach a height of nearly 35 ft. Their vertical channels, twenty to each column, emphasize the vertical elevation, and break the uniformity of the external surfaces. The channels are indeed shallow, but they are bounded by knife-sharp edges which form firm boundaries between bands of shade and of light on the shafts of the column. The columns themselves taper noticeably upwards. This contraction is more marked in the upper than the lower parts of the columns. It creates a curved line so that the columns from the middle downwards seem to have a slight swelling like that of a stretched muscle (entasis); their appearance thus becomes elastically taut, and the perspective of the colonnades acquires a wealth of subtle nuances.

The supreme expression of the function of the columns is, however, the capital. From the narrow upper part of the column, the neck, the capital rises upwards in a bowl-shaped section, the echinus. Its lower part is encircled by three fine horizontal lines, which as it were bind the column together to increase its supporting capacity. The contour of the echinus bends like a steel spring under the weight, first obliquely upwards, and then turns in a gradual curve upwards until at the top it is quickly drawn up. The uppermost part of the capital is in the shape of a rectangular plate, the abacus, which serves to form the transition to the architrave and the roof.

The upper part of the temple is much more elaborately executed than the lower. On the capitals rests the entablature, which consists of architrave and frieze. These two elements are separated by narrow projecting ridges. The frieze consists of triglyphs and metopes; the former are rectangular plaques with vertical channels, the latter are square and are indented in the angles of the triglyphs. On the Parthenon all the ninety-two metopes are decorated with figures in high relief.

Above the metopes comes the roof proper, which begins with a projecting course on all sides, the geison, which goes round the entire building in the form of a long projecting horizontal band sending out branches on the short sides which follow the low angles of the saddle-roof. The roof is also surrounded by a vertical gutter, the sima, which carries water-spouts in the form of lion-heads on the long sides.

The pedimental fields (in Greek, aetos=eagle) are occupied by great groups of sculpture: see Plate 80. The roof was covered with marble plaques in the form of tiles, which rested on an inner architrave of wood. While the horizontal lines of the long sides stressed the element of repose in the building, on the short sides the pedimental form provided an innate aspiration to height. This vertical line is counteracted by the fact that the top angle of the roof is very obtuse. In addition, the remaining upward-aspiring dominating lines on the tops of the pediments are picked up by floral ornaments, the acroteria, which permitted the soaring tendency to terminate in an easy and airy rhythm. Other smaller acroteria on the corners contributed to the impression of complete balance. The central acroteria on the Parthenon were in the form of large acanthus tendrils with palmettes. They are noteworthy as the first datable examples of the employment of the acanthus pattern in decorative art.

If one stands at one of the corners of the Parthenon and looks down the length of the sides of the floor it can be seen that the normal rules of perspective, which are customarily found in a building of this size in a horizontal plane, are lacking. The floor is not wholly level; the corners are some inches lower than the centre of the floor. This is not the result of chance arrangement. Careful measurement has shown that the columns and architraves are adapted to this irregularity. It gives life and movement to the great surface of floor, and may also have had a practical end: the rain-water ran away more easily.

Although the building is as much as 65 ft. high it gives an impression of calm and repose. This impression is in part effected by the fact that all the columns lean slightly inwards towards the central axis of the building. This inclination is strongest in the corner-columns.

The temple structure proper is two steps higher than the colonnade. It is terminated on each short side by six columns, and is thus an amphiprostylos. The original Doric form has only two columns between the antae. The antae of the Parthenon reach only half-way along the sides of the entrance halls.

Entrance to the interior of the temple was effected from the entrance-hall by two gigantic doors. These doors were the only

71. Kylix from Vulci by the Brygos-painter, ca. 590 B.C., ht. 0·144m.

72. Apollo and Artemis slaying the children of Niobe. Kylix-krater by the Niobid-painter, from Orvieto, ca. 560 B.C., ht. 0·54m.

73. Funerary lekythos from Eretria, ca. 420 B.C., total ht. 0·39m.

74. Pelops and Hippodameia, from an amphora, ca. 410 B.C.

75. Head of horse, from the chariot of Selene, east pediment of the Parthenon.

76. Detail of Parthenon – frieze, north side.

77. Parthenon, west pediment with frieze of cella.

78. Centaur and Lapith. Metope from south side of Parthenon.

79. Dying Niobid, ht. 1·49m.

80. Goddesses from east pediment of the Parthenon.

81. The slaughtered Niobids, marble copy probably of the relief on the base of Phidias' statue of Zeus at Olympia.

83. Nike adjusting her sandal. From the railing round the terrace of the Temple of Nike on the Acropolis, ca. 410 B.C., ht. 1·06m.

◄ 82. The Assault, relief from the 'Monument of the Nereids' at Xanthos.

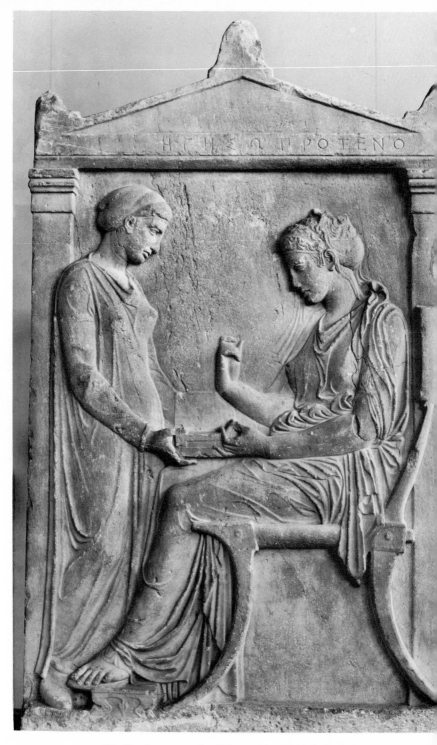

ΗΓΗΣΩ ΠΡΟΞΕΝΟ

84. The funerary stele of Hegeso, ca. 400 B.C., ht. 1·49m.

85. Bronze statue found in the sea off Marathon, ca. 340 B.C., ht. 1·3m. ▶

86. Heracles: detail from Scopas' pedimental sculpture of the Temple of Athena at Tegea. ht. from the snout of lion-skin to chin, 0·165m.

87. Plaster cast of amethyst cameo from Labraunda, ht. 0·032m.

88. Battle against the Amazons, probably the work of Scopas; detail of frieze from Mausoleum at Halicarnassus.

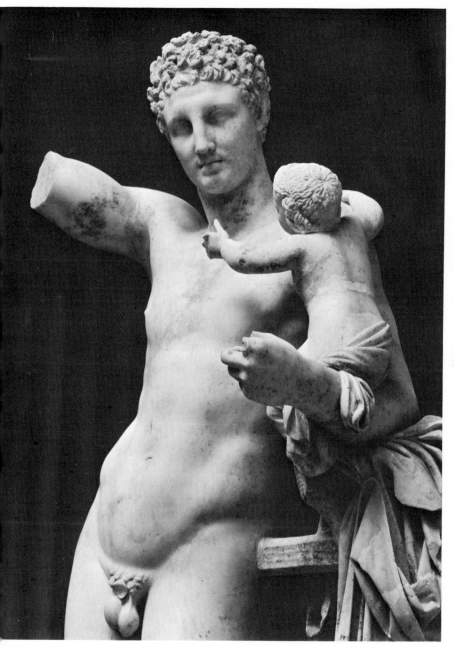

89. Hermes and the infant Dionysus, after Praxiteles, from the Temple of Hera in Olympia, ht. 2·15m.

90. Portrait-statue (of Maussollo[s])
from the Mausoleum at
Halicarnassus, ht. 2·75m.

91. Mausoleum at Halicarnass[us]
reconstruction of façade, by
Jeppesen. ▶

92. The sarcophagus of the
Mourning Women from Sidon.

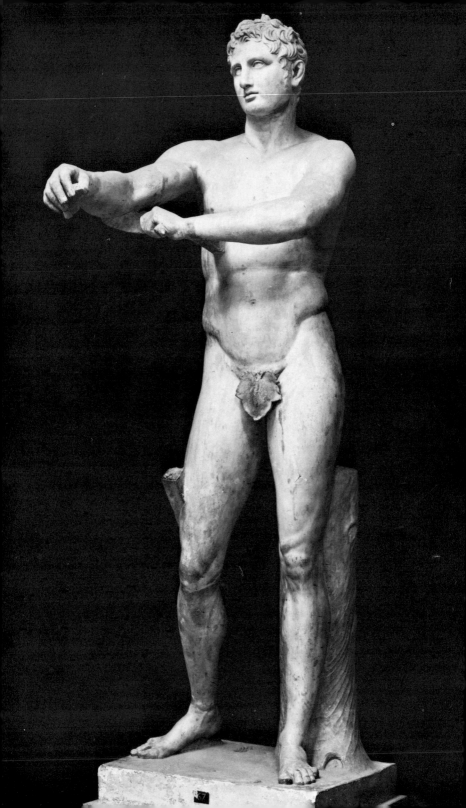

94. Grave stele from Ilissos, ca. 340 B.C., ht. 1·68m. The original architectural frame
is missing.

◄ 93. The 'Apoxyomenos' (scraper), Roman marble copy of Lysippos' bronze statue.

95. Sleeping satyr, the 'Barberini Faun', ca. 200 B.C., ht. 2·15m.

source of light; there were no windows. Although as a rule a Greek temple contained only one closed room, the Parthenon had two, wholly independent of each other. The larger of the two was to the east and formed the cella, with Phidias' great statue of Athena Parthenos, traces of the base of which can still be seen in the floor. The roof was of wood and divided into coffers. The inner colonnades, which formed an aisle round the interior of the cella, were Doric, and built into two courses, one above the other. This necessitated a horizontal architrave immediately above the half-way line of the room, the effect of which was to give the room greater cohesion. The columns thus appeared smaller, and the statue was brought into greater prominence. A comparison with the Temple of Zeus in Olympia shows that the architects of the Parthenon made a more deliberate effort to sustain the impression created by the statue of the deity. Phidias, the sculptor of the statue, was able to collaborate with the architects from the outset. In this respect the cella of the Parthenon represents a pioneer development in the history of Greek architecture.

The other room, according to the evidence of the inscriptions, was that which was actually called the Parthenon, the name which subsequently spread to the entire building. Its roof was supported by four Ionic columns, now wholly lost; the Ionic, being more delicate than the Doric, were more suited to internal use.

Round the cella, under the roof of the colonnade, ran the Ionic frieze which is the most famous part of the ornamentation of the Parthenon.

The effect of the decorative details was enhanced by the use of colours. The triglyphs on the Parthenon were blue, the ground of the metopes was red, and the drapery of the reliefs blue; the profiles which limited the triglyph-friezes on either side were also red. The tendency was to paint the upward-soaring parts in the upper part of the temple blue, and the horizontal, fluent parts, the details which expressed repose, red. The weightier elements in the construction, the columns and architrave, were unpainted.

A visually important part of the temple is the triglyph frieze, which runs round the entire building: see Plates 77 and 78. In comparison with the smooth architrave below, it constitutes a moving and lively element. Triglyphs and metopes are of the same size on all parts of the building. They thus form a regularly recurrent measure according to which the other parts of the building are

co-ordinated as in a set pattern. The triglyphs are placed above each
pillar and in the space between each pillar. To accommodate them
the distance between columns has been reduced at the corners
('corner-contraction': see Figure 31).

The Greek temple cannot be immediately associated with any
other building. It aspires to isolation just as much as the statues of
Polyclitus do. None of its sides dominates another. It was thought
at one time that the main entrance to the Parthenon lay on the west,
on the side of the Propylaea; in fact, however, it lay on the east, in
accordance with the general rule for Greek temples that the main
entrance should face the rising sun.

At first sight the Doric temple creates the impression of a simple
building with a row of vertical supports set between two horizontal
parts. In its fully developed form it is, however, a most subtly organized unity, all parts of which are formed according to the same
artistic laws. It is stamped with a harmony sufficient unto itself,
with a completeness which is a living expression of the moderation
of the Greeks. No lines project outside or above, nothing breaks the
impression of wholeness and completion. The temple bears its godhead within it, the statue, in which the god is thought to have his
being. The nature of the Greek temple is in absolute contrast to that
of the Gothic cathedral, which soars to the heights, as if it wishes to
annul all the laws of gravity and matter. By contrast the Greek temple
is the most sonorous expression of nature's own laws of equilibrium.
A Greek would have regarded it as hubris to attempt to storm the
heavens; he sought instead for the harmony of the universe and
created, according to the laws that he discovered, a complete plastic
likeness of a higher order of things.

It is not only the artistic form of the Parthenon which has aroused
the wonder of posterity: so also has its technical execution. The
ashlar technique is applied with extraordinary care. The joints
fit as tightly after 2,400 years as they did when they were new. Greek
builders did not employ mortar as a binding material. The column-
drums are held together by small pegs of wood, and the courses of
wall are kept in horizontal position by iron clamps. These were
mostly removed during the Middle Ages, which were in need of the
metal, and it is due to the quality of the work in stone that so much
of the building survives.

Art in Greece

The Ionic Order

The Ionic style of building is more directly inspired by oriental models than is the Doric. The differences are most apparent in the types of column and in the architrave: see Figures 26 and 29.

The Ionic column has a round base, the curved profile of which raises the column above the base-line of the building. Its flutings, usually twenty-four in number, are deeper and separated by wider edges. This column is markedly more delicate than the Doric. The capital is surrounded by a crown of hanging leaves or a 'kymation'. The taut-sprung part above this, with volutes falling down the sides, seems to have originated in the saddle-beam, which was set on wooden columns as a transition to the architrave. The architrave is divided into three horizontal bands, which diminish downwards, and thus create a much lighter impression than the massive Doric architrave. In Athens we find above the architrave a frieze decorated with reliefs, but this is normally lacking in later Ionic temples in the homeland of the style, Asia Minor; in its place there follows a row of dentils, which looks like a row of projecting beam-ends. Above this come the cornice and the sima as in the Doric order.

Reliefs may also be found in Ionic temples round the lower part of the columns and on the sima. Such is the case on the temple of Artemis at Ephesus.

Our knowledge of the earlier development of the Ionic style is largely derived from the great temples on Samos, at Ephesus and at Didyma south of Miletus. These had roofs above the colonnades only. The cella-walls surrounded an open court and stood, together with the outer hall of columns, on a high platform, to which a stairway led in the front. The Heraion at Samos had 123 large columns in the circular court and ten in the great open entrance-hall. The plan of the cella resembles that of a temple *in antis*.

The Aeolic style was related to the Ionian, but it was soon superseded by the latter. We know of forms of capitals, the volutes of which rise like calyxes of flowers vertically from the shaft of the column, and are thus closer to the Egyptian lotus-column and other oriental motives based on the lily, which can be seen in Babylon, Phoenicia and on Cyprus. The sima-reliefs on Ionian temples had predecessors of terracotta, such as were found in large numbers in the Swedish excavations on the acropolis of Larissa in the area north of

115

Smyrna. A capital of the Aeolic type was also discovered there: see Figure 27. The Siphnian Treasury in Delphi presents a perfect example of Ionic decorative architecture from the later part of the sixth century (cf. Figure 30 and Plate 32).

The Ionic style awoke to new life in Periclean Athens. The Erechtheion (see Figure 32), constructed during the Peloponnesian War, with its finely balanced decorative forms, was decisive for the future development of the style, and was even imitated in Asia. The

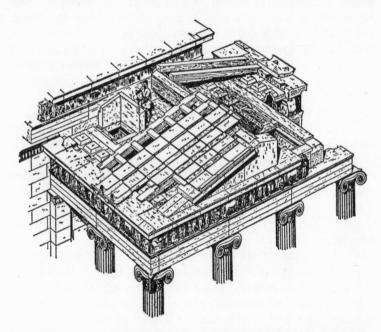

FIG. 32 Reconstruction of the roof-design of the North portico of the Erechtheion

Nereid Monument in Xanthos shows its influence. The decisive battle between the Doric and Ionic styles was fought in Athens. We have seen how the Ionic style penetrated the Parthenon. In the construction of the Propylaea its architect Mnesicles went a step further and interpolated Ionic columns in the inner part of the west hall, in front of the Doric façade.

The form of the Propylaea can also be regarded as an attempt to discover new ways in architecture. It was a portico which gave entrance to the Acropolis. A pair of wings projected on either side of the road, as it were to embrace and welcome the wanderer. When he entered the central hall, his eye was drawn up by the high Ionic columns; when he then passed the door-opening of the central wall, he saw through the eastern hall the whole Acropolis spread out before him. Mnesicles here created a living space, the impression created by which was altered as one advanced. The Propylaea represents an attempt to place a building in immediate contact with the exterior world, to embrace space instead of excluding it.

The art of town-planning was advanced by the great new construction of whole towns which was a consequence of the Persian War. Its most distinguished exponent was Hippodamos of Miletus, who constructed a plan for the Piraeus in the time of Pericles. Hippodamos' own city was also replanned at this period; after the old city was destroyed by the Persians, the new one was rebuilt on a better site. Hippodamos developed the system of streets lying at right angles to one another. The individual quarter consisted of an oblong rectangle. Certain quarters were left open, and thus became public places. The orientation of the street-plan took account of rational factors, such as the condition of the terrain and the direction of the prevailing winds. While Hippodamos' own book on the art of town-planning is almost entirely lost, a number of rules and indications on the theme are to be found in the writings of the doctor Hippocrates, who was active in the same century. Hippodamos' system was decisive for the development of city-planning right down to the Roman period. Priene, in Asia Minor, which was newly built in the time of Alexander the Great, presents the best-preserved example of its practical application: see Figure 33.

ii Myron

Like Phidias and Polyclitus, Myron is said to have been a pupil of the Argive bronze-caster Hageladas. He was an Athenian by birth, a native of Eleutherae, a village on the Attic frontier with Boeotia. His activity seems to have embraced the period from 480 to 440, to judge by the Olympic victors for whom he made statues. His works are said to have included the runner Ladas, on whose stone lips, it was reported, one could see the panting breath force its way out. Reliable copies of one of his works, a group of Athena and Marsyas, survive on a vase, in a little relief and also in statues. We hear also of figures of animals, among which that of a cow was particularly noted for its fidelity to nature. In addition, vessels in bronze or silver from the hand of Myron were highly prized in the Imperial period.

Myron prefers to portray figures in action. He is not content with a simple hasty movement forward as were Kritios and Nesiotes in the group of the Tyrant-Slayers; the movement is analysed, and the sculptor selects just those points at which it achieved its highest development. The Discobolus, 'The Discus-Thrower' (Plate 51), has just swung his discus as far back as possible so that at the next moment he can bring it forward in a curve and let his body follow through in a sweep. The composition is still in the style of a relief, and an Archaic rigidity is noticeable in certain anatomical details. The muscles of the trunk are flat and sharply distinguished from each other, but the powerful, swift movement is rendered with masterly skill.

For his Marsyas too the sculptor has chosen the moment in which a movement has reached its limit, to become the reverse action a moment later. The satyr recoils before Athena's repudiating gesture, when she forbids him to touch the pipes she has just cast aside. Both figures are clearly conceived to be looked at from only one angle, from which the whole movement can be easily comprehended. Athena's youth and charm and the subtle treatment of detail, which is evident even through the work of the copyists, refute many of the harsh judgements which ancient critics made concerning Myron's hard treatment of detail.

Myron brings the Archaic figure in movement to its final completion. He gives momentary pictures of events. His figures are concerned with what they are actually engaged in doing. While the figures created by his best contemporaries are full of meditation and quiet concentration, Myron's figures set about their task at once, and solve the problem—but they do no more.

iii Polyclitus

Tradition tells us that Polyclitus was also a pupil of Hageladas of Argos, though he was himself a native of Sicyon, where the art of bronze statue-making was at a very high level. He even moved to the city of his teacher and thus became the leader and greatest representative of the Argive school.

He was active after the middle of the fifth century. Towards the end of the century he executed a statue of Hera in gold and ivory for the new temple of Argos, which replaced that destroyed by fire in 423.

Polyclitus was a reflective artist; his greatness depends precisely

118

on his intellectual absorption in the mathematical problems, one might almost say, of the human form. For this reason his work possesses an internal firmness, and all later sculpture when portraying the human figure in its external appearance builds on his foundations. His aim was to seize not the casual elements in his model, but the elements which possess general validity for human stance and movement. He set down his theories about human proportions and on the technique of sculpture in a work entitled *Canon, The Rule*. The Doryphorus, the Spearsman (Plate 52), which posterity called 'The Canon', provides a synthesis of his art. A young man with a spear on his left shoulder has stopped still and stands at complete rest. The weight of the body rests on the right leg, and the hip is displaced to that side so that the centre of gravity will fall over the foot that carries the weight; the muscles of the trunk on the other side are gently flexed, and it is only on the left side that a certain tension is to be observed, caused by the light spear that rests upon it. A transverse positioning between the lines of strength is created, 'counterpoint', which gives life to the calm figure. All the details are carefully worked out, and the treatment of the hair is particularly characteristic: a thin 'calotte', or skull-cap, of delicately and fluently chased flat locks.

The Diadoumenos—he who binds a victor's wreath on his head—is softer and later than the Doryphorus, and completes the picture of Polyclitus' art. A gentle S-line goes through the entire figure and accentuates its rhythm.

The Argive master's statue of the Amazon has proved harder to identify than these statues of athletes. The problem has been continually discussed since there are three types of statue to choose from. Ancient sources record four contemporary statues of Amazons, including those of Polyclitus, Phidias and Cresilas. The most probable view is that which attributes the type of the 'Capitoline' Amazon, signed by the copyist Sosicles, to Cresilas, and the 'Mattei' to Phidias, while a third, in which the Amazon supports herself on a pillar (the 'Berlin' type), may be assigned to Polyclitus.

Antiquity spoke of 'statura quadrata' in connection with Polyclitus' work, referring thereby to its heavy proportions. But the expression can also be applied to his work in a different sense: he had not wholly liberated himself from the primitive quadrilateral technique of composition. His statues are constructed to be seen in a direct line from each of the four sides, and oblique views are not taken into account. But all the sides are carefully worked and balanced in themselves.

The influence of Polyclitus became enormous, not only through the Argive school, of which he was the second founder; it is already visible in his lifetime, for example in the sculptures of the Parthenon, and on vase-paintings.

iv Phidias and the Parthenon Sculptures

None of the sculptors of antiquity has received so much praise from posterity for his statues of gods as Phidias. The Roman writer Quintilian says that Phidias portrayed the gods in such a way that he added something new to the old religion. That religious outlook which saw the great ethical forces in the world of nature and of man embodied in the gods found its fullest expression in Phidias' work.

His personal biography is still in many respects obscure. He was a native of Athens, and is said to have been taught, like Myron and Polyclitus, by Hageladas of Argos. His activity was in the main transferred to Athens, but he also executed the great statue of Zeus for the temple of the god at Olympia, a statue of Aphrodite Urania for the city of Elis, and an Athena in Plataea. His great productivity is probably to be explained by the fact that his atelier contained many assistants and collaborators; Agoracritus, Alcamenes and Colotes are mentioned among his pupils. His brother, the painter Panainos, assisted him in his work on the statue of Zeus at Olympia.

Contradictory stories survive concerning the last stages of Phidias' life. According to one source he was prosecuted in Athens for embezzlement of the ivory issued for the statue of Athena Parthenos, and died subsequently in prison. Another source records that he went into exile, and died a prisoner in Elis. Plutarch states that Phidias assisted Pericles in the organization of the great building project on the Acropolis, and was immediately responsible for it. His name, however, does not occur in the preserved portions of the building accounts.

Even if it is true that the difference in style between the earliest sculptures in the metopes and the latest pedimental figures of the Parthenon is very considerable, the various stages nevertheless flow into each other in such a way that clear boundaries cannot be distinguished. Earlier stages of the style of drapery found in the pediments can be detected on some of the metopes and at many

120

points on the frieze. We are in fact in the presence of the work of a number of masters of different ages and ideas working under a common artistic leadership. The variations between the different schools gradually diminished as the work went on for sixteen years, and the magnificent drapery-style of the pediments is a result of this development. The lasting result of recent investigations seems to be that different parts, particularly the frieze, are the work of different hands. These investigations have also taught us a great deal about the method of work and about the fundamental differences between ancient and modern methods. The masters, who were directly responsible for the work, had considerable freedom not only in respect of details but also about the position of the figures and the treatment of perspective. It is evident that the leading sculptor gave his collaborators sketches and probably even models on a small scale, but these were not so mechanically reproduced as in more modern art; on the contrary, the individuality of the different sculptors had an opportunity to express itself.

A unified arrangement of the sides is already evident in the four rows of metopes. The theme is set—in the east, for example, the strife of the Gods with the Giants—the composition is unified, and there exists a balance between corresponding metopes. The north side is occupied with twenty-nine metopes containing the story of the destruction of Troy, bounded by the chariot of the rising sun in the east and that of the sinking moon in the west, and by three metopes with figures of gods. On the south side Theseus and the Lapiths are fighting the Centaurs (see Plate 78), on the west the Athenians strive with the Amazons. Only the metopes of the south side, and one of the north side are sufficiently well-preserved for stylistic comparisons to be possible. An older style of composition, which reminds one at times of Myron, and at times of other earlier works such as the west pediment of the temple of Zeus at Olympia, interchanges with a freer, more modern style, which characterizes both humans and beasts with feeling and ease. The height and width of the reliefs is about 4 ft.

Round the building, in front of the colonnade, ran the frieze, 524 ft. 2 ins. long and 3 ft. 2 ins. high. It represented the greatest of the festivals which Athens celebrated in honour of the goddess, the Great Panathenaea, which was held every four years, and on the occasion of which a peplos was brought to the goddess, woven by the noblest ladies of the city to clothe her primitive wooden statue.

In the middle of the eastern side we see the act of the presentation of the peplos to the priest; the scene is represented as taking place inside the temple. On either side of this scene sit six gods who look down from Olympus on the faithful people of Athens. The sitting figures are noticeably larger than the standing humans. On the outside of each group of gods are four elderly men, who are probably the legendary kings of Athens, and in addition some functionaries who await the procession, at the head of which are young women with offerings. On the long sides, we see the remainder of the procession with sacrificial beasts and other gifts. An important part of the festal procession consisted of racing-chariots, and more especially of horsemen, young men of leading Athenian families. These occupy about half of the frieze; the horses hurry forward with differently styled pacings and with an abundant variety of stances. On the west side the riders are in readiness to start, the horses are led out, some of them are rearing up, and some of the riders have mounted and begun the processional ride.

For the sake of artistic balance the humans here have been made relatively larger than the animals. Here and there riders race past one another; often they are so arranged that one partially conceals another. On the south side in particular the sculptor has tried to produce the impression of a closed group. The background is ideal, that is to say it does not attempt to give an impression either of a wall or of air; the figures speak for themselves by themselves. Artists and experts in horsemanship agree in giving the highest praise to the representations of the horses, which, in spite of the low relief, produce an impression of lively realism. Art has seldom portrayed in a single act such a blooming and handsome group of young men as here. The Doric ideal of youth, as we know it from Polyclitus, has been softened but not weakened in the milder spiritual climate of Athens.

While the metopes must have been completed by approximately 440, the work on the frieze may have lasted a few more years. This was followed by the work on the pediments, on which substantial sums were expended in 434 and 433.

The east pedimental group portrays the miraculous birth of Athena, when she springs fully armed from the head of her father Zeus, which Hephaestus opens with a blow of his hammer, and the reaction of the gods present to the wondrous event. The central group which contained Zeus, Athena and Hera, was already destroyed in the 1670's, when a Flemish artist made a sketch of what then remained of the pedimental figures together with some of the remaining sculptures of the temple. The scene is framed by the magnificent heads of the horses of the rising Sun God, and the plunging Goddess of the Moon. A goddess (Artemis?) hurries forward towards the spectator's left. Demeter and Persephone sit nearest to her and show their participation by gestures. Further off a youthful, handsome male figure, the so-called Dionysus, unconcernedly turns his back on them. His is the only head preserved. Far out in the opposite corner of the pediment there is a group of three goddesses, of whom two are sitting and the third (Aphrodite?), lies at full length, leaning with the upper part of her body on the knee of the one nearest to her. Her garments, and those of her companion, are so arranged that their beautiful shapes are visible without being exposed. The richly playing folds, which flow over the figures like ripples on water, reveal more than they conceal of the beauty of their bodies. But it is a beauty which befits the gods raised above the mortal sphere: see Plate 80.

The western pediment was better preserved than the eastern before the catastrophe which befell the Parthenon in 1687, and although it is now more damaged we consequently know its composition better by means of the drawings made at that time. Athena contends with Poseidon for dominion over Attica, and each strives to win the victory by valuable gifts and proofs of their power. Athena causes an olive tree to spring up and thereby becomes victor. In vain Poseidon strikes his trident in the rock with a mighty gesture, and calls forth a spring of salt-water. The treatment of the drapery in the west pediment shows a tendency towards a refined style; the figures are also enlivened by an unbelievable play of sharply defined folds.

In Athens three statues by the master were recorded: the Athena Lemnia and Athena Promachos of bronze, and the Athena Parthenos of gold and ivory, all on the Acropolis. The first of these portrayed the goddess without her helmet; we are fortunate enough to know it from two copies. They exhibit a softer and richer charm than that of Myron's Athena. The drapery is less stiff and richer in folds, and the bend of the head freer.

The statue of the Parthenos was dedicated in 438, after nearly ten years' work by the sculptor. It was conspicuous, as was the statue of Zeus in Olympia, for a prolific wealth both of material and of secondary artistic decoration. The goddess stood upright, wearing an Attic peplos. She stretched her right hand forwards and supported it on a pillar, so as to hold a figure of Nike which was 6½ ft. high but gave an impression of smallness beside the 33 ft. tall Athena. By the left side of the statue rested the shield, from beneath which crept out a large snake—there was always a sacred snake with its own shrine on the Acropolis. A lance stood on the ground, supported by the left shoulder of the goddess. The helmet bore three crests decorated with a sphinx and two griffins. On the outside of the shield was portrayed a battle between Greeks and Amazons, and on the inside the battle of the Gods and the Giants. Even the edges of her sandals were decorated with reliefs. On the front of the base Phidias carved the birth of Pandora.

A large number of copies enable us to form an impression of the statue. The best of the larger copies, though only one-sixth of the size of the original, is the 'Minerve au Collier' in the Louvre; the most complete is a statuette in Athens, only 3¼ ft. high, which is a dry and pedantic piece of factory-workmanship. The strength and beauty of the head shine most clearly in a sadly damaged head in Copenhagen, where there is also a copy of a scene from the battle of the Amazons on the shield, which can be identified as a copy of Phidias' work thanks to the find of similar copies in Piraeus. Cameos and some gold medallions provide important information about the decoration of the helmet.

Among Phidias' own work the statue of Zeus at Olympia was the most famous, although critics remarked that it was too large for the temple. Pausanias has left us a detailed description of it, and representations on coins of Elis give an impression of its appearance and style. When Phidias was asked how he found the inspiration for this statue it is said that he recited the lines from the *Iliad*:

> Thus spake Cronos' son, and bent his dark-hued brow,
> And the ambrosian hair round the god's immortal head
> Swung billowing forward; and all Olympus shook.

The naked parts of the statue were of ivory, the rest of gold plate on a core of wood. Fragments of the raw material and moulds for the details of the drapery have been discovered in the excavation of the building which was still pointed out as Phidias' workshop in Pausanias' time. From these discoveries we know that the statue of Zeus belonged to a later phase than the statue of Athena.

The god was represented seated on a throne. The height of the statue without its base was, according to the poet Callimachus (Iamb. VI) 42 ft. or 25 cubits, and traces of the base indicate that it was about 33 ft. deep and 19½ ft. wide. The height of the cella has been estimated about 46 ft. So Strabo—as R. Pfeiffer has pointed out—was right in saying that the image of Zeus, though seated, almost touched the roof with his head. On his right hand there stood a Nike, and in the other he held his sceptre. His gold mantle was decorated with figures of animals and lilies. His throne was covered with gold, precious stones, ebony and ivory, and bore a number of sculptured figures, reliefs and paintings, among them Apollo and Artemis slaughtering the children of Niobe with their arrows. The footstool under his feet was ornamented with reliefs, and the railing which surrounded the statue was decorated on three sides and ornamented with paintings by Panainos, the brother of Phidias. A number of reliefs of the Niobids, preserved in many variant forms, of which the best is in Leningrad, can be regarded as copies of the corresponding relief on the throne. The association is confirmed by the copies of figures on the shield of Athena Parthenos, found in the harbour of Piraeus, which are stylistically close to the Niobid relief in Leningrad.

Zeus' face was framed by curly hair and beard; his expression was stamped with such sublimity and gentleness that it was said that his gaze could give consolation in the deepest sorrow. This type of the father of the gods long preserved its power over the minds of men. It was adopted by a number of ancient sculptors, varied to suit the taste of time and special requirements, and found its last artistic form in the Byzantine figure of Christ. Thus the genius of Phidias has shone through the ages, borne by the work of other masters, even after his own work was destroyed.

Phidias' most important contribution lay in the new spiritual dimension which he gave his work. His figures of gods had an ethical sublimity which no previous sculptor could express.

In Classic art in its prime an image of man was created which was purified and liberated from all fortuitous elements. It aimed at creating its figures as they were in and for themselves, to use an expression which frequently occurs in Socratic philosophy. The figures are conceived independently of all external chance factors.

Art in Greece

The nature of the godhead itself was interpreted in the same way, and this was expressed in terms of the most sublime humanity. The great names of Polyclitus and Myron put all others in the shade during this period, but they had rivals who went their own ways. One of these was Cresilas, of whose work we know, apart from an Amazon, a portrait of Pericles, which portrays the great statesman in a stylized form as a general wearing a Corinthian helmet. One of the masters independent of those we have named created a group of dying Niobids, of which an original statue was discovered in Rome: see Plate 79. The fragile tone in the moulding of the young woman, who has been pierced by an arrow and sinks on one knee, is perhaps more moving than in any other Classic work.

THE FOLLOWERS OF PHIDIAS (430–375)

The outbreak of the Peloponnesian War in 431 marks a sharp break in the spiritual life of Greece. The old religious and political ideals disintegrated in the external storms and internal strife. While the preceding age had aimed at completeness, at the universal, this was now all denied by the sophists, who proclaimed instead the relativity of everything. 'Man is the measure of all things', was the epitome of their varied message. When the universal norms, the supremacy of the laws and the authority of the gods were declared valueless, it was the individual with his own thoughts and fancies who was placed in the highest place. In literature Euripides studied the human propensity for good and evil; Aristophanes caricatured his contemporaries on the stage, and Thucydides portrayed the tendencies and struggles of interests of politicians and parties as they appeared to the sophists' view of the world. In art the study of the individual was a new and important task. Alcibiades was the first to put into practice the new theory of life, and he recognized no personal restrictions either in public or in private life. He was also apparently the first person to commission a well-known artist to decorate his house.

While on one hand critically probing, sceptical intelligence took the lead, those who were unwilling or unable to follow in its footsteps had recourse to superstition of one sort or another. The religious requirements of the masses were satisfied by miracles and omens in newly introduced cults. Among the deities whose worship now spread

126

rapidly were the god of healing, Asclepius, and the foreign gods who were closer to the life of nature than were the Olympians, for example Cybele from Asia Minor. It was the task of the artist to give Hellenic form to these foreign figures.

Athens indeed lost her empire and her income from tribute as a result of the Peloponnesian War, but still remained the leading cultural centre of Greece. The city set the tone in intellectual and literary matters and was the home of important artists. It was a lasting fruit of Pericles' cultural policy that the Athenian public was foremost in general education and cultural interests throughout all of Greece.

At his death Phidias left a group of pupils and assistants who continued to work in the style he had developed. Tradition records that Alcamenes and Agoracritus were the most important. The latter executed a colossal statue of Nemesis in Rhamnus, in north-east Attica, which local tradition ascribed, certainly wrongly, to Phidias himself. A fragment of the head of the statue has been found, with a treatment of the hair which stylistically agrees closely with the 'Laborde' head from the east pediment of the Parthenon.

Among Alcamenes' works we hear of an Aphrodite erected in the Gardens of Athens, a group of Hephaestus and Athena, and a statue of the goddess Hecate, who possessed three heads in one.

We also possess a Hermes of Alcamenes in the Archaic form of a rectangular pillar with a sculptured head, which received its name from the god. An ancient copy of this 'Hermes Propylaios' has been discovered in Pergamon.

Work on the magnificent buildings on the Acropolis was suspended as soon as the Peloponnesian War broke out. The walls of the Propylaea were never finally smoothed off. And the works which were subsequently undertaken were far smaller in extent than the constructions of Pericles. The army of workers in marble, who had been employed there, now had to find other tasks, partly in other places. The marble-style elaborated on the Parthenon, with its effective use of draperies which at one and the same time concealed and emphasized the lines of the body, and its linear treatment of folds, now became universal. It was practised on all decorative reliefs and marble sculpture throughout Greece, even though local variants can be detected. It became the dominating style from Asia Minor in the east to Italy in the west right down to the middle of the fourth century. The style developed increasingly in a purely ornamental direction with emphasis on an expressive play of lines. The previous age had concentrated on the main features of man's spiritual and physical image; the sculptors now filled in the details at the same time as they laid emphasis on grace and harmonious movement.

In Athens the first stages of the style's development can be followed on the little temple of Nike, which was constructed on the Acropolis after the Peace of Nikias in 421. At the same time work was begun on the Erechtheion; the famous Porch of the Caryatids belonging to this temple seems to have been finished a few years later. The frieze on the temple was an experiment in colour: figures of white marble were set on a ground of bluey-grey limestone from Eleusis. Previously a similar colour-effect had been achieved by painting the background blue. The reliefs from the balustrade which surrounded the temple of Nike portray the goddesses of victory making offerings and hanging the enemy's arms, wreaths and fillets on trophies; one of them, the best preserved, is tying up her sandals: see Plate 83. As on the figure of Aphrodite in the east pediment of the Parthenon, the beautiful lines of the female figures stand out clearly under the drapery, the folds of which, however, are more billowy, and follow and emphasize with greater refinement the position and movement of the body. The linear rhythm of the folds of the drapery has become a complete means of expression in itself. In spite of the sculptural depth of individual figures this style comes more and more to stress the external lines; it is a form of sketching, the aim of which is to organize the surface with its beautiful play of curves. When this technique is applied to sculpture in the round it is intended that the work should be regarded from only one side.

Outside Athens we may note the sculpture on the temple of Hera at Argos, where Polyclitus' statue of the goddess of gold and ivory, to which reference has already been made, was installed. From Bassae in Arcadia we have a frieze on which Centaurs steal women and Amazons fight Greeks. The wild spirit and the heavy proportions of the figures do not create an impression of Attic work, but the technique of the drapery reveals strong Attic influence. The folds stand like sharp lines which are stretched by the movement of the limbs, and the ends of the mantles float like streamers against the background.

In Asia the native dynasts, who were under Persian rule, also employed Greek sculptors. Some sarcophagi from the royal cemetery in Sidon in Phoenicia cover nearly two hundred years, from the Persian Wars till the end of the fourth century. Four of them are works of art of high quality. The oldest, known as 'The Satrap's Sarcophagus', still preserves some older features but nevertheless is probably of later date than the Parthenon frieze. The next oldest of the four has a type of roof which is characteristic of Lycian graves, and is therefore called 'Lycian'. The pediments are decorated with sphinxes, and the long sides with riders and hunting-scenes in relief. The chariots are represented in oblique perspective and there is an evident attempt at spatial impression. The other two sarcophagi from Sidon belong to the following period.

The Attic decorative relief-style recurs in a more superficial form on the Nereid Monument from Xanthos (see Plate 82). This monument derives its name from the statues of women portrayed in violent movement, set in the colonnades; but they probably symbolize winds and not nereids at all. In the reliefs from this splendid monument decorative skill has degenerated into mechanically-adapted mannerism. A building resembling a temple stood on a high platform decorated with relief-friezes. The fluttering draperies of the statues form a continuation of the style of which Paionios' Nike sculpted between 420 and 430 is the foremost example. The reliefs represent battle-scenes between Lycians and other Orientals, a siege and capture of a city and other events in the life of a great man of Asia Minor. Although the wishes of the customer were in this respect decisive for the choice of theme, the style is nevertheless entirely Greek. Here also we are struck by the depth of space. The architecture of the Nereid Monument is a comprehensive copy of the forms of the Erechtheion, and it therefore cannot be dated earlier than the last decade of the fifth century, and it was probably executed some time in the first decades of the following century. The statues are, however, of an older style than the sculptures from the temple of Asclepius at Epidaurus, which were carved, with the assistance of the Athenian Timotheos and others, in the 'seventies of the fourth century.

The evolution of the style can also be traced from the end of the fourth century on Athenian grave-reliefs. The custom of adorning the graves of the deceased, which was already common in Athens in the Archaic period, lapsed in the Classic period, probably because this type of luxury was forbidden. The decoration of graves with valuable works of art, which drew attention to the resting-places of the rich and the powerful was hardly consonant with the highly developed spirit of citizenship. The city erected large common monuments only for those who fell in battle on behalf of the father-land. During the Peloponnesian War private grave-reliefs again appeared, and the oldest are of the same style as the Parthenon-frieze. Many come from a cemetery laid out in 394 by the stream of Eridanos near the main city-gate. To this cemetery belongs the fam-ous relief of Hegeso: see Plate 84. A seated woman draws her treas-ures out of a box, which a servant standing in front of her holds out to her. By reason of its context the motif has been elevated into a religious sphere. We recall Alcestis' preparations for her death, as narrated by the serving-woman in Euripides' drama:

> When she knew that the hour had come
> she washed her white body in the river
> and took from her cedar-chests her jewels forth
> and her clothes, and attired herself as for a feast.

THE TRIUMPH OF THE ART OF PAINTING

The great reputation which Polygnotos and his collaborators achieved by their work, and which echoes through the descriptions of the Roman period, did not prevent many critics of later times from considering that their paintings had an Archaic stiffness. Many later critics regarded the painters of the following generation, that is the last third of the fifth century, as the founders of this branch of art. Agatharchus of Samos, who assisted Aeschylus with decorations for his tragedies and decorated Alcibiades' house in about 420, was apparently an original and fashionable artist, but the decisive step was taken by his younger contemporary, the Athenian Apollodorus, while full mastery in this respect seems to have been achieved by Zeuxis and Parrhasius. Their school is customarily called the 'Asiatic' school, since at least Parrhasius was a native of Asia Minor, but Athens was clearly the centre of their activity, and it was there that the decisive steps were taken.

Lack of paintings makes it difficult to exemplify in detail the ad-vances made by these masters. But an analysis of reliefs and vase-paintings, together with information provided by ancient art-historians, give an idea of the types of innovation which were now adopted in painting, and remained fundamental until the end of antiquity. Of these the most important was that the portrayal of space now won central significance in the composition of the picture. Compare, for example, a piece of the Parthenon-frieze with the Hegeso relief: see Plates 77 and 84. If we look at them carefully we see that the position of the figures and the effect of the silhouette on the frieze make no impression at all of a representation of space. The figures stand as if portrayed against the air, but this air-space nevertheless creates no notion of illimitability. The background on the Parthenon-frieze makes no attempt at an illusion of sky or of earth or even of a wall. It is neutral, or as the theorists of art say, ideal. The impression created by the Hegeso-relief is different. This is principally the result of the frame round the sides with its high profiles, which creates in itself a feeling of space. The relief encroaches slightly on the frame on both sides; and from the depth of the frame we derive the sense of depth within.

One medium by which space may be represented as a unity in a picture is by light. A thorough impression of light in a painting is most simply created by the shadows cast by the bodies. Previous painters had utilized the shading of individual sunken parts, such as the depressions in the folds of drapery, the inner sides of shields, etc., but at the end of the fifth century a painter discovered the importance of shadow for the picture as a whole. This was the above-named Apollodorus of Athens, surnamed 'the Shadow-Painter', 'Skiagraphos'. His discovery gave rise to a lively debate between those who thought that art should aim at truth and reproduce bodies as they really were, and those who maintained that it should reproduce the appearance of reality as the eye saw it. The Socratic philosophers supported the former thesis, but the latter won the day among artists.

The new conception of space found expression more easily on a small than on a large scale, and was better suited to compositions with few figures than to those with many. Artists devoted themselves rather to canvas-painting than to frescos. The usual technique was tempera upon wood. Zeuxis is said especially to have developed the art of reproducing shadows, while Parrhasius won praise for the perfect lines and delicate sweet colouring of his canvases. It was said of his portrait of Theseus that the hero was clearly nourished on roses.

The new conception of space is best exemplified by a contemporary painting: the Pelops Amphora: see Plate 74. The theme is the end of

the race, the preliminaries to which we saw on the east pediment
at Olympia. The course crosses the sea, which is represented by
waves and a dolphin; the landscape close at hand is shown by a tree
or two and the view is limited by distant heights. The vase represents
an advance by comparison with the Polygnotan Orvieto-crater, but
it does not approach the perspective in depth, the internal opening
of landscape which is common among the painters of the early
Renaissance in Italy. We possess copies and imitations of the works
of Zeuxis and his contemporaries in wall-paintings of the so-called
'Second Decorative Style' at Pompeii, Herculaneum and Rome.

Vase-painting gradually divorced itself from painting properly
so-called. Its function became more and more purely decorative, and
the artist was no longer content with the colour-contrast of red and
black, but instead made frequent use of white and gold.

The white grave-lekythi are a class by themselves. On the white
ground scenes were painted—usually representing sacrifices and
scenes of lamentation at the grave—in blue, red, brown and gold,
in different gradations, as in Plate 73.

In the painting of the decades immediately before and after 400
we can observe a change in the artist's view of the individual. Man is
no longer regarded as an isolated being, but is seen as a part of a
larger whole, in which he is assimilated and to whose laws and
structure he has to subordinate himself.

THE LATER CLASSIC PERIOD

i Praxiteles

In sculpture the successors of Phidias and Polyclitus long followed
in the footsteps of their masters. They had tested the possibilities
to which the impulses of the great artists showed the way, and varied
the motifs both in respect of draped figures and statues of naked
athletes.

In about 370 a bronze statue, the work of Cephisodotus, was set
up in the agora in Athens, representing Eirene, the goddess of peace,
with the child Ploutos, wealth, in her arms. The statue has been
identified with a type which is represented both on Athenian coins
of the Roman period and in Roman copies in marble, the two best
of which are in Munich and New York (though the identification
has been questioned).

Here we find the features of the new age, but in a negative manner. We no longer see the sharply contoured figure with its firmly delineated form, which we observed in the works of Phidias and Polyclitus. Everything has become softer whether it be the contour lines or the softly billowing form of the surface. The face expresses mildness rather than sublimity, and the figure of the child with its graceful movements gives the whole group the flavour of an idyll. It is the first Classic example of the mother-and-child group, which reappears later in the innumerable Madonnas of Christian art.

Cephisodotus' work was soon overshadowed by that of his great son, Praxiteles. Praxiteles introduced a new divine ideal. Gravity was replaced by charm. The stances adopted became softer. The gods approached more closely to human beings, becoming, as it were, handsome mortals. His statues of the divinities of love, Aphrodite and Eros, were his most famous works. With him monumental art learnt to play upon a new scale of feelings. No ancient sculptor enjoyed such popularity, and people made long journeys to see his work. A small city such as Cnidos would not part with his statue of Aphrodite for all the money in the world. Praxiteles' works were copied in large numbers, and it has been possible to identify certain ancient statues as copies of his work. Some of the originals were of bronze, but the majority, and the most famous, were of marble.

Praxiteles portrayed Apollo, who had been conceived a century earlier as the grave and stern avenger, as a gentle youth with a soft feminine face. His Apollo Sauroktonos is just such a youth, supporting himself with his left hand against a tree-trunk. His body thus acquires a soft and pliant curve and the contours become more fluid than in Polyclitus' work. In his right hand he has an arrow, with which he is aiming at a lizard climbing up the tree-trunk. The representation is inspired by an old story, but the choice of this precise moment to characterize the god is revealing. By giving his figures a prop at the side Praxiteles overcomes the rigidity present in the figures of Polyclitus and his successors. A prop of this sort occurs in his famous Satyr and in his statue of Hermes at Olympia. The whole figure becomes inscribed in a given space by the turning of the head and the movement of the limbs forward and to the sides. In this way he attempted to adapt sculpture to the conception of space achieved in contemporary painting.

As regards stance Praxiteles' Satyr was closely related to his Apollo Sauroktonos: he is the ennobled creature of nature. While earlier art had portrayed the satyrs as wild and savage beings with large tails and animal eyes, Praxiteles has made his satyr a strong and active youth; only the pointed ears and a small stub of a tail betray his origin. In the features of his face there shines nevertheless a fresh and powerful sensuality. The characterization has thus been made subtler.

Antiquity praised Praxiteles for his subtle treatment of the surface of the marble. It has long been believed that his technique can be particularly studied on one of his works, the statue of Hermes in Olympia: see Plate 89. It is modulated and worked with great feeling. The various planes of the surface and the living muscles pass from one to the other with the greatest possible softness. This is a refinement which is not otherwise encountered before the Hellenistic age. The back is partly unworked. The grooves caused by the round-chisel can still be seen in a number of places: but in the fourth century the naked parts of all marble statuary of the better quality were executed with a pointed chisel. Another disturbing element is the prop, which binds the figure with the tree-trunk, and which one is reluctant to ascribe to a master of the class of Praxiteles. All this has led scholars to suppose that the work in question is either an original of a younger Praxiteles, or a copy made to replace the original after this had been carried off to Italy by some Roman governor, as not infrequently occurred. The statue was discovered in the temple of Hera. However, in his description of it Pausanias says, 'among other works which were erected as gifts in the Heraion, is a Hermes of marble, who is carrying the child Dionysus; it is the art (*techne*) of Praxiteles.' The riddle of the statue of Hermes continues to be the subject of numerous attempted solutions.

Praxiteles was also a pioneer in the art of portraying the female body as fundamentally different from the ideal of the athlete. We can see this in his famous statue of the Cnidian Aphrodite. This is known from numerous copies. Aphrodite is represented at the moment in which she is removing her clothes before stepping into the bath. Her gaze is turned to the left. She sees something far away, which is not of this earth. She holds her right hand very naturally and quite unconsciously in front of her. Her body is stamped with feminine softness. Her calm, large beauty is raised above all coquetry. The statue was set up in a small shrine in Cnidos, and so that it could be seen from all sides a door was opened in the back of the temple. The back of the statue was the part which was especially admired.

Apart from the Cnidian Aphrodite Praxiteles also executed other statues of the goddess. One of them, we know, which was on the island of Cos, represented the goddess fully clad. The beautiful Aphrodite from Arles, who raises her mantle to her hips, is among the works assigned to him on stylistic grounds.

Praxiteles also executed some statues of Eros, the son of Aphrodite. The most famous of these was a gift of the hetaera Phryne, the model and mistress of the sculptor, to her native city, Thespiae. It is significant for the outlook of the time that Phryne's own statue was allowed to stand next to that of the goddess. Apart from this she had commissioned the gilt portrait-statue of herself in the guise of Aphrodite, also the work of Praxiteles, to be erected in Delphi.

The influence of Praxiteles on his contemporaries and on posterity was very great; the exquisite charm of his figures never ceased to demand imitation. The features of the faces of his young ideal figures became almost canonical, and were reproduced endlessly by the sculptors of the Hellenistic, and still more of the Roman period. The inspiration he provided for the portrayal of the female figure was exploited above that of any other artist. His sons and grandsons, among whom the names of Praxiteles and Cephisodotus re-appear, continued to work in his manner. The great number of works in his style make it difficult to distinguish the work of the master from that of his pupils.

Among the important draped figures which attest the influence of Praxiteles, are the figures on the sarcophagus of the Mourning Women from Sidon. Between the Ionic pilasters on the temple-shaped sarcophagus stand women in different styles of drapery, who in varying gestures and poses express their sorrow over the death of the ruler laid in the sarcophagus: see Plate 92.

A type of a youth in the style of Praxiteles' school is represented by the fine bronze statue which was discovered in the sea off Marathon in 1925: see Plate 85. The body is stamped with a certain feebleness in the movements and shaping, but the face is strikingly alive and expressive.

Industrial art was also strongly influenced by Praxiteles. The numerous clay statuettes which were produced in Tanagra from the middle of the fourth to the end of the third century are largely inspired by his style. The same impulses were also transplanted to other centres where a similar industry rapidly grew up, from Asia Minor in the east to Sicily in the west.

ii Scopas and the Sculptures of the Mausoleum

Scopas was a contemporary and a rival of Praxiteles He worked primarily in marble, but he also enjoyed a considerable reputation as an architect. He was a native of Paros, and his work took him to both the Peloponnese and Asia Minor.

The greatest temple in the Peloponnese was that of Athena Alea at Tegea, in Arcadia. It was built as a replacement for an older temple which was destroyed in the 390's, and Scopas was both its architect and sculptor. The date of the building can only be approximately determined. Both historical grounds—the fate of Tegea during this period—and stylistic arguments suggest that a few decades passed between the destruction of the old temple by fire and the building of the new one. This gives us the years around 370 as the earliest date for the beginning of Scopas' activity in Tegea.

The pediments of the temple were the work of this master. The eastern pediment, of which the most important fragments remain, portrayed the hunt of the Calydonian boar with Atalanta and Meleager. Some heads, a large part of the body of the boar and otherwise only some insignificant fragments survive. The heads are all of a similar and very unusual type; they are almost cubic; the brows are low and wide and rise straight from the bridge of the nose and the deeply set eyes. By means of shadowing and the twist given to the very bulging eyeballs the glances are directed upwards with an expression of the deepest pain. The curves of the cheeks are wide, and the mouth is formed in a sensual curve: see the head of Heracles from the pedimental sculpture, Plate 86.

The powerful expression of emotion was something new in art, and ancient critics emphasize Scopas' pathos as one of the most characteristic features of his work. He seems also to have succeeded in expressing finer variations of character and feeling. This is attested by his group of Love, Desire and Lust. His Bacchant was famous for its ecstatic expression and for the illusion of movement which the statue created. It has been identified in a small marble copy in Dresden.

Scopas' reputation in antiquity rested also on the fact that Augustus caused a statue by him of Apollo Citharoedus to be brought to Rome, and installed in the great temple on the Palatine which he dedicated to the god. The general appearance of the statue is known from small reproductions on coins and reliefs.

Scopas' male figures are heavier and more massive than those of Praxiteles, and he associates himself in this way with the tradition

136

of Polyclitus. But there is no direct statement to the effect that he belonged to any of the Peloponnesian schools of sculptors in Argos or Sicyon. While Praxiteles was the interpreter of the joyful soft emotions, Scopas introduced suffering and passion, pathos, into sculpture.

Scopas was already a famous sculptor when he and three other sculptors received the commission to collaborate in the ornamentation of the sepulchral monument of the Carian ruler Maussollos and his wife Artemisia.

While Athens was no longer in a position to offer sculptors undertakings on a monumental scale, a new field of activity opened in Asia Minor in the fourth century. The Greek cities there had grown rapidly in prosperity after the downfall of the Athenian empire, and could afford large building programmes. Moreover, the native princes wished to beautify their cities through the work of Greek artists and thereby glorify themselves.

From the typological point of view the tomb which Maussollos of Caria caused to be built in his residence Halicarnassus is a continuation of the tradition of the Nereid Monument, but it outstrips all its predecessors in size and splendour: see Plate 91. It was reckoned among the seven wonders of the world. Its ground-plan was almost square. The grave-chamber stood on a high platform surrounded by an Ionic colonnade. The whole, instead of being completed by a roof of the usual type, was surmounted by a step-pyramid, on the top of which a huge four-horse chariot carrying statues of the prince and his wife was set. This crowning group was the work of the architect Pytheos. The rest of the decoration consisted of statues in the colonnades, and three relief-friezes, which were probably placed round the platform. It was so divided that each of four sculptors, Scopas, Timotheos, Leochares and Bryaxis was responsible for his own side.

The best preserved of the friezes are those which portray the battle of the Greeks and the Amazons. The plaques from the different sides of the building reveal certain stylistic differences, and on this formation attempts have been made to determine the sculptors of each, and to co-ordinate the reliefs with the other works of the sculptors. The problem is, however, not yet solved. The relief-plaques from the east side, which Pliny says were the work of Scopas, surpass the others in the fresh rhythm of the composition and the effective execution of the figures.

On the Mausoleum friezes the reliefs no longer occupy the entire
height of the plaque as they do on the friezes of the Parthenon and at
Bassae. There is air above their heads. The artists have abandoned
the attempt to achieve an impression of depth by crowding the
figures together in tight groups; they are loosely distributed over the
field. The contestants move sideways from the viewpoint of the
onlooker and make no attempt to move outwards from or inwards
into the relief. They act as if on a narrow stage. The Classic relief
has won for itself just that amount of space necessary for a continuous epic portrayal of a battle-scene. An air of one of Homer's
battle-scenes hangs over this frieze. The individual warriors are
portrayed plastically and graphically against the background; it is
here clear that by replacing the ideal background by one with a more
realistic stress the artists have also profited in the representation
of the individual figures. The Mausoleum frieze thus marks one of
the high-points in Greek relief-style. Just as the Parthenon frieze is
the fullest expression of the pure Classic style, so the style of the
second Classic period is reflected in the Mausoleum frieze.

Some statues and fragments of statues with portrait-features
have survived from the north side of the monument, and have on
that account been ascribed to Bryaxis. The most distinguished of
these portraits, commonly taken to represent Maussollos, is now
dated by some archaeologists to the second century B.C., but this
can hardly be right: see Plate 90.

When Maussollos died in 353, his wife Artemisia continued the
work on the tomb. At her death in 351 it was not finally completed,
but each artist is said to have completed his share of the work
without further payment.

We have already mentioned the Athenian Timotheos as among the
artists who worked with Scopas on the Mausoleum; he was perhaps
the same sculptor who worked in Epidaurus. He was apparently
older than Scopas, while the other two, Leochares and Bryaxis, were
pupils of Scopas.

Among Timotheos' works is a 'Leda and the Swan', which is
stylistically near to the acroteria from Epidaurus.

His fellow-countryman Leochares enjoyed a considerable reputation. About 350 B.C. he worked on the Mausoleum. Later (after
338 B.C.) he received the commission to make portraits of the
members of the Macedonian royal family in gold and ivory, which
were erected in the Philippeion in Olympia: see Plate 101.

The famous Apollo Belvedere, the original of which used to be attributed to Leochares, is a Roman copy of a Hellenistic original.

Scopas' influence can be seen on many Attic grave-reliefs. The expression of sorrow becomes stronger, and a preference developed for large groups of whole families assembled for the leave-taking. The relief is deeper than on the stele of Hegeso. The frame round the sides and the upper piece are separately worked and create a niche, within which the scene is portrayed: see Plate 94.

The generation of artists of around 350 inherited all the psychological and formal consequences of the ground gained in the pure Classic period. These artists were able to play on the whole range of human emotions from the most passionate sorrow to the most tender utterances of the soul. By the side of the sublimity and majesty of the gods, which Phidias portrayed in an unrivalled manner, they knew how to portray gaiety, charm and a sympathetic mildness. The stances have become softer and artists have discovered immediate means of expressing movement, both when it was required to be stormy and wild, and gentle as a ripple on water on a summer's day. The Goddess of Love herself had stepped down to earth and revealed herself in art.

iii Lysippos

The Greek art of sculpture had advanced step by step on its voyage of discovery. It had freed itself from the bonds of frontality, and in the person of Polyclitus it had taught itself to portray an isolated, ideal figure of a man. Phidias had expressed in plastic form the majesty of the gods, Praxiteles had portrayed their grace. Again, Scopas had personified the passions and powerful surges of emotion. In the external arts, particularly painting, and subsequently also in relief-sculpture, a conception of space was worked out, which less stressed the individual figures than co-ordinated them as parts of a larger whole. Scopas and still more Praxiteles adapted their work to this notion of space.

It fell to Lysippos consciously to grapple with the task of executing statues according to the painters' catch-word, namely to represent objects as they appeared to be, not as they were. Lysippos was born and worked in Sicyon, where important artists had been active for a full century before, in both sculpture and in painting. He denied that he was any artist's pupil, and declared that nature had been his teacher. On another occasion he described Polyclitus' statue, the

Doryphorus, as the school in which he had been formed. He stressed his independence by the pronouncement that Polyclitus had portrayed humans as they were, but that he made them as they appeared to be.

Lysippos devoted himself entirely to the production of bronze statues and was extremely productive within this field. He is said in all to have made fifteen hundred statues. He produced primarily statues of athletes and portrait-figures; statues of gods from his hand are by no means so common.

The most famous of his statues of athletes was the 'Apoxyo-menos', or 'Athlete scraping himself clean', the best copy of which is in the Vatican: see Plate 93. His athletic exercise over, a naked young man stands and scrapes the dust and oil from himself. His arms are out stretched, and the weight of his body is unequally distributed on the legs, which are elastically bent. The musculature of the trunk is well-developed.

The difference between it and the Doryphorus (see Plate 52) is clear. The head is smaller; it occupies only a tenth part of the total length of the figure as against an eighth of that of the Doryphorus. The legs and arms are relatively longer, the trunk shorter. The whole figure presents a more elegant and smoother appearance. Pliny says (*NH*. 34, 65) that Lysippos made his bodies *graciliora siccioraque*— 'more slender and firm'. While the different limbs and muscular parts of the Doryphorus are sharply separated and modelled in large level, unified surfaces, in the Apoxyomenos—also the figure of an athlete with powerful muscles—the different limbs and muscles flow into each other without sharp divisions. The surface parts are irregularly curved, and blend with one another like waves, and there are no firm surfaces or lines for the eye to fix on. In the place of Polyclitus' scientific analysis we have an attempt at an ocular synthesis of the whole figure. But behind this synthesis there lies a deep and fundamental anatomical knowledge.

The different sides of the figures are no more sharply demarcated against each other than the individual muscular areas. On whichever side one stands a number of lines lead over to the neighbouring sides. No side gives a wholly complete view; the viewer is continually encouraged to walk all round the statue. The round form of the trunk and the arms outstretched in a curve are the formal means by which this result is most obviously achieved.

The 'Scraper' with his outstretched arms seems to embrace a part of the space around him. He has a more direct and lively contact with the surrounding atmosphere than any of his predecessors in the history of Greek art. This is further stressed by the mobile modelling of the surface, whose lights and shades are directly linked with the space around the figure.

Lysippos made a number of statues of Heracles and portrayed the hero in different situations and moods. The most famous was the statue which portrayed him in middle age, his Labours completed, leaning exhausted on his club. There are many copies of this statue, of which the most distinguished is the colossal Hercules Farnese in Naples.

The most famous of Lysippos' statues was, however, that of Alexander the Great. He succeeded in exploiting certain abnormalities in the appearance of the king—the twist in the neck, and the consequent bend of the head—to heighten the heroic element in his expression, and he is said on this account to have been granted the sole right to sculpture his likeness. There exist a very large number of portraits of Alexander, but the majority are idealized transformations of the following periods.

The art of portraiture had been practised in Greece before Lysippos. The first attempts at realistic portraiture are attributed to Demetrios of Alopeke, and are said to have been contemporary with Euripides' realistic dramas. In the middle of the fourth century it became increasingly common to honour distinguished men with portrait-statues. One of the first to receive such an honour was the philosopher Plato.

His realism makes Lysippos the authentic founder of the art of portraiture. In his school realism went so far that his brother Lysistratus took casts of living models, which he subsequently cast in bronze after the necessary retouching.

Lysippos marks the consummation of the attempt of Greek sculpture to plumb the physical nature of man. He thus opened the way for the new age which began for the Greeks and for Greek culture with the conquests of Alexander the Great, the age of Hellenism.

4. THE HELLENISTIC AGE
(330–27 B.C.)

The conquests of Alexander the Great brought with them changes of profound significance for Greek culture. The East as far as the frontiers of India was opened to Greek civilization, and the old centres had to yield place to the new: Alexandria, Antioch and Pergamon. Many foreign peoples now shared in Greek culture, and participated in the new development to the extent that they could appropriate to themselves the Greek cultural inheritance. Culture, which had previously had national limits, now became international.

The internationalism of the upper classes had grown out of the individualistic trend in the philosophy of the fourth century. Individualism gave birth to a morality of the Superman. To the men who followed Alexander the Great on his wonderful expedition, and then were his heirs, nothing seemed impossible. In a brief time their careers led them to heights of power and wealth which were unthinkable when the Macedonians had first crossed over into Asia. The boundaries between the divine and the human were removed. The old Greek fear of hubris, excessive pride, was now despised. And what is true of the leaders themselves is also true, although to a lesser extent, of their subordinates.

The task of art in the new society was first and foremost to pay homage to the new rulers, who, whether they allowed themselves to be worshipped as gods or not, demanded to be portrayed as superior to ordinary mortals. The portraits of Alexander the Great by Lysippos and Apelles set the tone for this. Other artists were ready to follow suit.

Both the material and psychological presuppositions of art were thus altered by the conquests of Alexander. The experience of the previous age had also prepared artists to undertake new tasks.

The great new monarchies had incomparably greater economic resources than the old Greek city-states. The rulers wished to adorn their newly built palaces with splendid works of art, worthy of the Hellenic culture of which the Macedonians too were proud. They spared no expense when it was a question of acquiring famous works of art or of associating outstanding artists with their courts. They also exhibited their liberality towards the old Greek shrines, and by gifts, architectural undertakings and statues attempted to win the sympathies of the surviving free states. Athens continued to be an important artistic centre, and Rhodes became of great consequence since, as a result of a clever and courageous foreign policy, she managed to maintain her independence between the great powers.

Lysippos' school survived for a time in Sicyon, and enjoyed commissions from all quarters. Painting seems especially to have developed in Asia Minor, though the artists were also employed at different princely courts elsewhere.

LATE CLASSIC AND HELLENISTIC ARCHITECTURE

In the field of architecture the completion of the building operations on the Acropolis at Athens at the end of the fifth century marks an epoch. Both the Doric and the Ionic styles had received a classic form in the Parthenon and the Erechtheion respectively. In the Propylaea the two styles had indeed begun to come closer to one another. The characteristics of the great age were clarity and sharpness of line in contours as well as in decorative details. The next generations attempted to find richer forms within the field they had inherited; the two styles, Doric and Ionic, came to stand in a very close relation to one another, as we can see from the temples of Bassae, Tegea and Labraunda, where Ionic forms are found side by side with the Doric.

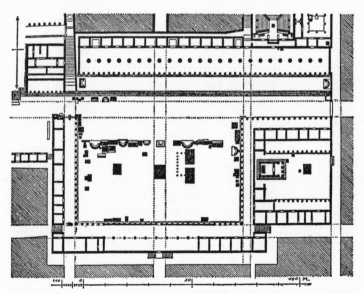

FIG. 33 Agora of Priene with surrounding colonnades. In the Agora are bases for statues in honour of individuals and other objects

With the Mausoleum and the Temple of Artemis in Ephesus, dating from the middle of the fourth century, we can observe a renaissance of the Asiatic-Ionic style. At the same time decorative forms emerge in Greece itself which attest a new feeling for form and style. This new element received its final expression in the Hellenistic age.

The political and social revolutions of the age were of outstanding importance for architecture, since the situation demanded that the new capitals in Syria, Egypt and Asia Minor were constructed according to Greek architectural requirements. Alexandria was

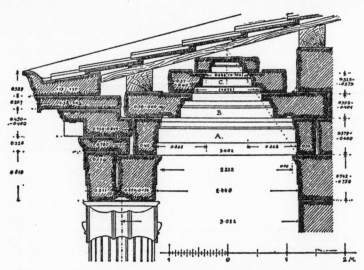

FIG. 34 Construction of entablature and roof of Ionic order. Temple of Athena at Priene (von Gerkan's reconstruction)

regarded as the most magnificent of the Hellenistic capitals. It had been planned on the classic system of Hippodamos, with straight streets and rectangular quarters. The main street was particularly renowned for its width (33 yards) and length (4½ miles).

This type of street-plan (see *Figure* 33) was characteristic of Hellenistic town-planning. The cities had large squares, wholly surrounded by colonnades behind which were rows of shops. The public buildings for the Council and Assembly and the temples were mostly built in the open squares.

The simple harmony of the Doric style was too uniform to please

Demosthenes, Roman
copy of a statue that
erected in Athens, ca.
280 B.C.

97. The Nike of Samothrace, ca. 190 B.C., ht. 2·45m.

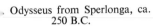
Odysseus from Sperlonga, ca. 250 B.C.

. Zeus striving with the Giants, om the Great Frieze of the Altar at Pergamon, ht. 2·3m.

100. Hellenistic ruler in heroic s[...]
bronze, ht. 2·37m., staff mod[...]

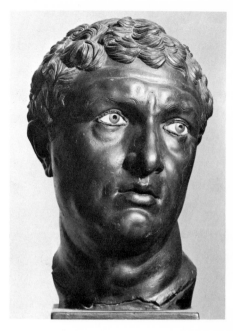

101. Alexander the Great, probably the work of Leochares, ca. 330 B.C.

102. Late Hellenistic portrait from Delos.

103 (*left*). Homer, idealized portrait, replica of a late Hellenistic work, ca. 150 B.C.

104. A silver coin of Lysimachus, King of Thrace, 286–281 B.C., representing the head of Alexander the Great deified.

105. Laocoon and his sons, ht. 2·42m. The group was discovered in 1506 near the Baths of Trajan.

106. Funerary urn of the 'Canopic' type from Chiusi, ca. 600 B.C.

107. A hut-urn from Vulci, seventh century B.C.

108. Askos of grey earthenware (impasto) from N. Etruria, ca. 600 B.C., ht. 0·177m.

109. Gold fibula from the Regolini-Galassi tomb at Caere, 600 B.C.

110. 'Tomba del Barone', Tarquinia, end of the sixth century B.C.
111. 'Tomba dei Tori', Tarquinia, second half of the sixth century B.C.

112. Bronze detail of an Etruscan war-chariot, 550–540 B.C.

113. Bronze fitting on a war-chariot (biga) found near Monteleone, 550–540 B.C.

114. Satyr and maenad, terracotta antefix from Satricum, early fifth century B.C. ▶

115. The Capitoline wolf, Etrus
bronze—the twins were added
more modern times—ca. 500 B

116. Apollo, terracotta statue fr
Veii, ca. 500 B.C.

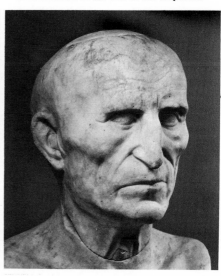

117. 'Brutus', Etruscan bronze head of the third century B.C.

118. Late Etruscan portrait in terracotta from sarcophagus, first century B.C.

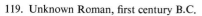

119. Unknown Roman, first century B.C.

120. Portrait of the end of the Republic.

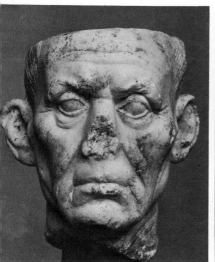

121. The Round Temple at Tivoli (Tibur).

122. Augustus as Pontifex Maximus.

123. Acanthus scroll: detail of relief-decoration on the Ara Pacis, Rome.

124. Stucco-relief: ritual of initiation, from the Villa Farnese in Rome.

125. Detail of relief from the Ara Pacis, Rome.

126. Detail of relief from the Ara Pacis, Rome.

127. Interior of the Pantheon, Rome.

the new age. Architects frequently disregarded its strict scheme and simplified a number of its parts, with the result that, for example, the echinos lost its curve and its contour became almost vertical, and the architrave became smaller than the triglyph-frieze so that the whole upper structure had a lighter appearance.

As a general rule the preference was for the Ionic style or its off-shoot, the Corinthian. Among monumental Ionic buildings we may notice especially the temple of Artemis in Ephesus, which was begun as early as the 350's, and the temple of Apollo at Didyma,

FIG. 35 Temple of Athena at Priene, by Pytheos

which was under construction throughout the entire period and was never completely finished. Even in the earliest stages of these temples a clear distinction is made between the side containing the entrance, and the rear; in the Doric temple there was no such distinction of sides. This emphasis on one direction was developed to extremes in Hellenistic architecture. Pytheos was one of the leading architects of the fourth century. He was the master of the Mausoleum (see Plate 91) and of the temple of Athena at Priene. In these he returned to the older form of Ionic column, while the temple of Artemis at Ephesus is partly influenced by Attic models. Neither of Pytheos' buildings had friezes; in their place the dentil-moulding decoration, which supported the projecting geison, played a prominent role. The sima is high and with its impressive ornament of acanthus-wreaths, palmettes and lions-heads, wholly dominates the narrow geison.

The whole Mausoleum, the lower part of which was 130 feet long and 108 feet wide, was set on a high platform, ornamented with the sculptured friezes already described. Above the colonnade and the architrave was the roof, which took the form of a step-pyramid, crowned by the statuary-group of the ruler and his consort standing in a four-horse chariot.

Pytheos probably also collaborated in the transformation of the sanctuary of Zeus at Labraunda in the time of Maussollos and his brother Idrieus.

Hermogenes, whose work was regarded in the Roman period as

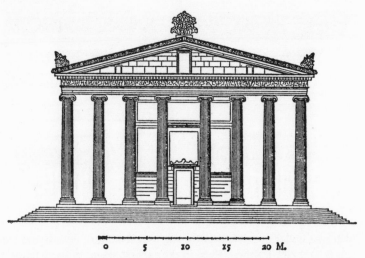

FIG. 36 Temple of Artemis at Magnesia, by Hermogenes. Reconstruction

classic, was active around 150 B.C. He built the temple of Artemis at Magnesia, see Figure 36. Hermogenes here adopted the frieze ornamented with figures above the architrave in the Athenian manner (cf. the Erechtheion), evidently to achieve a stronger emphasis on the horizontal areas at the expense of the columns. His successors retained the frieze, but replaced the human figures with an ornamental decoration, wreaths of leaves, flowers, etc. They clearly discovered that the figures of Hellenistic sculpture lacked the firm stance which is desirable in an architectural decorative scheme. Hermogenes further stressed the entrance by making the distance between the central columns of the short side substantially greater than that between the other columns. The width of the sur-

146

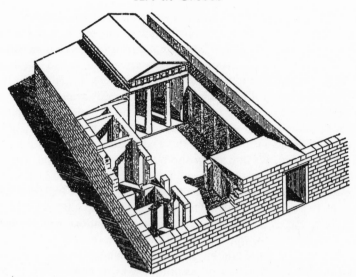

FIG. 37 Private house at Priene, about 300 B.C. Reconstruction in perspective

rounding colonnade was twice as great as usual, and the front entrance hall twice as deep as the back one. In this way Hermogenes associated himself with the tendency to give the temple a particular defined frontage, to stress its direction, as was done in the colossal temples of the old Ionic style.

The volutes of the Ionic columns were set nearer one another, and the horizontal band between them became narrower and lost its elasticity. It is clear that the feeling for its original function had been largely lost; this found external expression in the fact that the forms of the column lost their clarity through more profuse plastic decoration. Vegetable-ornaments and figure-reliefs were placed in the centre of the volutes.

The Corinthian Style
This style is not independent in the same way as the other two architectural styles, each of which was the expression of a particular mentality and had its own laws of development. The Corinthian is a branch of the Ionic style, whose general construction it follows, and differs from it only in the form of the column-capital.

The Ionic capital had a peculiarity which complicated its use: there was a marked difference between the long and the short sides.

The result was that it was necessary to employ a modified form for the corner columns so that the one volute sprang out from the building in a diagonal direction. This was not satisfactory; a column which was the same on all four sides was necessary.

The Corinthian capital is said to have been invented by the Athenian sculptor Callimachus, who was active around 400. The oldest preserved Corinthian capital occurs on a single column in the cella of the temple of Apollo at Bassae. Then there are others on a ring of columns in the cella of the Tholos at Delphi (beginning of fourth century). We find a new and richer version of it in the Tholos at Epidaurus, the work of the younger Polyclitus (second half of the fourth century). The outer ring of columns in all these buildings was Doric. In the tholos-shaped Philippeion at Olympia (about 335 B.C.) the outer ring of columns was Doric, while Corinthian half-columns were engaged in the inner façade of the cella wall.

The core of the Corinthian capital is round. The lower part is surrounded by two rows of acanthus-leaves, a remodelling of the palmette-wreath of the Ionic column. Above the acanthus-leaves rise small volutes, the largest of which supports the out-turned corner of the rectangular abacus. The sides between the horizontal corner-volutes are decorated with smaller volutes, acanthus-leaves and rosettes.

The Corinthian order of columns stresses still more than the Ionic the soaring element in the building, and in an age that loved splendour it provided a structure with greater opportunities for rich decoration. The architects employed it with great freedom, and a whole series of different forms arose. This type of capital first found its fullest expression in the Roman period. It provided the model for the late-Roman leaf-capitals and through them for the capitals of the Byzantine and Romanesque styles.

Both the fourth century and the first century of the Hellenistic age were periods of greatly increasing economic prosperity. Even if cities such as Athens suffered from economic difficulties, private individuals possessed considerable wealth, and the standard of living rose. The development of private houses benefited from this. The houses of Olynthus, on the coast of Macedonia, which can be dated by the destruction of the city in 348, provide the most thoroughly investigated examples of this. We can there see the emergence of mosaic floors and painted walls. In Priene well-preserved structures of the close of the fourth century have been identified. The fundamental plan of the house is of the old megaron-house, but this has been expanded by the addition of side-rooms; in addition, in the more prosperous houses an important element consisted of the courtyard, or peristyle surrounded by colonnades. These peristyle courtyards are characteristic of the plan of the royal palace at Pergamon. The finds from Priene are supported by the excavations at Delos, where the discoveries form a transition to the Roman period.

SCULPTURE

We know much about the immediate predecessors of the Hellenistic sculptors, Praxiteles, Scopas and Lysippos, and we also know the names of a considerable number of the masters of the period itself. In addition a large number of works of art have been preserved either in the original or in copies. Yet for all this the history of Hellenistic art is a comparatively obscure chapter. There are many works which lack a master, and many masters whose works are lost. The greatest difficulty of all in this period, however, is the absence of a secure chronology. Between about 300 and the twenties of the third century there are no large-scale monumental sculptures which can be securely dated. Recently, however, a magnificent Rhodian marble group portraying the blinding of Polyphemus has been recognized among the sculptures from the 'Cave of Tiberius' at Sperlonga near Sorrento; it can be dated on stylistic grounds to the middle of the third century B.C. (See plate 98).

From about 230 for some sixty years we have a firm basis in' the great Pergamene monuments, the groups of the Gaulish warriors, and the reliefs from the altar of Zeus. This period marks the climax of Hellenistic art. For the following period we are again ill-informed, though the discoveries on Delos, which was destroyed in 69 B.C., give us some clues for dating. The artistic trends of the Hellenistic age are mirrored in a class of monuments where there is fortunately no uncertainty with regard to chronology, namely the coins with their powerful portraits of the Hellenistic rulers: see Plate 104.

The task of arranging and sorting the abundant material is rendered more difficult by the freedom and variety of the artists' works. The masters of the age were able to use freely all the achievements and advances of their great predecessors of the two Classic epochs.

They were masters of anatomy and of the theory of perspective; they were familiar with the representation of the most difficult twists and bends. Scopas and Praxiteles had shown them how the sculptor could express human feelings and moods from deep suffering to soft charm. Lysippos' realism had given them possibilities of discovering intermediate tones. They had also learnt from Lysippos how to place sculpture within a given space.

The artists of the Hellenistic age strove to surpass their predecessors in all directions. Suffering was heightened to anguish, happiness became joy, and the gentle smile became ever sweeter. Their work is based on a careful study of reality. In the hands of the Greeks realism became primarily a means of creating and deepening the expression; it never became, as in Italy, an end in itself.

The repertoire of the artist was extended. Certainly statues of athletes became less common now, when professionalism began to predominate in athletics, and in place of them we have representations of the great men of the period in the guise of heroes. Statues of gods were necessary for the temples of the new cities. Art also had a part to play in the decoration of private houses and gardens. Scenes of daily life were portrayed, sometimes with a pleasing charm, sometimes with lively realism. Caricatures of both humans and animals were also very popular.

The 'Alexander-sarcophagus' from Sidon (about 300 B.C.) shows how sculptors succeeded in assembling close groups of figures to form a living unit. This sarcophagus is the latest of the sculptured chests from the royal cemetery at Sidon, and probably contained the remains of the native prince who was appointed ruler of Phoenicia by Alexander. Its rich and well-preserved colours are particularly striking. In the use of colour artists strove more for harmony and decorative effect than for fidelity to nature. The main shades were violet and yellow, and in addition pale blue and pale red. At times armour was gilded.

The scene was represented within a small area, which appears rather deeper than in the frieze of the Mausoleum by reason of the closer positioning of the figures, but there is no trace of an attempt to represent either infinite depth or perspective in depth. The conception of space on the sarcophagus is typical of the age; it does not depend on the technical assumptions of the relief. The same conception of space is also conspicuous in contemporary vase-painting.

Polyeuctus' statue of Demosthenes (Plate 96) was erected in

Art in Greece

Athens following a decree of the people in 280. The orator stands calmly with lowered arms; his hands, as we know from a fragment of a copy, were folded in front of the body: a gesture of inward strain and sorrow. The lower part of the body and the trunk form a slight angle with one another, which is emphasized by the stance of the legs. By these means the impression of frontality is avoided; this is a lesson learnt from Lysippos, though the statue creates a more angular and harder impression than do his works. The spiral movement round the figure, which originates in the oblique fold of the mantle from the right leg upwards, is checked by the perpendicular fold at the left shoulder and by the sharply accentuated gathered portion of the mantle below the breast. The artist has tried to achieve an equilibrium of movement. The horizontal folds bind the statue in the horizontal plane and we are reminded in that connection of 'The Scraper', whose outstretched arms perform a similar function. It may serve as an illustration of what the theorists of the Hellenistic period called the 'strict rhythm', in contrast to the more graceful 'eurythmia' which the well-known statue of Sophocles in the Lateran Museum exemplifies.

The muscles in the dry and sinewy body, as well as in the face, stand out as clearly defined ridges; they tell of an intense inner life. The deep shadow over the eyes and the mouth adds an air of relentless suffering. The statue is an act of homage to the great patriot, whose every admonition to unity and to a decisive struggle against the approaching enemy had to die away unheard.

The statue of Demosthenes gives us an insight into the principles of composition of statues and of the employment of musculature and drapery as a means of expression at the beginning of the Hellenistic age. It is, more than that, a masterpiece of portraiture.

Eutychides' famous statue of the City-Goddess of Antioch is a typical Hellenistic composition; the goddess is represented sitting with her arms resting on her knees. Here we see a play of oblique lines, broken up by an emphatic vertical. Eutychides was a pupil of Lysippos, and of his son Boidas, of whom we know a 'Praying Youth' from an excellent bronze copy in Berlin. This expresses in every line an aspiration upwards, without the employment of the spiral composition usual later.

The most famous of all Hellenistic statues is the Nike of Samothrace (Plate 97), which can be dated to immediately after 200 B.C. A tall woman has just alighted on a ship's deck towards the bows.

151

Art in Greece

The horizontally placed wings give a balance to the figure, which would otherwise appear to fall forward. The current of air drives her clothes against the body, so that her noble figure stands out. The ends of her garments flutter behind her. The joy of victory and the play of winds in the Aegean have probably never received a more sonorous expression than in this statue, which now forms one of the greatest treasures of the Louvre. The spiral composition is clear in the folds of the drapery and in the movements of the body. This constitutes the foundation of the unified expression.

An excellent example of the skill with which artists portrayed variations in the different material of garments is provided by the 'Girl from Anzio', preserved in a good marble copy, probably based on an original in bronze. Here too we observe that the spiral composition has been thoroughly worked out.

Praxiteles' Cnidian Aphrodite was the starting-point for a long series of figures of Aphrodite, more or less naked. The goddess was portrayed increasingly like a mortal. The Capitoline Aphrodite seems, like the famous Venus Medici, to be only too conscious both of her beauty and of her nakedness. A refined treatment of the surface emphasized the feminine curves of the figure.

Variations in the stance of the goddess also occur. Diodalsas portrayed the goddess bending her knee as she dries herself after her bath.

Many statues portray her half-naked. The finest of these is the Aphrodite of Melos, the strongly emphasized spiral movement of which is of significance for Hellenistic art in the second century B.C.

In the great bronze statue in Rome of a Hellenistic ruler heroically idealized (Plate 100) this aspiring tendency is expressed by the fact that the body throughout all its limbs constitutes a rising spiral terminating in the raised left hand. With this statue we have already entered the middle period of Hellenistic art, when Pergamon set the fashion. The artists of this period did not attempt, like those of the Classic period, to find the permanent element in things, but wished to express movement. The forms are stretched to breaking-point, and the composition is never rounded off. The Hellenistic age is not searching for the elevated equilibrium of the Classic period; its art rather issues in dissonance, and finds its artistic expression in the 'centrifugal style' of the second century B.C.

In the Pergamene kingdom art and culture were under royal patronage. Attalus I (241–197 B.C.) and Eumenes II (197–159 B.C.)

the successors of Eumenes I, who had secured his throne by his victories over the Gallic hordes which had settled in Asia Minor, commemorated this event by splendid monuments. We possess fragments of two different series. One consists of larger-than-life bronze groups. Copies of 'The Dying Gaul' and 'The Gaul and his Wife' may be seen in Rome. In addition there are other figures which on stylistic grounds belong to the same series. The Barbarians are distinguished by their tufty hair and their necklaces, but in accordance with the conventions of Greek art they are portrayed naked. A grievous composure in the face of approaching death is stamped on the face of the dying Gaul. His fellow-countryman who has murdered his wife, and now plunges the sword in his own breast, to avoid the

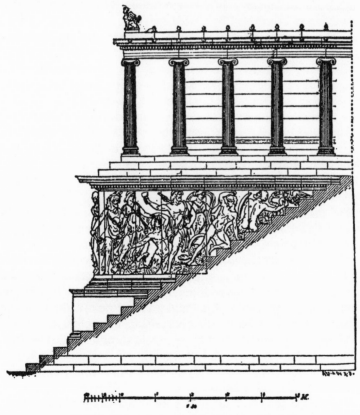

FIG. 38 The Altar at Pergamon. Section through stairway

shame of captivity, has a more extroverted pathos, which is brought out by the strong contrast in the patterns of movement in the component parts of the group. The portrayal of the defeated enemy is marked by a truly Greek humanity of conception.

The unrivalled 'Barberini Faun' in Munich, found in Rome (Plate 95), also belongs to the earlier Pergamene tradition. This portrayal of a satyr in a blissful Dionysiac sleep is characterized not only by naturalistic intensity, but also by an almost Phidian power.

It was probably under Attalus' successor, Eumenes II, that Pergamon acquired its most outstanding artistic adornment, the great Altar of Zeus: see Figure 38. It lay on a terrace of the high citadel, and was visible from afar on all sides. It consisted of a mighty walled, almost square, platform, 115 feet by 124½ feet. On one long side this was interrupted by a wide stairway, which led to the level area on which the Altar itself stood. This area was surrounded on all sides by Ionic columns.

The platform stood on a base as tall as a man, which was surrounded by a long relief-frieze, 7½ feet high and 142 yards long, representing the War of the Gods and the Giants. The age-old myth here formed an allusion to the Pergamene victories over the Gauls.

The Altar, which was excavated by German archaeologists, was reconstructed in the period between the two World Wars in the Pergamon Museum in Berlin. The names of the artists who worked on the Altar were engraved below the relief. One of them is Menecrates.

The frieze of the altar is not only the largest monumental sculpture of Greek art to survive; the War of the Giants (see Plate 99) also constitutes a sculptural expression of an entire period of culture.

It is an unparalleled confusion of figures. The legs of the giants terminate in snakes, whose biting heads participate in the strife, and whose spirals entwine the gods and occupy all the space between the contestants. Expressions of joy and pride in victory alternate with expressions of pain, care, fear, compassion and nobility.

The dimensions of the bodies are powerful, with swelling muscles; the female deities and the female kinsfolk of the giants mostly wear clothes, which with their richly folded surfaces form an effective contrast to the naked figures.

The composition is continuous, without any sharp break from one side of the stairway right round the structure to the other side. Distinct groups can, however, be distinguished, among which that of Zeus and Athena with their opponents is particularly conspicuous by reason of their magnificent execution. Mature male strength has probably seldom received a more complete expression than in the mighty figure of Zeus, which reminds us of that of Poseidon in the west pediment of the Parthenon. The figure of the moon-goddess, Selene, provokes particular admiration for its fine work.

A few irregularities apart, the work is of surprisingly high quality when one considers the vast extent of the undertaking, which must have required a whole force of collaborators.

The background wholly disappears behind the welter of figures, and the relief is so deep that the bodies stand free from the back-ground.

The style of this relief has often been compared with that of European Baroque art, and it has been called 'Greek Baroque'. The comparison is just in so far as the details of the forms and the external composition are concerned, but the composition in depth, the treatment of air and light on the Altar-relief are very unlike that encountered in Baroque art, and the spirit which inspires it is different.

A relief which represented Telephos' fate and deeds ran round the Ionic colonnade, which enclosed the level area above the platform like a railing. Telephos was a son of Heracles and was regarded as the founder of the city of Pergamon. This frieze is smaller than the frieze of the Giants; the figures are still smaller, and do not reach to the top edge of the relief. They are for the most part sparsely set, and the landscape round about them is given in detail. It is on this account that the Telephos-frieze is the most important document in the history of Greek landscape representation. The ground is shown as generally rising, rocks and buildings conceal the horizon, and delineate the space.

The different scenes on the frieze are divided only by such objects as trees and buildings which form part of the representation. The story is thus continuous. This method of composition was later developed in the historical reliefs of the Roman period.

Discoveries in Pergamon also included a large number of statues. Many of these reveal an extremely subtle treatment of drapery, which even reaches the point where the folds of the under-garments were made visible through those of the upper garments.

By about 200 B.C. the Romans had already begun to intervene in the quarrels of the Greek states, and soon occupied the culturally important areas of the Balkan peninsula. The subjection of Pergamon to Rome in 133 marked the end of independent artistic production there. Syria was torn to pieces by internal strife, and the power of Egypt was on the decline. Artists found a refuge in Rhodes and in other Greek centres, including Delos. The Rhodian sculptors continued an indigenous tradition with pathetic groups such as 'The Death of Dirce', by Apollonius and Tauriscus, the 'Farnese Bull', the 'Scylla' group in Sperlonga, and the Laocoon group by Athanodoros, Hagesandros and Polydoros (Plate 105).

These groups are proof of an extraordinarily clever sense of composition, and the Laocoon manifests in addition an effective treatment of detail which awoke the wonder of the Renaissance and of the Baroque period. Even after the middle of the eighteenth century Lessing called his outline of aesthetics, *Laocoon*. By contrast with earlier Hellenistic groups such as 'The Gaul and his Wife', the 'Farnese Bull' and other pieces, Laocoon and his Sons are set side by side, as in a relief. This too is a sign of incipient classicism.

The naturalistic treatment, which the Hellenistic age inherited from Lysippos, had been a way of heightening the potentialities of expression. The pronounced pathos of the Pergamene period had given naturalism an idealistic character. Artists did not, however, refrain from themes of a more agonizing nature: the torments and mental anguish of Marsyas induced more than one Hellenistic artist to show his skill in portraying suffering. Towards the end of the Hellenistic period a realism emerges which is self-sufficient. The spiritual element yields to representations of the infirmities of old age, and other themes which a Classic sculptor wholly passed by. Old fishermen and labourers, a drunken old woman, a begging philosopher and similar figures are now subjects for treatment by skilful artists.

Through all the phases of the Hellenistic age there exists an art which is dominated by an idyllic 'rococo' tendency with a strong emphasis both on the sentimental, and on the games and pranks of the children of nature, fauns and nymphs. To this group belongs the 'Boy with a Goose', the work of Boethos, which was particularly popular in the Roman period.

THE ART OF PORTRAITURE

The Hellenistic age was a golden age of portraiture. Early Classic and Phidian art had nourished the interest in, and the ability to portray, physiognomical features. Another prerequisite for the art of portraiture was the new attitude to human beings as individuals, which operates from the end of the Periclean epoch. Individualism, which had such triumphs to celebrate in the Hellenistic age, emerges in Athens already a century before Alexander the Great, as witnessed not least by such dominating and colourful personalities as Pericles and Alcibiades.

The statues of Cleobis and Biton at Delphi, of Kroisos from Anavysos, and of Harmodios and Aristogeiton in Athens, and even Cresilas' famous statue of Pericles, may have been regarded as portraits by their contemporaries; to our eyes they are still ideal representations. The first genuine portrait-statues in the Greek world seem to have been executed in the cities of Asia Minor under Persian sway, on the orders of, or as an act of homage to, the Persian satraps. It is scarcely a matter of chance that the series of Greek monumental portraits of rulers is inaugurated by the portrait-statues from the Mausoleum (about 350 B.C.): see Plate 90.

Until the middle of the fifth century all Greek art was religious. In the first place even portrait-statues belonged to the religious sphere, as votive-statues in temples and sanctuaries, or as statues of heroes closely associated with a hero-cult. Thus Cresilas' statue of Pericles was a votive-offering which took its place in the fortress-sanctuary of Pallas Athene. Silanion's portrait of Plato, which was placed in the Academy, carried a votive-inscription to the Muses.

As heroes of Athenian democracy, Harmodios and Aristogeiton were commemorated by statues erected in the Athenian Agora. In the same way a statue of Themistocles, portrayed in heroic nudity, was set up in the market-place of Magnesia; beside the statue stood a sacrificial altar. The disciples of the philosopher Epicurus also offered sacrifice before his statue on commemorative days.

The art of portraiture finally emerged in Athens in the fourth century, when portraits of living persons began to appear. Copies of honorific statues of, for example, Aeschines and Demosthenes are preserved (Plate 96).

Before the Hellenistic age only a very limited class of persons was honoured with portrait-statues: kings, statesmen, orators, poets, philosophers and victors in the athletic contests. But when cities became more and more dependent for their existence on the spirit of self-sacrifice of wealthy private citizens, there was an inflation in honorific statues, which became the most usual way for the public to thank its benefactors.

Another important group of portraits is represented by the ideal portraits of long dead luminaries of Greek culture, executed by artists on the basis of the ideal conception of the age. Such ideal portraits were, for example, Silanion's portrait of Sappho and the various Hellenistic portraits of Homer (Plate 103).

In spite of this ever-increasing ability to portray individuality, the Hellenistic portrait-sculptors never wholly abandoned the idealization of their subject. In this respect their portraits, even those which portray Romans, may be distinguished from the veristic portraits which were executed outside the sphere of Greek influence, in Etruria and in Republican Rome.

PAINTING

The later part of the fourth century was regarded by critics of the Roman period as the true golden age of painting. The name of Apelles always shone brightest in the artistic firmament, and it was not even overshadowed by the names of the greatest sculptors. By the side of Apelles were many other painters of distinction, Protogenes, Aetion, Antiphilos and others. The ancient paintings preserved from the cities devastated by Vesuvius in A.D. 79 lend support to the impression to be derived from literature. The paintings found there are largely copies and variations of Greek originals from the later part of the fourth century and the early Hellenistic period, the Classic period of ancient painting.

Since the material at our disposal is not sufficient to enable us to distinguish clearly defined stages of development within this rich period, it will be convenient to combine a sketch of the age of Apelles with a survey of Hellenistic painting.

With Apelles the leadership in painting passed from Greece proper to Ionia. Apelles himself had indeed been a student in Sicyon, but his style and method of work were wholly unlike those of the Sicyonian school. After his student-years he settled in the flourishing city of Ephesus, in his native Ionia.

His status is revealed by the statement that he was the only painter who had the privilege of painting Alexander from life, just as Lysippos had a corresponding privilege among sculptors. Apelles portrayed the King with the attribute of Zeus, the shaft of lightning.

The artist's most notable canvas was that of Aphrodite Anadyomene, which represented the goddess standing in the water, while she wrung out her hair. Some of Apelles' pictures were compositions with a number of persons, but for the most part the number of figures seems to have been few. With regard to the range of colours on his palette he is said to have remained faithful to the four used by Polygnotos, but he seems to have understood how to extract from them a large number of shades, for he was particularly notable for his rich and attractive colours. He preferred the tempera-technique to the use of wax colours. Apelles was famed for his ability to portray clearly his characters' moods and attitudes of mind, however varying they may have been. At the same time charm was reckoned as the pre-eminent quality of his paintings.

No faithful copy survives to furnish us with a direct impression of Apelles' style. It is true of him, as of painters contemporary with him, that the human being formed the main element in his canvases. Landscape played only a very subordinate role, and was represented instead by nymphs and other appropriate substitutes. The range of theme was extended to include, in addition to mythology and history, genre-motifs and even occasionally still-life; some artists show an interest in the problems of light and illumination. Pliny tells us of a canvas of Antiphilos representing a boy blowing on a sacrificial fire, in which the reflection of the fire in the boy's face was particularly admired.

Of all the many paintings from Pompeii and the neighbouring cities, which go back to originals of Apelles and his immediate successors, it appears that the great mosaic representing the confrontation in battle of Alexander and Darius is the truest to its original. It has been suggested that it is a copy of the original by Philoxenos, who painted this subject for Cassander of Macedon who was active in Athens shortly after the death of Alexander. The same original probably inspired the master of the Alexander-sarcophagus from Sidon of which we have already spoken. The copy of the mosaic (Plate 137) has certainly lost some of the figures which were in the original, but the overall impression of the composition seems to be faithfully retained. The scene is depicted from a low-lying vantage-point. The foremost groups in the *mêlée* consequently conceal those in the further distance. Above the heads of the combatants the lances of the Macedonian infantry stand out against the sky. Because of this the picture has very little depth, but within the available space it is a mass of movements criss-crossing in different directions from left to right, inwards towards the background and out towards the spectator. Darius dominates the picture on one side, where he rises in his great chariot, full of compassion for the faithful Persians who fall under Alexander's lance beside his chariot. The other half of the picture is dominated by the figure of the Macedonian King, who rushes forward to the attack. The artist has contrived with great skill to draw the onlooker's attention to him: Alexander is the centre of force that dominates the action. Colour and line-composition combine to create such an impression. The ground-colour of the picture is a warm yellow tone which, together with the other colours, brown, black and red, creates a rich colour-symphony. Lust of battle and will to conquer, faithfulness unto death, and compassion for the fallen, all find place within this picture, so rich in human and artistic values.

Portrayals of the human figure continue to be the dominant subject of Hellenistic painting. In some paintings from Herculaneum and Boscoreale we find figures placed to form a small scene with a wall as background. The figures stand out plastically against their surroundings. The use of colour and the treatment of light combine to bring the different figures into prominence. The brush-work has a plastic, modelling character.

The great salon in the 'Villa dei Misteri' outside the walls of Pompeii has given us a large composition with figures in monumental, plastic style. The painting has been adapted to an architectural decoration in the Second Pompeian style. On three of the walls of the room there are scenes connected with the Dionysiac mysteries (Plate 132). In the centre of the back wall sits the god himself beside an enthroned goddess. In this frieze with its figures of natural size the means of expression usual in painting have been subordinated to the presentation of the plastic value of the figures. The figures make an impression as of living statues.

Only in the later Hellenistic period did landscape achieve a more independent development, such as we see in the paintings with motives from the Odyssey, from a house in Rome (now in the Vatican). The figures are small in comparison with the surrounding landscape. The action in the foreground is viewed from above, as if the onlooker stood on a look-out post. The view within the landscape is for the most part shut off by the high-piled, rugged rocks. Only

here and there the prospect opens towards a distant sea, the horizon
of which lies high up towards the upper edge of the picture: Plate
135.

As a result of the fragmentary nature of the material available for
study we can only follow the purely aesthetic and technical development of Hellenistic painting in a very incomplete way. On the other
hand we know that the range of themes became much richer within
this sphere. Among the large number of most delightful and gracious
representations of Eros, in which the houses of Pompeii were so
rich, there are certainly many which reproduce Hellenistic forms
more or less directly.

Hellenistic art developed and enriched the inheritance it received
from Classic art. Its wealth of forms enabled it to be used for the
most varied tasks. It glorified the power of the world-states, gave
expression to the Greek myths and sagas of heroes, and gave space
and atmosphere to the private house. If we look back from this
final point over the complete development of Greek art, its course
may in some degree seem to be finished. All possibilities in the
artistic representation of the human form seem to have been exploited. The Hellenistic age mastered in sovereign style the canons
for the execution of statues in all conceivable postures, and for the
most difficult group-compositions with extension in height, width
and depth. But the evolution was not complete. Greek art still
carried within itself the seed of a new and imposing development.
There were still many problems unsolved when, as the masters of the
world, the Romans took possession of Greek art, along with the other
elements of Greek culture, and exploited it for their own special
requirements.

III · The Art of the Etruscans

FROM the earliest times the Apennine peninsula had absorbed impulses deriving from the higher cultures of the east. In addition, links existed with Central Europe by way of the eastern Alps. Before the Greek colonial epoch the culture of the Apennine peninsula was essentially an offshoot of the Middle European and Balkan culture. Sicily and the most southern part of the peninsula belonged, on the other hand, to the world of Mediterranean culture. The Tyrrhene coastal zone, which had already had links with the world of Aegean culture (as is shown, for example, by the remarkable excavations at Luni in Etruria), was increasingly drawn into the sphere of influence of the Aegean and the eastern Mediterranean. A culture, which differed in important respects from the Bronze Age culture, now made its entry into Italy. The carriers of this 'Tyrrheno-Archaic' culture originally occupied only a few bases on the Tyrrhene coast. A first wave of immigrants buried their dead in rectangular shaft-graves which were kept together in special necropoleis; a somewhat later wave is characterized by its fields of urn-graves; in certain places, especially in Latium and southern Etruria, the two rites existed side by side. These immigrations occurred not long before the true Hellenic colonization, in the course of the eighth century.

The immigrants clearly came principally by sea, and various factors indicate that they embarked in the Aegean area. Beside the grave-types they brought with them a new type of settlement, and by their choice of sites laid the foundations of the later Etruscan urban development.

Some carefully selected plateaux in the region of the Etruscan coast now became thickly populated with an agricultural population, concentrated in villages and skilled in the use and even manufacture of weapons. It is this society which in a relatively short time developed into the well-known major Etruscan cities, Tarquinii, Vulci, Caere, Veii and others. The same development occurred also in the settlements on the Roman hills. At the end of the seventh century the Proto-Etruscan village-communities had already taken on the character of cities. From this time we may legitimately speak of an

ETRUSCAN ITALY

0   10   20   30   40   50 MILES

The Art of the Etruscans

Etruscan nation and an Etruscan culture. To the same date also belong the oldest inscriptions in the Etruscan language.

Through its increased prosperity, the result primarily of its wealth of iron-ore and other metals and its abundance of forest, through its intensified commercial connections with the eastern Mediterranean, and not least through the direct collaboration of immigrant Greeks, Etruria was now finally brought within the world of eastern Mediterranean urban civilization.

In their turn the south Etruscan metropoleis founded new cities in north Etruria, in the Po-Valley, especially Felsina (Bologna), and on the Adriatic coast, as also in Latium and Campania. The village-communities on the Roman hills were transformed around 575 to a city of Etruscan character, and in part with Etruscan kings, while Capua became the political and cultural centre of Campania. In the sixth century the Etruscan union of cities dominated culturally and politically the greater part of the Apennine peninsula north of Paestum. The Etruscans now competed with the Greeks and Carthaginians for the supremacy of the western part of the Mediterranean. But in 474 Hieron I, tyrant of Syracuse, inflicted a crushing blow on them at sea. Split as they now were into numerous city-states, they could not in the long run withstand the growing power of Rome. In the fourth and third centuries their land was finally incorporated into the Roman state.

The development of Etruscan art was fundamentally determined by influences from the cultural regions of the east. In their new homeland the Tyrrheno-Archaic pioneers had lit upon a comparatively sparse population, whose culture was most closely associated with both the Balkan peninsula and Central Europe. It practised both agriculture and stock-raising, and decorated its better type of clay vessels with carved or hollowed-out geometric designs, frequently emphasized by the application of a white chalky material as a contrast to the grey-black clay: see Figure 39.

It is probable that the new inhabitants of Etruria learnt from their predecessors in technical matters. But by and large the Tyrrheno-Archaic pottery of Etruria is clearly distinguishable from the previous, 'Apennine', in respect both of decoration and of the shapes of vases. One of the principal new forms is the double-coned grave-urn with horizontal handle. It is often undecorated, but is sometimes embellished with patterns which appear to be inspired by the incised geometric decoration on contemporary arms and ornaments

164

FIG. 39 Decorative patterns on Apennine pottery of the Bronze Age, ca. 1400–1100 B.C. (by Puglisi)

in metal: cf. Plate 107. Variants of the meander and swastika play an important part in it. The principle of the decoration is for the most part tectonic.

A landed class of country gentlemen very soon developed, which made far greater demands on art than did the people of the urn-burials and the shaft-graves. The Etruscan 'Lucumones' were not only yeomen-farmers, they were also mine-owners, industrialists and merchants on a large scale with their own mercantile fleets. Their pretentions to a luxurious life were no longer satisfied by the products handed down from the Central European Iron Age culture. It was the Greeks, and more briefly also the Phoenicians, who gave the Lucumones what they desired in the way of artistic festal trappings in life and in death. In the seventh century Etruria became a peripheral province of the great oriental cultural-world, but a province nevertheless with its own striking, and sometimes rather barbaric character.

Corinthian influence predominated until the middle of the sixth century. This is matched in the literary tradition by the story of how the leading Corinthian, Damaratos, migrated to Tarquinii with four artists, 'who conveyed the plastic art to Italy' (Plin. *NH*, 35, 152). After about 550 Ionian and Attic influences were dominant.

Circumstances have led to our knowing Etruscan art mainly from the graves and their contents, and also to some extent from the surviving fragments of decoration of Etruscan temples. We know less of secular architecture, usually tufa ashlar work. The Italian excavations in Marzabotto, and also indeed the Swedish excavations at San Giovenale have, however, provided valuable data regarding the construction of Etruscan cities. The chamber-graves give us some information regarding the inside of houses: see Plates 110, 111.

The Etruscan temple long retained a more primitive form than the Greek. Wood and mud remained the dominant building materials, save in foundations, which were usually of squares of tufa. The woodwork of the upper part of the structure was dressed with terracotta as in the oldest Greek temples. In Etruscan columns the echinos has a more level curve than on Doric columns. On the other hand the Etruscan columns also have a separate base.

Since the upper part of the temple was not of stone, the Etruscans did not need to set their columns so close as Greek architects. Instead of a peristyle-form an entrance-porch was usual, so deep that the threshold in the cella door formed the centre of the entire ground-plan. This ground-plan was determined by religious considerations, since the threshold-stone was intended to be used in divination, which played so important a part in Etruscan religion. The whole temple was set on a high podium with a large free-standing staircase in the front face.

The type of temple which the Romans regarded as typically Etruscan had three cellae side by side, which were sometimes open to the front.

In contrast to the Doric temple, its Etruscan counterpart empha-

FIG. 40 Tomba delle Sedie, Caere. Section through the entrance chamber

sized the façade, a trait which the Romans retained. There are also examples of the Etruscan temple being axially orientated within a sanctuary in such a way that it was placed against the back-wall of the sanctuary, in the same way as, for example, the 'Capitolium' (Temple of Jupiter) in the forum of Ostia or of Pompeii.

The other type of architectural monument which the Etruscans left behind are graves.

The Etruscan monumental graves fall into two main types, the tumulus-grave and the rock-cut grave. The tumulus-grave is the predominant type in the coastal area, while the rock-cut grave is characteristic of a limited area in central Etruria. Natural conditions favoured there the development of this type of grave.

The tumulus-grave consists of one or more chambers over which was erected a conical grave-mound resting on a circular base. The grave-chamber might be either of masonry or cut out of the tolerably soft tufa-stone. It was also, sometimes, particularly in graves of a later date, given a richly architectonic form; this can be seen especially in the well-preserved and instructive necropolis of Caere. The earliest tumulus-graves are of the seventh century. Similar grave-types also occur in the Aegean area in the sub-Mycenaean period.

The rock-cut graves belong to a class which has characteristic and magnificent representatives in an area which stretches from western Asia Minor to Persia, although it cannot be demonstrated that the Etruscan variety has any close link with any of the Asiatic varieties. The rock-cut grave, which in its simplest form consists of one chamber cut in the vertical rock-face, was the most natural form for a chamber-grave in the area of Etruria where it occurs: the region between Sovana, Norchia and Blera, with its deeply

167

The Art of the Etruscans

scored river-valleys flanked by steep rising cliffs of tufa, now covered with an almost impenetrable vegetation of ground-ivy, broom and honeysuckle. This is, in the most fundamental sense, a Dionysiac landscape. At a later stage of their development, in the Hellenistic period, the chamber-graves are adorned with richly worked architectural façades.

The grave-chambers, especially those in the tumulus-graves, are often ornamented with fresco-paintings. These are priceless witnesses to the mind and outlook of the Etruscans, at least those of the upper classes (they also provide an admittedly provincial and crude substitute for large-scale Greek painting of the corresponding period,

FIG. 41 Etruscan rock-cut tomb,
Hellenistic date

which has been entirely lost). The most important discoveries of grave-paintings have been made at Tarquinia, but Vulci, Chiusi and other places in Etruria also have tumulus-graves with important paintings. In Veii there is a tomb, the 'Tomba Campana', with paintings in the orientalized style from about 600 B.C. The majority of the paintings otherwise belong to the period from the middle of the sixth to the end of the fourth century.

The artists who executed these paintings were certainly native Etruscans as well as Italians and immigrant Greeks. In the 'Tomba del Barone' (see Plate 110) the existence of signatures of Greek artists has been established. The patterns which the artists copied were in any case certainly Greek: in the sixth century primarily Ionic, later especially Attic. In general, the way of life of the Etruscan Lucumones in the Archaic period seems to have corresponded most closely to the culture of the Ionic and Aeolic landed gentry.

The Art of the Etruscans

FIG. 42 Fresco from the 'Tomba Campana' at Veii, orientalizing style

As is natural in this Dionysiac domain the grave-paintings in the Archaic period centre mainly on Bacchic themes: drinking-parties and ecstatic dances are portrayed in a framework of ivy and Elysian trees. Sports, often of a very bloody kind, are also a favourite theme: the Roman gladiatorial games were themselves an Etruscan invention. Themes, usually bloodthirsty ones, from the Greek myths and sagas also occur. Less frequent are representations from the brighter side of everyday life, such as the charming fishing and hunting scenes in the 'Tomba della Caccia e della Pesca' in Tarquinia. Scenes of the Underworld dominate the later period of Etruscan grave-painting. It is a far cry here from the Elysian happiness of the earlier graves—the mood is macabre, and reminds us of Lucretius' description of the 'Acherusian horror'.

The best of the paintings in the Archaic graves are of such a quality that they can help us to form an impression of the style and means of expression of contemporary Greek painting. The air and damp have had a disastrous effect on some of the graves, but many of them still impart a strong impression of the original gaiety of the colours. A number of the more outstanding grave-paintings have recently been transferred to the appropriate museums.

The contents of the graves were often extremely rich, and included

169

both foreign and native valuables. The 'Regolini-Galassi' tomb yielded a splendid gold buckle, or 'fibula' (Plate 109). The decoration of the disc which is 7¾ ins. wide, consists of a lion and palmettes in oriental style. The work is, however, certainly Etruscan, since this sort of buckle was never fashionable elsewhere than in Etruria. The Etruscans were unsurpassed masters of the technique of granulation.

The well-known She-Wolf in Rome, dated around 500 B.C. (Plate 115) is an outstanding proof of Etruscan skill in bronzework. It became Rome's coat-of arms; the wolf was sacred to the god Mars. The figure was struck by lightning in 65 B.C., and as a result

FIG. 43 Painting from Tomba del Cardinale, Tarquinia, ca. 300 B.C. (From an old sketch)

was buried within the sacred area on the Capitolium. According to ancient notions anything struck by lightning in this way must be sacred to the god. The She-Wolf has a wild strength of expression which we also see in the terracotta groups from the temple of Apollo at Veii, among which the statue of Apollo (Plate 116) is the finest. The modelling of the muscular play of the face and legs and of the folds of the mantle of Apollo is stylized with an expressive sharpness to which there is no counterpart in Greek art. The group, which also includes a goddess carrying a little boy (Leto with Apollo?), and Hermes and Heracles with the Cerynian hind, was probably placed on the actual ridge-pole of the temple.

At about the time that the temple of Apollo at Veii was built, an artist called Vulca—an Etruscan name—was summoned to Rome to decorate the temple of Jupiter on the Capitoline with pedimental figures of terracotta.

As a result of the lack of marble and suitable limestone the Etruscans continued to use terracotta as plastic material both for the

170

pediments and acroteria of temples and for the free-standing statues. Thus there survive groups of satyrs and maenads from a late Archaic temple in Satricum, which are stamped with a robust expressiveness (Plate 114). Outstanding evidence of this terracotta plastic art is to be further found in the temple-sculptures from Falerii and Tarquinii, which are purely Hellenistic in style.

In those parts of Etruria in which cremation was practised, for example in the north of the country, funerary urns of stone or terracotta were manufactured, which retained the traditional form of the sarcophagus, but on a smaller scale. The front sides were decorated with reliefs, which are rarely of great artistic merit. Battle-scenes such as the duel between Eteocles and his brother Polyneices, are among the most popular themes.

Art in Italy had become an offshoot of the great art-centres of the eastern Mediterranean. In spite of its dependence in purely stylistic matters, Etruscan art has a veristic tendency, which lay deep in the character of that people and subsequently came to be an important factor in the development of art in the Roman Empire. This is clearly visible in the Etruscan portraiture which had an intimate link from its earliest days with sepulchral art (cf. Plate 106).

In other parts of Italy Greek influence becomes stronger the further south one goes. At the end of the fifth century Apulia, Lucania and Campania developed the manufacture of painted pottery on the pattern of the Athenian. In fineness of technique, in colour and in the quality of the clay they do not rival their models, but there are nevertheless very many extremely decorative and splendid vases among them. The Second Punic War (218-201) destroyed the economic prosperity of Southern Italy, and with it the basis of an independent manufacture of works of art.

IV · Art in the World Empire of Rome

THE defeat of the Hellenistic powers by Rome altered the entire foundations of art. In the earlier periods of its history Rome had not been an independent centre of artistic production. The leading class in Rome, the aristocracy, had little interest for anything other than military matters, politics and money.

The Romans took over Hellenistic art when it was fully developed. Its formal language, and its way of looking at the world and at human beings had been evolved in a world in which the Romans had not exercised any artistic influence. But Roman taste became a matter of importance, not only in regard to the choice of themes, but also for the stylistic form which was decisive in the early stages. When the Romans first employed Greek artists they naturally attempted to acquire the contemporary features of their civilization, and many Hellenistic portraits, which were previously believed on stylistic grounds to portray Greeks, are in fact portraits of Romans. But when the Romans became more familiar with Greek art of different periods, they began to select, independently of current fashions, the styles which appealed most to them, and the artists had to adjust themselves to the requirements of their customers. The same situation existed in the field of literature: Cicero began to develop his rhetorical skill under the influence of the 'Asiatic' current fashion, but later preferred more classic models. Catullus, Virgil and Horace followed similar lines of development in poetry.

What the Romans of the last century B.C. admired above all in Greek art were the sublime gravity of Phidias and his contemporaries and the grace of Praxiteles. They thus accepted a Classic current, which already existed within Hellenistic art, and which helped this latter to win the day. This course of development is most clear in the field of sculpture, but is also visible in painting and architecture.

On the other hand Hellenistic art survived more unchanged in the provinces of the East; thus two parallel streams began to flow, which influenced each other until they finally formed one great river, the

172

ANCIENT ITALY

0   50   100 MILES

art of the Roman Empire, the expression of the unifying cultural policy of the world empire of Rome.

FROM AUGUSTUS TO TRAJAN

Hellenistic art had made its way into Rome in an unbroken stream ever since the Greek cities of south Italy had come under Roman sway. Some nationalistic circles had certainly resisted the import of luxury wares from the east. Cato the Elder (d. 149 B.C.) conducted a fruitless struggle against the process of hellenization, and punished a prominent Roman by expelling him from the Senate, on the ground that he owned a large collection of silver plate. But the Romans had nothing of their own to set against the products of Hellenistic art, and the steady growth of wealth and booty made all sumptuary legislation useless. The need for the masters of the world to create a milieu worthy of their position was ever more widely felt. Greek artists were the only people who could give Roman life such a sumptuous setting.

Marcellus' sack of Syracuse in 212 B.C., the wars against the Hellenistic Kings in the East, Sulla's sack of Athens in 88 B.C., in which he removed the columns of the Temple of Olympian Zeus to the Roman Capitol, were events of great importance for Roman art. Pompey and Caesar inaugurated large building-programmes for the adornment of Rome, but the reign of Augustus marks the real turning-point, the moment at which the Roman spirit set its mark on the art which was created for the embellishment of the capital and of the cities of the provinces.

The age of Augustus (27 B.C.–A.D. 14) marks a conscious reaction in all aspects of culture against the increasingly uncontrolled inflow of Hellenistic impulses. The Romans held the reins also in the cultural sphere.

The Roman Empire had given the world peace, after the continual wars of the Hellenistic age and the long death-struggle of the Roman Republic. In the first century of the Empire, down to the middle of the second century A.D., a general increase of prosperity is discernible in the different parts of the Empire, but Italy was pre-eminent in wealth. An artistic style now developed there which exercised a fruitful influence on the provinces. In the western provinces Rome eclipsed all other centres of art. Even the eastern provinces, which

174

had previously been the home of Hellenistic art, now received powerful influences from Rome, which helped to obliterate provincial peculiarities.

Ancient literary sources for the history of Roman art are very scanty. The architect Vitruvius wrote his work on architecture as early as the reign of Augustus, and Pliny the Elder (A.D. 79) primarily used Greek sources. Buildings and monuments are mentioned casually by the historians, but the most important source of knowledge lies in the monuments themselves, which survive in large numbers; they are moreover frequently dated either by inscriptions or in some other way. Apart from monumental sculpture the portraits of members of the Imperial family also enable us to follow stylistic development from decade to decade.

i Architecture

The art of building in the Roman period disposed of new materials and methods of construction, which completely altered its funda-

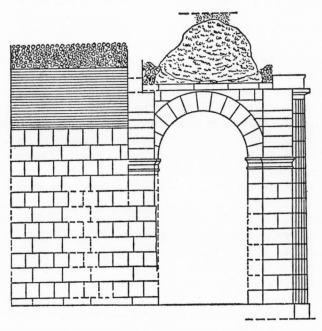

FIG. 44 Tabularium. Cross-section through portico on first floor. Opus quadratum and opus caementicium (concrete)

mental conditions. In the Hellenistic period the technique of preparing mortar of lime and volcanic soil, the 'pozzolana', had been evolved. The mortar was mixed with stone-splinters, and was dressed with ashlar or small wedge-shaped blocks of tufa; from the first century of the Empire burnt bricks were mainly used as facing for the mortar core.

The other important new feature was the true arch, constructed of wedge-shaped cut stones. This technique had already been employed by the Greeks in buildings with a purely practical aim, but its artistic possibilities were first discovered by Roman architects. The Greek columnar architecture was, however, retained as a form of decoration.

The first example of the use of the arch in combination with decorative columns is the Tabularium in the Roman Forum, constructed around 80 B.C. The Tabularium is one of the most distinguished examples of the monumental architecture of Roman Hellenism. We may assign to this period those parts of the old Republican city-wall which were rebuilt in contemporary technique in the 'eighties of the first century.

It was after the Second Punic War and the campaigns against the Hellenistic kingdoms in the first half of the second century that the leading aristocratic families seriously began to re-design Rome on Hellenistic models. Basilicas such as the Basilica Aemilia, and porticos, quays and bridges were now built. The whole area near the Tiber between the Capitol and the Aventine was formalized and enlarged by harbour installations; market-trading was regulated and transferred to a special market-place surrounded with porticos. Aqueducts were constructed across the Roman Campagna on numerous arches of ashlar.

Monumental architecture was by no means restricted to the capital. Imposing indications are to be seen at different places in Latium: in Ferentinum with its market-places and its fortifications of masonry, in Terracina with its shrine of Jupiter built on huge foundations of concrete faced with small tufa-stones ('opus incertum'). In Cora and Tibur there are well-preserved and elegant temples in the late Doric and Corinthian styles. At Tibur also, and especially at Praeneste, we come across complicated and elaborate temple-structures: see Figure 45. The temple of Fortuna at Praeneste, which was exposed by an intensive bombardment in the last war, is constructed on the steep slope of the city in a spaciously conceived

128. Augustus, marble statue found in the Villa of Livia at Prima Porta, ht. 2m.

129. Park landscape: wall-painting from the Villa of Livia at Prima Porta.

130. The 'Portland Vase', b
and white glass, early Impe
date, ht. 0·247m., lower f
missing.

131. 'Casa dei Grifi' on the Palatine, Rome; early stage of 'Second Style'.

132. Dionysiac rites, wall-painting from the 'Villa dei Misteri', Pompeii.

133. (*top*). Walls from
cubiculum of a villa
Boscoreale, near Pom
first century B.C

134. (*centre*). Wall dec
in the 'Second Style',
a villa in Boscoreale
Pompeii.

135. Landscape of s
from the *Odyssey*, fr
house on the Esqui
Rome.

136. Wall decorated in the 'Third Style',
Lucretius Fronto's house in Pompeii.

137. The Alexander Mosaic, the House
of the Faun in Pompeii, based on a
painting of ca. 320 B.C.

138. Seaside villa, from Pompeii.

139. The 'Aldobrandini wedding scene', detail of wall-painting, ht. 0·7m.

140. Achilles on Scyrus, from the House of the Dioscuri, Pompeii, ht. 1·3m.

141. Detail of wall decorated in the 'Fourth Style', from Herculaneum.

42. Relief from Trajan's column,
Rome.

3. Relief from column of Marcus
Aurelius, Rome.

144. The Theatre of Marcellus, Rome.

145. (*below*). The Flavian Amphitheatre (Colosseum), Rome.

146. The gateway of the South Market at Miletus, Antonine date (second century A.D.). ▶

147. Plan of the large sanctuary at Baalbek, with forecourts and propylaea. (*below*). ▶

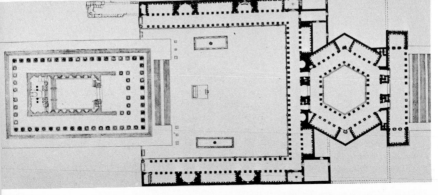

148. The Arch of Severus in the Forum Romanum, A.D. 203.

149. The 'Ludovisi Sarcophagus', A.D. 230–240. (*top*). ▶

150. Relief on Arch of Constantine, Rome, A.D. 345. (*middle*). ▶

151. Relief on base of the Obelisk of Theodosius in Constantinople, A.D. 390. (*bottom*). ▶

152. Agrippa.

153. Virgil (?).

154. Tiberius.

155. Caligula.

156. Claudius.

157. Nero.

8. Lucius Caecilius Jucundus, a banker
   from Pompeii, bronze.

159. Vespasian.

160. Titus.

161. Domitian.

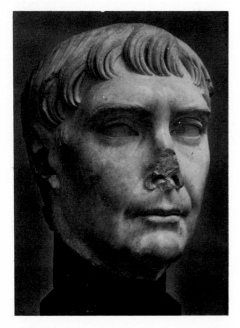

162. Trajan.

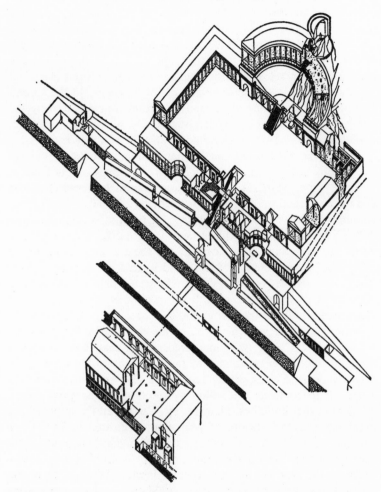

FIG. 45 The Sanctuary of Fortuna Primigenia at Praeneste, axonometric reconstruction, by Fasolo

system of ramps and porticos, leading up to a large semi-circular colonnade, which surmounts a cavea and encircles the temple itself. It is a plan conceived in the same spirit as the large villas of the Italian Renaissance and Baroque Age.

In the Hellenistic period the defensive system of Rome was enlarged by newly-built fortifications outside Rome itself. The first strong ring-walls of the military colonies such as Norba and Mons

Circaeus in the region of the Volsci, and Cosa in Etruria, were erected in the first half of the third century B.C. The earliest portions of the impressive walls of Praeneste and Aletrium with their façades of polygonal stones belong to the same period. In the Sullan age the use of a concrete core with a facing of ashlar or 'opus incertum' became general in the construction of fortifications. In the second half of the first century B.C. 'opus incertum' was replaced by the regular 'opus reticulatum', which was in turn, in the Julio-Claudian period, superseded by, or combined with, tile as a façade-covering.

Among the most important Roman buildings of the period between Sulla and Augustus is the Theatre of Pompey on the Field of Mars (Campus Martius). The old Roman spirit had resisted to the end the construction of permanent theatrical buildings, but Pompey circumvented the embargo by constructing the theatre on the analogy of the plan elaborated in the Hellenistic period for the complex of curia and comitium. The cavea of the theatre was placed like a comitium below a temple which could if need be serve as a curia. The temple was dedicated to Venus. The scenic structure constituted one side of a large portico-area. It became one of the most favoured promenades and rendezvous of the elegant society of Rome.

Pompey's Curia was the scene of the meeting of the Senate at which Julius Caesar was murdered. With that deed, Caesar's splendid building-plans, aimed at raising Rome to the level of the great Hellenistic cities of the East, were also cut short. It fell to Augustus to complete the building-projects of his adoptive father.

Among the buildings planned by Caesar and completed by Augustus was the Theatre of Marcellus, dedicated in 11 B.C., a brilliant example of the use of Greek forms in combination with the new technique. The constructional element in the building is provided by the arcades; the half-columns inserted between the arches support (or appear to support) entablatures which, with their friezes and ledges, divide the floors. The lower floor has Doric half-columns, while the upper floor is decorated with Ionic half-columns. The original third arcade with Corinthian half-columns has been entirely destroyed. The whole decoration is expressive of a classic and simple form, and provides at the same time a rational division of the building: see Plate 144.

As we see from the Colosseum, which belongs to the Flavian period (A.D. 79–80), the tendency was towards an ever-increasing wealth of forms (Plate 145). Above the Doric and Ionic orders of columns, as in the Theatre of Marcellus, there is also a floor with Corinthian half-columns, and on top of that finally a floor with a row of Corinthian pilasters. Rectangular windows and large round shields (clipei) alternated between the pilasters. Vaulted constructions are employed here even more than in earlier buildings. A system of barrel-vaults running in a circular direction is intersected by other barrel-vaults which are constructed radially: a cross-vault is formed at the point of intersection. The weight from the rising rows of spectators' seats inside the building is taken up and distributed by this means. This system of archways, linked by staircases, facilitated the swift movement of the large crowds to and from the spectacle. The whole building was 603 feet long and 500 feet wide. The external walls have a height of 157 feet. The auditorium itself was open, like ancient theatres in general, and could accommodate about 45,000 spectators.

The supporting capacity of Roman vault-structures is most clearly visible in bridges and aqueducts. The great 'Pont du Gard' near Nîmes has a vault with a span of 79 feet.

The best preserved of all Roman temples is the 'Maison Carrée' in Nîmes, of Augustan date. It is a Corinthian pseudo-peripteros with a podium, a wide front flight of steps and a deep entrance-hall, like the Etruscan temples. The profiling of the podium, with mouldings above and below, indicates a link with Greek architecture. The elegant columns support capitals with thick acanthus-ornament in a softer and more luxurious style than that employed by Hellenistic architects. The frieze is decorated with leaf-tendrils.

The well-preserved buildings from the provinces should not be allowed to conceal the fact that Rome was the leading centre of art. Nero's 'Golden House' marks an epoch not so much by reason of the lavish splendour of its decoration as by its siting: it was a royal villa in a natural landscape, conjured forth with subtle art in the midst of Rome. The 'Golden House' can be described as a consummation of the late Republican tradition of villas, exemplified by Sallust's and Maecenas' villas which were surrounded by parks. The work of construction was broken off by the death of the emperor, and the parts already completed were adapted for purposes other than those originally intended.

The great Flavian Imperial Palace on the summit of the Palatine indicates a new departure in palace-architecture: see Figure 46. The plan is more self-contained and more strictly axial than that of the

'Golden House'. The architect was a certain Rabirius. It stood on a large terrace, the foundations of which buried the palace of Nero and many other aristocratic dwellings on the south-eastern slope of the original Palatine Hill. The palace, the size and splendour of which made an unparalleled impression on the contemporary world, con-

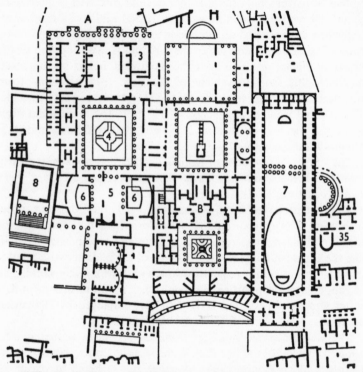

FIG. 46 The Flavian Palace on the Palatine. A: Ceremonial Section. B: Residential Quarters. 1: Vestibulum (Tablinum). 2: Basilica. 3: Lararium. 4: Atrium. 5: Triclinium. 6: Nymphaea. 7: Hippodrome. 8: Temple of Apollo

sisted of three main sections: the ceremonial part in the west, the actual residential area in the centre, and lastly, the garden area (the hippodrome).

The ceremonial area was dominated by the great audience-suite (1–5 on the plan) consisting of a large hall (the so-called 'Aula regia'), a courtyard surrounded by colonnades of two storeys (the 'atrium' or 'peristylium') and finally the throne-room itself, the 'triclinium'.

On either side of the 'Aula regia' was a hall of basilical form (2), and a smaller rectangular room, the 'lararium' (3).

The walls of the 'Aula regia' were divided into niches and colonnades of the type that may be seen in contemporary architectural painting (the 'Fourth Style'). The vaulted roof of the hall had the enormous width of 111½ feet. Its construction is a matter of dispute.

In the middle of the courtyard (4) was an octagon of flower-beds and fountains. Round the circumference were niches for statues, fountains and ornamental beds.

The courtyard gave access to a series of rooms of varying sizes. Those to the west, which are of a notably baroque plan, were roofed with cupolas and semi-cupolas.

The entrance to the triclinium consisted of a monumental pediment supported on five granite columns, between which there probably hung richly decorated draperies. At the back of the hall was an apse. Its patterned marble floor, heated from below by a warm-air apparatus which can still be seen, has been preserved. Two nymphaea were visible through low openings in the side-walls of the triclinium. The palace was ornamented with fine sculptures, and the walls were decorated in intarsia of precious stones.

The residential part of the palace was built round a peristyle courtyard placed at a considerably lower level. This part of the palace faced in the opposite direction to the ceremonial part, that is, towards the valley of the Circus Maximus. It rose here in a mighty façade—like Pelion on Ossa, according to Martial—in the form of a huge semi-circular exedra between rectangular wings.

On the north side, between the ceremonial wing and the hippodrome, there was another courtyard surrounded by pillars, at the same level as the ceremonial section. In this courtyard there was a lake with an artificial island, on which there was a summer-house in the form of a temple, and which was linked with the shore by a bridge. The edge of the lake was elaborately constructed with niches and projecting features in a regular alternating pattern.

The villa-element in the plan of the Flavian palace was emphasized by the courtyard, in the form of a hippodrome. This type of layout recurs on a larger scale in Hadrian's villa at Tivoli (Tibur). Pliny the Younger gives a detailed description of a hippodrome of this type in one of his letters; he relates how the ancient art of landscape gardening made its greatest effort to achieve a suitable and worthy framework for the *otium* of the owner of the house and his guests by a harmonious combination of trees, plants, water and architecture.

It is instructive to compare the Flavian palace with the Hellenistic royal palace in Pergamon (see Figure 47). The peristyle courtyard forms the main element of both. But in Pergamon the grouping of the surrounding rooms is loose and unsymmetrical, while in the

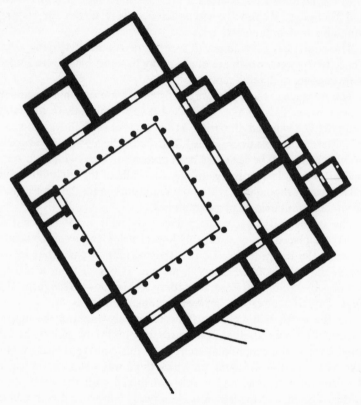

FIG. 47 The later palace at Pergamon

Flavian palace the plan is determined by a comprehensive axial system with a symmetrical arrangement of the various groups of rooms.

The classicism of the early Imperial period had been repulsed. The taste now was for ornament fit to vie in magnificence with the plan and construction of the building. The same tendency recurs in other buildings of the period; thus in the temple of Vespasian in the Forum the number of decoratively worked mouldings which surmount the structure is increased in comparison with previous buildings, and each element is more strongly emphasized by the greater height of the relief-work. The aim was to create lively and mobile exteriors with strong contrasts between light and shade.

In this respect the 'Forum of Nerva', which may be said to mark the last stage in the development of the Flavian style, goes still further. The engaged columns convey a strong impression of relief to the inner façade of the Forum wall.

In the early Imperial period there also developed a particular monumental form, namely the triumphal arch, which, however, has no connection with the actual celebration of a triumph. Its purpose

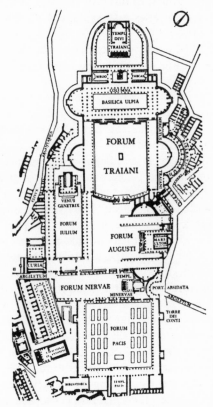

FIG. 48 The Imperial fora in Rome (Courtesy: Graphic Arts Society, Boston, from *Roman Art* by G. Hanfmann)

was partly to immortalize the heroic deeds of a general and partly to mark an important point in the city-plan, such as the entrance to the forum, an intersection of the main streets or a city-gate. The arches are always surrounded by columns with an associated architrave, and a high attic which supports statues. The simple type, of which the Arch of Titus in Rome and the Arch of Trajan at Beneventum are the best known examples, have simply an arched passage. The more developed type has two smaller arched openings on either side of the larger central one. This type is continued by the Arches of Septimius Severus and Constantine in Rome and the Arch of Galerius in Thessalonica (Plate 148).

In Rome the emperors attempted to surpass the great Hellenistic cities by laying out elaborate open places which met the requirements and status of the city as the capital of a world empire better than the narrow and irregular Forum Romanum. In this way the Fora of the Caesars found their place in a long series east of the old Forum: see Figure 48.

The Forum of Augustus formed a sort of entrance-courtyard to the Temple of Mars Ultor, which was directly linked with the back wall of the Forum. The long sides had an absidal form on both sides of the temple, with colonnades in front of them. We have already seen that the tendency to subordinate an open space to a specific aspect of a building occurs among the Etruscans, but the Corinthian columnar architecture of the Temple of Mars derives ultimately from Greece. The Forum of Nerva is a comparatively narrow passage, dominated by a temple in the background. None of the open spaces of antiquity could, however, rival the Forum of Trajan. The plan aimed at a continuous increase in effects. The visitor passed through a gate-house and over a vast square courtyard, 313¼ feet square, to the colossal Basilica Ulpia, with its double colonnades surrounding the central hall. After that the space between the two libraries tapers off, and is concentrated on Trajan's Column, which contained the ashes of the Emperor. Thereafter a broad staircase led up to the temple where the image of Trajan was worshipped. The apses on the sides of both the open court and the basilica repeated a motif which we have already encountered in the Forum of Augustus.

The architectural decoration of the Hellenistic market-place had usually been confined to emphasizing the particular feature of the open square as a separate limited space. By so siting the market-place that the main streets ran down its sides, the square was absorbed in

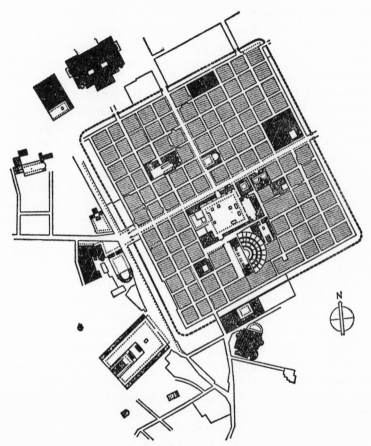

FIG. 49 Timgad. City-plan

the traffic system of the city. The splendid Roman Forum was not intended to be incorporated in a street-system; it leads the visitor on to an especially venerated building and compels him to halt before it.

The plan of the Roman military camp was based on principles which had consequences for the town-planning both of antiquity and of more recent times. The plan of the camp is rectangular, with central streets, the cardo and the decumanus, which intersect at right angles in the centre of the camp. The headquarters lie at the point of intersection in such a way that it is crossed by one of the

185

two main roads. In front of the headquarters there is a tribunal for the general and his staff. In the blocks on each side sections were removed so than an open space was created, dominated by the headquarters. In the fora of some Italic cities which were modelled on the camp-system the position of the headquarters of the camp was taken by a temple of Jupiter, which was so sited that it dominated the forum. Prominence was given to the points at which the streets flowed into the market-place by the construction of imposing archways. A classic example of a camp-plan adapted to a city-plan survives at Timgad on the southern frontier of the empire, near the Sahara: see Figure 49. Here the forum has actually been shifted to a slightly higher level than the surrounding streets, and is thus even more emphasized as the central point. While Greek architecture and city-planning aimed at a harmonious whole, the parts of which are all of equal significance, the Romans aimed at superior and inferior degrees; a just expression of the bureaucratic state.

ii Sculpture

The sculpture of the Roman period is particularly responsible for the opinion which is sometimes expressed that art of the Roman period is derivative, and as compared with its Greek counterpart lacks spirituality. The actual quality of the work of Roman sculptors often seems inferior to that of Greek sculptors; the work was more summary, and was executed with tools and methods which were more economical of time than those employed by Greeks of the Archaic and Classic periods. The work had become industrialized; the taste for Classic Greek art led to a considerable demand for copies of works of the great period, and sculptors' workshops produced these in bulk.

It must not, however, be forgotten that side by side with this industrial production of works of art there existed another in which the emphasis was laid on quality. There were discerning connoisseurs of art even among Roman statesmen. There is certainly no lack of work of high quality from the Imperial period: this is especially true of the art of portraiture.

Once again, we must not employ anachronistic arguments with regard to the independence of Roman sculpture. The close approximation to known themes of Greek statuary is deliberate, and must essentially be judged by the same standard as Virgil's and Horace's employment of classic literary forms and motives. We must above all try and learn from the work itself what effect the artist is striving to attain in the different phases of Roman art. Roman sculpture of high quality is an independent expression of the ideas and intentions of the age.

In the reliefs of the altar of Domitius Ahenobarbus, which probably belong to the beginning of the first century B.C., we see on one side a purely Hellenistic representation of the marriage-procession of Poseidon and Amphitrite among Tritons and Nereids, and on the other a realistic scene of sacrifice. This side is heavy and massive with large simple forms; but the wedding-scene on the other is full of grace and movement, and the artist had Hellenistic models available for this.

In the great relief-plaques of Augustus' 'Altar of Peace' (Ara Pacis), which was dedicated in 9 B.C., the Roman harshness has been refined (Plates 123, 125, 126). The Emperor and his family and senators and priests have assembled to perform the dedicatory sacrifices. A noble dignity characterizes the figures. Two of the scenes represent Aeneas' sacrifice, and Mother Earth surrounded by 'Jupiter's health-bringing breezes' (Plate 125). They glorify Augustus' political programme. The reliefs decorated the wall which surrounded the actual altar on all sides. This wall was divided into separate panels by pilasters, and was in addition ornamented with leaf-tendrils in relief of an especially noble style (Plate 123). On the inside widely-hung garlands of a free yet full style were carved. Similar motifs of garlands occur also in painting, for example in the House of Livia on the Palatine. The artist shows a complete mastery over his material in the decoration of the Altar of Peace. He controls the whole composition no less than the details. With this work there was born an entirely new type of pictorial representation, the realistic historical, representative relief.

Augustus here chose to be represented not as the autocrat, but as the first citizen in the circle of his family and of the leading men of the state. The Altar of Peace is thus the most distinguished exposition of the form of government embodied in the Principate, as evolved by Augustus.

The Altar of Peace provides the proof of a living classicism, capable of taking the types of the great period of Greek art, and moulding them to a new and independent style, which truly expresses the feelings of the contemporary world. The gravity and the calm dignity which the Romans made their ideal, are here magnificently expressed. The impression of space is especially convincing, particularly in the reliefs with a background of landscape.

Some reliefs on which the background is worked in detail belong stylistically with these representations of landscape on the altar. In these the background acquires a value of its own beside the figures. Such relief-plaques with a landscape background were popular for more than a century as decoration for fountains and wall-surfaces.

In contrast to this modern style there stood another, which carried the classicism of the age to such a point that it consciously worked in an archaistic style. The 'Neo-Attic' artists created pastiches in the style of the fifth and fourth centuries. The decoration of luxury vases and candelabra with relief-figures drawn from ancient models was especially fashionable. The tides of fashion changed so that at times this archaic art itself became popular and was industriously copied. This archaistic current is to be detected through almost the entire Imperial period.

The general classicism of the period dominated portraiture as well, though artists did not slavishly copy old models. Some portraits of the Emperor Augustus illustrate the stylistic ideal of the period. His statue in full armour from Prima Porta outside Rome (Plate 128), discovered in a villa which belonged to his wife Livia, is strongly influenced in its stance by the Doryphorus of Polyclitus. The relief-decoration on the breastplate, which portrays how the standards captured by the Parthians were handed back, emphasizes the political character of the statue. A small figure of Eros, who sits astride a dolphin at the Emperor's feet, is a discreet reminder of Venus, the divine ancestress of the Julian race. The firm and clear construction and the sure fine lines of the contours are unmistakable indications of Classic influence, but within that framework there is a wealth of lively detail. The marble statue discovered in the Via Labicana in Rome gives a moving representation of the physically worn emperor. Augustus is here portrayed as pontifex maximus with his toga drawn up over his head (Plate 122).

The Greeks always regarded a portrait as having a public, representative character, constituting either an act of homage on the part of the city or forming a dedication either in a temple or on a funerary monument. Consequently portraits had invariably been in the form of statues. In Rome the custom of preserving waxen masks of deceased ancestors in the home, and of placing portraits of the head of the family in the house, which was under his protection, and, no less, the desire to adorn residences, libraries and parks with the portraits of famous men, led to a demand for simpler and cheaper forms of portraiture. In the first place herms, previously reserved for deities, and busts were used for this purpose. In the age of Augustus busts were still very small, and only reached as far as the hollow of the neck and the beginning of the shoulders at the side of the neck. Gradually they became larger, and in the Flavian period reached as far as the curve of the shoulders; in the following century they even included part of the upper arm and the trunk as far as the diaphragm: see Plate 166.

Augustan classicism produced a number of distinguished decorative works apart from the great ornamental wreathes on the Altar of Peace. Among these are the pillar-ornamentation and bases from the Basilica Aemilia in the Forum. The manufacture of pottery also flourished in the early Imperial period, at Arezzo, which produced vessels of glazed red ware with fine moulded reliefs. These elegant vases rival and even surpass Hellenistic wares. Their decoration is related to that of silver work with relief decoration, of which numerous important finds have been made in Boscoreale, near Pompeii, at Bernay, at Hildesheim and as far north as Hoby in Lolland (Denmark).

The numerous stucco-reliefs, which were used as decoration for walls in graves and houses are also characteristic of the period. The relief reproduced in Plate 124 is particularly charming on account of the easy, airy treatment of the landscape, which marks a step on the road to the independent evolution of landscape drawing.

Sculptural style developed during the following reigns in the direction of increasing mobility; the classic framework was broken through, and from the end of the reign of Nero an impressionistic technique developed, the aim of which was to give an illusory image of things by means of a rich interplay of light and shade. This style was at its peak during the reigns of the Flavian emperors (A.D. 70–96). The most distinguished works in the style are the reliefs from Titus' Triumphal Arch and the grave of the Haterii and, not least, a series of outstanding portrait-heads.

Behind this new style there lies a desire to grasp reality more immediately; it is a product of the veristic sense of the Romans. It reaches back to and develops the realism of late Hellenistic art, but it operates with more visual effects than the latter. In portraits we

189

observe a clear and organic construction of the skeleton linked with a modelling of the exterior which brings out in particular the mobile musculature of the face. Less attractive details in the appearance of the subject are also introduced in the interests of truth: see for example the portrait of the banker Lucius Caecilius Jucundus (Plate 158). Here the characterization is almost indiscreetly sharp, with the abrupt furrows and lively play of muscles in the face, but these details are nevertheless subordinated to the firmly constructed whole. The strong brow and the clear modelling of the temples, the oval skull, the prominent nose and the jutting line of the jaw, all help us to see the organic unity of the portrait.

The contours are slacker than in works of the Augustan period. The firm skeleton has, as it were, been contracted inwards, and the muscles of the face have acquired an increased importance for the expression of the face. But already in the reign of Trajan the restless vitality of Flavian art encountered a reaction, which clearly derived its inspiration from Classic Greek art.

At the centre of this reaction stands the decoration of the Forum of Trajan in Rome. From here survives a large collection of barbaric types of a faithful ethnographical style, with faces full of character. Four panels of large reliefs with battle-scenes, which were re-used in the Arch of Constantine, have been assigned to the temple of the deified Trajan. The portrayal of the press of battle rivals that of the Mosaic of Alexander. When the attacking Roman army storms obliquely forwards out of the depth of the scene, the spectator is put in mind of a great abyss from which the mass of troops streams forth.

The most remarkable sculptural representation in Trajan's Forum is, however, the 98 ft. high column with its spiral reliefs, which portray the Emperor's two Dacian Wars (A.D. 101–107): see Plate 142. The idea of adorning a columnar monument with a relief-band running spirally round it is without known precedent, but it was not infrequently imitated.

The representations on the relief are continuous; one scene follows another without a frame such as would break the unified impression of the band. The different scenes are, however, distinguished from one another by the grouping of the figures, by alterations in the scenery, and by the introduction of objects belonging to the terrain. The principal theme is the discipline and bravery of the Romans, their skill in bridge-building and trench-digging—in a word the high quality of the Roman army.

The scenes with cities, fortified camps, woods, the river Danube and others are given in detail, but the representation of landscape is less detailed than that found on the relief-pictures of the previous age. The human beings dominate the whole portrayal. They are concentrated in tight groups which form, with the compact mass, the decisive elements of the composition. On closer study we discern in these tight groups a number of brilliantly designed heads, which give the impression of portraits.

The new classicism which characterizes the age of Trajan, emerges even more clearly on the Emperor's Arch at Beneventum, almost the whole surface of which is studded with reliefs on a grand scale.

iii Painting and Room Decoration

The finds at Pompeii and Herculaneum have provided us with such a full picture of the artistic form of the Roman private house that they require separate treatment. The picture is completed by paintings from contemporary buildings in Rome.

The type of house which we encounter in the dwellings of the upper classes in Pompeii forms a combination of Italian and Hellenistic elements. The Italian atrium-house is identified by its large central hall, the atrium, with an opening in the roof and a water-tank in the floor beneath it. In the rear the hall ends in the tablinum, a room which was open in the front, and which according to an old tradition was originally designed to be the bedroom. But increasing demands of space led to the atrium being provided with side-rooms for members of the family, and the tablinum became the dining-room; when later a peristyle type of construction was added as a further feature in the architecture of the house, the private rooms of the family were moved to the new parts of the house and the atrium together with the tablinum became a typical reception-room and office for the master of the house. The primitive central significance of the atrium in the house is further indicated by the shrine of the lares in a side-niche and by the altar beside the water-tank in the centre.

The oldest houses in Pompeii preserve styles of wall-decoration of the Hellenistic period. In this style the wall is decorated with stucco and divided into rectangular fields in different colours, in imitation of rectangular stone blocks of different materials. This style of decoration, known as the 'First Style' was apparently in vogue until the beginning of the first century B.C.

The 'Second Style' exhibits a painted colonnade-architecture set

191

on a low base round the room: see Plate 134. The walls are, as it were, pushed backwards, and the upper sections appear to consist of open galleries, through which there is a view of cities and columned courtyards with shrines in a long perspective. This style, which passes through several stages until the age of Augustus, is marked by great dignity. Among the finest examples of it are the 'Villa dei Misteri' in Pompeii and the Boscoreale Villa. The paintings set in the walls include mythological scenes, genre-paintings and landscapes, as well as still-lifes. To a large extent they derive from the works of Greek artists of the fourth and third centuries B.C. Comparisons between various Pompeian paintings which clearly go back to a common original show that the copyists made very free use of their originals; it is characteristic that the styles of the copyists are quite different within the various styles of decoration.

In the 'Third Style', which marks a reaction against the 'Second Style', the walls are broken up into an increasingly fantastic combination of landscape and architecture. They are once more composed of large, quiet fields; a brilliant, warm red colour combined with black predominates. The architectural decoration is resolved into delicate ornamentation, such as candelabra, which are not intended to be realistic, but are simply employed as ornament, and as a means of dividing limited wall space. The inset pictures are in light, clear colours, and landscape occupies a large place in comparison with figures. There is a cool aristocratic air over a room in the 'Third Style': see Plate 136. The Villa Farnese in Rome is a fine example of this style.

But this style forms only an episode in the general evolution. The 'Fourth Style', which reigned supreme at Pompeii in the last two decades before the disaster, develops the tendencies of the 'Second Style', but with still greater dynamism: see Plate 141. The surfaces of the walls are full of violent agitation, and there are no points of rest. The actual technique of painting is stamped by a conspicuous impressionism. The style is marked by brilliant contrasts of light and shade, and chiaroscuro painting. The inset painted plaques also aim at similar stylistic effects. The fantastic architectural forms of the 'Fourth Style' and the resolution of the wall into niches and projections betrays remarkable similarities with the scenery-walls of the Roman theatre.

The development of this kind of decorative painting was unquestionably centred in Rome.

The painted plaques inserted in the mural paintings are normally imitations of Greek originals, but the method of painting is not always the same. In the 'Second' and 'Third' Styles different originals are frequently fused together to form new paintings. The best known example of this eclectic taste is the 'Aldobrandini Wedding Scene' (Plate 139), in which elements from the fourth century and the Hellenistic age are utilized side by side. Preference in colour is given to pale violet, green and yellow. Only the figure of Hymenaios with its dark browny-red tone forms an exception to the range of colour. Large parts of the figure are in shadow, but a sharp contrast of light and shade brings into prominence the parts which are most important for the modelling.

The 'Third Style' has a fondness for placing figures borrowed from classical originals in bright and dainty landscape scenes, in which the figures often appear as intruders. These paintings thus correspond to the reliefs with landscape-motifs, which have already been mentioned.

In the 'Fourth Style' the 'impressionistic' technique again emerges. One of its finest products is the 'Achilles on Scyrus' from the 'House of the Dioscuri' (Plate 140). The same theme was treated by a painter of the 'Second Style', and both paintings evidently reproduce the same original. In the painting from the 'House of the Dioscuri' the colours are dominated by the dark, browny-red shade of the figures in the foreground. Apart from this, there is a scale of increasingly pale shades of the same basic colour which passes through the figures in the middle ground to those in the background. The necessary contrast is provided by the pale green and pale violet mantles worn by Achilles and a woman respectively. It is a style of painting based on the effect of colour-values instead of the old variety of colour. The treatment of light and shade gives the whole painting an uncommon interest, and raises it far above the rank and file of simple and faithful copies. The treatment of drapery and the movements of the figures are full of high dramatic tension. The moment portrayed is that in which the young Achilles seizes his weapon at the sound of a trumpet, and thereby reveals his identity, after he had long been cherished disguised in women's clothes in the women's quarters of King Lycomedes.

The 'impressionistic' technique distinguishes the majority of the better paintings in rooms of the 'Fourth Style', though scarcely any are of the masterly quality of the Achilles-painting. The 'House of the Vettii', for example, provides a rich series of both mythological paintings and genre-scenes. We encounter here the enchanting small friezes with *amorini* engaged in a large number of different occupations and professions. In addition there are landscape-paintings and seascapes. Still-life also has some distinguished representatives at Pompeii, which can stand comparison with the best of this class from Baroque and Rococo periods.

We do not know for certain the extent to which canvases were produced with paintings in the same style as the wall-paintings. The familiar mummy-portraits from Fayyum in Egypt of Claudian and Flavian date show the influence of Roman painting in their pasty application of colour, the use of sharp lustrous lights and the contrast between light and dark. Subsequently in the Antonine period the method of expression is increasingly simplified. We see the influence of monumental art with its expressionistic tendencies. The eye is unnaturally enlarged and the contours become harder, while the areas of colour are more sharply juxtaposed: see Plate 186.

Wall-painting such as we have seen at Pompeii was soon displaced by other forms of ornamentation. In the decoration of the Imperial palaces and large public buildings its place was taken by a more costly method, and the walls were covered with plaques of different coloured stones. More modest rooms were covered with painted relief-ornamentation in stucco.

The first 150 years of the Imperial age had remoulded Hellenistic art to make it an expression of the spirit of the Roman Empire. Artists had discovered in historical reliefs and in triumphal arches a medium which was especially suited to express the nature of the State. But the beginning of the Imperial age is also a decisive point in the development of style; new tendencies begin to make their appearance and finally emerge in all their purity.

THE AGE OF HADRIAN AND THE ANTONINES

During this period the Roman principate was transformed into an autocracy. It is true that under Marcus Aurelius the Stoic doctrine that the Ruler was the chosen servant of the State set its mark on the Emperor's conception of his vocation, but the theories of the philosophers and of educated circles could not withstand the practical arguments of the soldiers. The pre-eminence of Italy was reduced,

194

since the country had lost that primacy in economic development which it had long enjoyed vis-à-vis the western provinces of the Empire. An incipient depopulation and a corresponding decline in husbandry were among the prime causes of Italy's economic decay. The provinces of the eastern Mediterranean region now experienced a great prosperity, which led to the increasing deplacement of the centre of gravity of the Empire to the east. Rome nevertheless continued to be an important centre of art.

The Oriental religions gained an ever tighter grip over the great mass of the population in the different parts of the Empire. The armies recruited in the different frontier regions of the Empire compelled the introduction of a policy of taxation which ruined the highly cultivated element. The general standard of culture sank noticeably, at least if considered from the old Greek point of view, which had previously dominated Rome. On the other hand men were now active within the Christian Church and they began to make it felt as a cultural force.

If we consider the external conditions of the production of works of art, we can see that it was not limited in scope. The interest of the state and of individuals in art did not diminish. No period of antiquity has left so many monumental buildings as the second and third centuries of the Empire. Similarly there was no decline in the technical ability of artists as compared with previous periods. This is shown by a number of works of high quality, which are of greater evidential value than the products of industrial art. The differences between the leading works of this period and of those which precede it lies not in the quality of the work but in its artistic purpose.

i Architecture

The aesthetic construction of the enclosed space is the most important contribution of the Romans to the history of art. The new aspect of a room was essentially provided by the construction of arches. The barrel-vault had already been in use at the end of the Republic; the age of Hadrian gives us the first example of a monumental building entirely roofed by a cupola, the Pantheon in Rome (Plate 127). The main element consists of a circular structure with a diameter of 143 feet. Light was admitted through a large round opening in the top of the cupola. The proportions are as simple as possible. The vault forms an exact semi-circle, and rests on a circular wall, which is of the same height as the radius of the circle. The lower part of the wall is interrupted by eight alternately rectangular and semi-circular niches, enclosed by flying-buttresses which help to absorb the side-pressure from the cupola. The niches are enlivened by a series of columns the architrave of which runs like a containing zone round the inside of the hall.

The mighty vault creates a light and airy impression thanks to the light pouring in from above and the harmonious proportions between the mass borne and the supporting forces. The combination of strength and grandeur in execution with airiness and space makes the Pantheon the finest room of classical art.

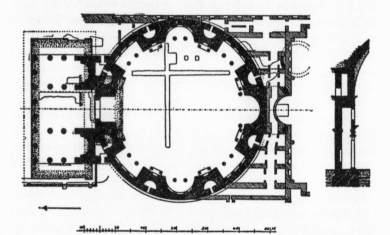

FIG. 50 Pantheon, plan and section. (Based on von Gerkan)

The building with central cupola did not, however, entirely replace other forms of buildings. In Venus' and Rome's double-temple in Rome, Hadrian, said himself to have been its architect, adapted the hall-type with an apse in one of the short sides, which we have encountered in the basilica of the Flavian palace, and so arranged the two buildings that the apses lay back to back. It is not certain to what extent the roof was vaulted from the outset, or whether this was the result of a later reconstruction.

Since arch and vault constructions now enabled the weight to be focused on a small number of points, with the result that the inter-mediate parts became unimportant from an architectural point of view, the walls could now be designed with greater freedom and variation than hitherto. For example in Hadrian's Villa at Tivoli

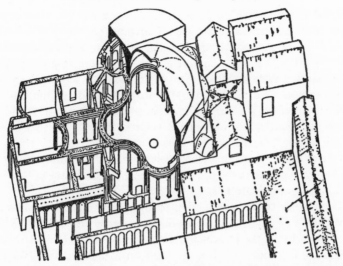

FIG. 51 Hadrian's Villa at Tivoli, the 'Piazza d'Oro'. Axonometric reconstruction, by Kähler

there is a hall the roof of which is supported by large pillars. The intervening space is occupied by slender pillars set in a curved row, which swing outwards and inwards on either side; the whole plan of the room comes to resemble a Greek cross with rounded arms. It is as capricious and diversified as a rococo pavilion: see Figure 51.

Hadrian's Villa constitutes an attempt to fuse natural landscape and architecture. The whole complex reveals a striving after variation: halls of pillars, loggias, open and enclosed courtyards and fountains have been fused to a unity with the beautiful landscape at the edge of the Roman Campagna. The whole is populated with gods and the spirits of nature in marble. The real aim of the whole construction was a mythological landscape, as being the only worthy setting for the Divine Caesar.

The Mausoleum of the Emperor Hadrian has withstood the destruction of the ages; its core served in the Middle Ages as the papal bulwark against the attacks of their enemies. Its type had already been introduced into Rome by Augustus. The Mausolea are associated by their size and rich decoration, now lost, with the original Mausoleum in Halicarnassus (see Plate 91), but its ground-plan is that of the grave-mound, which we have already encountered in the graves of Etruscan nobles, for example at Caere.

The breaking up of the walls of houses by niches and projecting

197

groups of columns with canopies, already current in the Flavian age, became a leading characteristic of architecture in the Antonine period. More particularly the oriental provinces and North Africa became the scenes of a comprehensive architectural activity. The great Market Gate at Miletus (see Plate 146) may serve as a significant example of a richly decorated Roman façade of the time of Marcus Aurelius. The same style of decoration is also to be found on the great theatrical façades of the Imperial period, i.e. that aspect of the scenery which faced the spectators.

One of the most striking memorials of the architectural activity of the Imperial period in the provinces is the great sanctuary of Baalbek (Heliopolis): see Plate 147.

The history of its construction occupies well nigh two centuries. The temple of Jupiter—a pseudodipteron—rivals in size the largest temples of Ionia, the Didymaion and the Artemision (height 150 ft., length 177 ft., width 177 ft.). It stood on a high podium, for the terrace-walls of which stone blocks over sixty tons in weight were used. The temple structure seems to have been begun in the first century, but it was not completed until the reign of Antoninus Pius (138–161). The propylaea were built during the reign of Septimius Severus, the hexagonal court not until the middle of the third century. In the second half of the second century the sanctuary was extended by the addition of the temple of 'Bacchus' and of a circular temple (of 'Tyche', or 'Venus'). Their styles reveal a mixture of purely Roman and Hellenistic influences. The temple of 'Bacchus' has a peripteral colonnade of Corinthian columns, with double colonnades in the front, set on a high podium. The entrance is flanked by two towers which support stairs to the roof level. The cella walls are adorned with Corinthian pilasters and fluted half-columns on pedestals. Between these are niches in two tiers, the lower with rounded, the upper with triangular pediments. All the decorative parts, for instance the carving in the ceiling of the portico which contains busts of different deities, are executed with great wealth of detail.

The Temple of 'Tyche' (or 'Venus') does not impress by its sheer size as do the other temples in Baalbek, but it has an extremely original form. It has a circular plan, but a quarter of the circle has been removed on the front face. In its place an entrance hall has been constructed. The round walls are surrounded by Corinthian columns, which however do not constitute a circular hall; the architraves swing in arches from the wall to the columns and back again. We are reminded of a rococo-pavilion.

Palmyra, not far off in the Syrian desert, experienced its greatest prosperity and its decline in the second and third centuries respectively. The mighty colonnades down the main streets are particularly noteworthy; the streets themselves intersected in the centre of the city, on the regular Roman camp-system. The point of intersection was marked by richly designed arches. Streets adorned with columns are frequent in the city-plans of the Imperial period.

Towards the end of this period the art of vault-construction celebrated a new triumph in the construction of the Baths of Caracalla in Rome. This was a public bath of unparalleled size, with rooms for cold, luke-warm and hot baths, arranged in a series of rooms across the width of the building. The room which catered for luke-warm baths, the central hall (tepidarium), which had a width of 180 ft., occupied most of the longitudinal axis. It was covered by intersecting barrel-vaults, which reached a height of 108 ft. from the ground.

While the outer façades of the Baths of Caracalla were relatively simple, the inside was decorated with the utmost lavishness. The Baths had a long architectural history before they reached this final form, which was at once both clear and imposing.

The appearance of the cities was altered in other ways than by the construction of these luxurious public buildings. A type of city like the Hellenistic Pompeii, with spacious patrician houses which had an internal plan and were closed externally, was long since out of date. Already during the Punic Wars the great mass of artisans and other members of the Roman plebs had been compelled to crowd together in dwellings which were more like those of a large city, with varying numbers of floors and windows facing on to the street. The ground floor of these buildings was mostly occupied by shops and workshops, tabernae. Rows of shops of this sort are a form of building familiar from a very early date in the Mediterranean area. In Rome they were certainly to be found in the Etruscan period. Streets like the Vicus Tuscus and the Vicus Iugarius, the 'Etruscan Street' and the 'Street of the Yoke-Maker', in the valley between the Capitol and the Palatine, were undoubtedly flanked by such workshops.

The continually increasing population of Rome compelled the construction of tall houses, which were constructed simply in several floors on the whole length of the tabernae. The Rome which largely disappeared in flames in the Neronian conflagration must, with its tall houses of brick and half-timber, or mud, and narrow streets and lanes, have presented an appearance similar to that which some Arab and North African cities still have today.

In the new city, 'nova urbs', which Nero wished to build on the ruins of the old, the danger of fire was to be reduced by the construction of wider streets and improved methods of building. We see the realization and completion of Nero's ideal in Ostia. Here and there we may still see an old patrician house surviving from the old aristocratic world of Ostia—two, which date from the time of

FIG. 52 Reconstruction of a street in Ostia, by Gismondi

Augustus, are imposing structures—but for the most part the form of tenement house which became the norm in Rome and Ostia in the second century of the Empire is predominant here. The faulty and inflammable houses of pre-Neronian type have finally been abandoned. The houses turn their tiled façades, usually furnished with a balcony, on to streets richly paved with basalt paving stones. The ground floor is occupied by tabernae, with wide porches on the street. In the main thoroughfares, the ground floor buildings often have porticos, such as we later find, for example, in the north Italian cities: see Figure 52.

The upper floors, which had a separate stairway, were divided into groups of rooms which were lit by large windows on the street-side and also from light-wells on the inside. The usual height of tenements in Ostia seems to have been three or four floors, and the maximum height allowed by the civic authorities was 65½ feet. This particularly functional type of city-dwelling found a direct continuation in the domestic dwellings of the mediaeval period in Italy and the neighbouring countries.

ii Sculpture

The age of Hadrian, like that of Trajan, is customarily designated as classicistic in taste, but it does not only turn back to the past. It holds firmly to the forms of the classic age, but new tendencies appear against this background. A soft sentimentality permeates the age. The taste of the time is revealed in its figures of young men of languishing beauty, an Antinous for example or an Endymion. The usual observation that these figures are copies of Greek originals does not get to the core of the problem. The significant feature from the point of view of artistic history is not the extent to which they resemble their models, but how much they differ from them. The statues of Antinous have indeed very little in common with the statues of athletes of the early part of the fifth century B.C., of which they seem to be copies. The softness, the muscles which merge into one another in gentle almost invisible waves, the dreamy expression, all give the portrait an extremely weak character. The figure of Antinous almost lacks form; the treatment of the surface is such that the light seems to find its way into the stone. It is the fine variations on the surface which the artist wished above all to evoke, and which are his principal means of expression.

In the Antonine period the pictorial style is also represented by the best of the portraits. The altered technique does not give less reality to the portraits than the method of work prevalent in the preceding period did. The new feeling for style and the philosophical classicism are also to be seen in a far-reaching change of fashion. It again became customary from the time of Hadrian to wear a full beard, a fashion which had been characteristic of philosophers, especially of Stoics and Cynics, from the time of Alexander the Great. The pupils of the eye were now represented by a depression in marble sculpture. A projecting ridge reflected the brilliance of the light as it entered the eye. Hair and beard were often very bushy, and their character was indicated by closely set, deeply bored holes and grooves. A strong contrast was created between the rugged exterior of the hair and the beard, and the delicately modelled features. Thus during the Antonine period the softness which was characteristic of the Antinous-type was gradually abandoned, and the features became livelier, but interest was still concentrated on the expressive and picturesque portrayal of the actual surface, and its light-effects were still further emphasized by polishing. The portrait of Commodus (see Plate 166) shows how the artist sought by means of drilling in the hair and beard to create a contrast with the face, the polished surface of which gives the impression of porcelain. The rich decorative embellishment marks the Emperor as the ruler of the world and the benefactor of mankind. According to the Stoics Hercules personified the ideal emperor.

This Hadrianic and Antonine style was suitable for the intimacy of the boudoir and for the shady arbours of private parks. It was exceptionally picturesque, and subordinated sculpture wholly to the treatment of light. The refined and subtle treatment of the details was not suitable for monumental sculpture, in the production of which the traditions of representative art of the Trajanic period were still accepted.

On the column of Marcus Aurelius, the subject of which is the war against the Marcomanni, we can observe how the artists attempted to outstrip their predecessors. The figures are somewhat larger than on Trajan's Column, and the relief stands out more clearly against its background, both by reason of its greater depth, and by reason of a simplification of the landscape details. The groups of figures are formed into more compact groups than before, and thus possess a greater weight in the composition as a whole. By way of contrast the individual figures are treated more summarily. The assiduous use of the drill helps to give the details of the figures a harder stamp. Where Trajan's Column expresses calm and dignity, that of Marcus expresses disturbed feelings. Its artists had a penchant for emotional scenes; the brutality of war and the grim suffering of the defeated tribes are treated in extenso. When opportunity occurs, the figures make pathetic gestures, and their faces are twisted in anguish, pain, lust of battle or recklessness.

The representation of landscape, which is less conspicuous on the Column of Marcus Aurelius, is again prominent on the reliefs from the Triumphal Arch of Septimius Severus in the Roman Forum

(Plate 148). They are large panoramic scenes, in which the same scene portrays the whole course of a battle from the first deployment till the final pursuit of the enemy. Here too we see an attempt to group the figures in larger crowds, which determines the whole character of the composition. As we approach the end of the period the portraits express increasingly a nervous unease.

The evolution of style culminates in such portraits as that of Caracalla (Plate 168). The 'pictorial' technique of sculpture has been used to express the extreme of inquietude. The reflections of light intersect one another across the face, the different parts of which are emphasized by sharply-contoured furrows. The hair and beard, though not long, have a curious wildness. The artist has not been afraid to show the weaknesses of the Emperor's character; grimness matched with cowardice are written on his features.

Some of the copies of Greek originals erected in the Baths of Caracalla give us in addition a view of the style of contemporary statuary. It is no less restless and ostentatious than the portraits. The swollen muscles of the Hercules Farnese in Naples show how a copyist of this period transformed Lysippos' admittedly powerful, but not bombastic style. The age of Caracalla can be described as the Baroque of Antiquity with more justice than can the Pergamene period.

In the second century A.D. the practice of burial in sarcophagi returned to fashion. The lid often took the form of a bed, as in oriental models, on which the deceased was portrayed in a lying position, while the chest itself was decorated with reliefs, the themes of which were largely drawn from Greek mythology. On stylistic grounds an Italian and a Greek series can be distinguished. The latter includes in particular the sarcophagi surrounded with arched colonnades.

In the Imperial period the centre of the artist's interest in regard to the portrayal of the human form was increasingly displaced from the centre to the periphery. While in the Augustan period the internal structure, the skeleton, is so emphasized that it gives position and firmness to the figure, the artists of the Flavian period portray the musculature in a lively and illusionistic manner. The internal constructional strength which was inherited from the previous period survived. The Antonine age goes so far in its interest for optical effects that it foregoes the inner structure of the figure. It seems as if it was precisely the interest of Roman veristic art in effects which caused art to lose its feeling for and interest in the anatomical foundations.

In the third century the dominating political factor was that of the armies and the defence of frontiers. The emperors were increasingly dependent on the soldiers, who regarded with satisfaction frequent changes of the occupants of the throne, since they thus were in a position to enjoy the payments which newly enthroned emperors were in the habit of doling out. Conspiracies, the assassination of emperors, and repeated civil wars followed. The economic strength of the Empire sank rapidly, and Italy became less and less important in the life of the Empire. In the oriental and African provinces, which were less exposed to the German assaults, the decline was less evident than elsewhere. In spite of the ever-growing economic difficulties, however, the money was found to continue the financing of large building operations. The external status of the Imperial throne and the splendour of the court even increased at the expense of the tax-loaded subjects. State projects and the need for propaganda created an increasing need for art and artists.

i Architecture

After the great reorganization of the Empire under Diocletian two large new Baths were erected in Rome; that of Diocletian is still largely standing. Its main room was transformed by Michelangelo

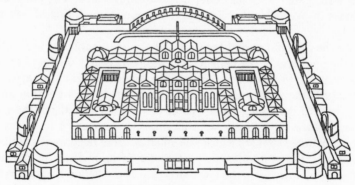

FIG. 53 The Baths of Diocletian in Rome

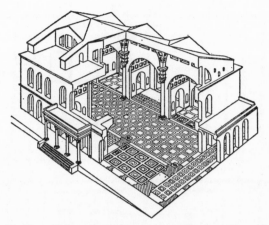

FIG. 54 The Basilica of Maxentius in Rome, reconstruction. The main entrance is
is on the right short side

FIG. 55 The Frigidarium in the 'Imperial Baths' at Trier. Reconstruction by
Krencker

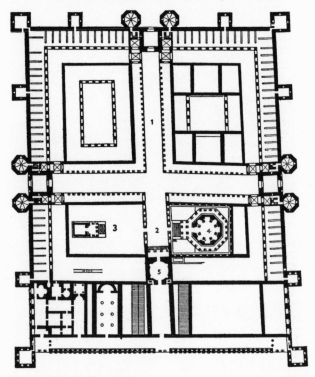

FIG. 56 The Palace of Diocletian in Split. 1: Main street. 2: Peristyle court.
3: Temple of Jupiter. 4: Mausoleum of Diocletian. 5: Vestibulum

into a Church, Santa Maria degli Angeli, which provides a lively
impression of the vast space of the building. The interior of the
Basilica of Maxentius in the Forum, completed by Constantine,
must have been even more impressive. The central of the three naves
reached a height of 115 ft., and the span of the vault was 79 ft. The
whole hall had a floor area of 19,685 sq. ft. In spite of the devasta-
tion which has ruined the central nave and the southern side-nave,
the simple majesty of the proportions of this basilica make it one of
the most overwhelming of all Rome's ruins.

In the Imperial city of Trier, once the residence of Constantius
Chlorus and his son Constantine the Great, Porta Nigra bears
witness to the ability of the architects of the late Empire to achieve
a monumental effect with relatively small means. Trier also has
the remains of two Baths, which are second only in size to those of

Rome herself. Another very remarkable building is the 'Basilica', which now encloses a church within its ancient walls. The great single-naved hall has now been identified as the Aula Palatina, the Audience-Chamber of the Constantinian palace.

Split in Dalmatia is built inside the ruins of the great palace which Diocletian built as a residence for his old age. It is not only, like the Imperial palace on the Palatine, a building for receptions and festivals, but a powerful fortress. The plan (Figure 56) approximates to that of the Roman camp, and forms a rectangle with a length of 626 ft. and a width of 515 ft. Two main streets, which intersect in the middle, divide the area into four approximately equal parts. In one of these lay a temple of the Imperial Cult, in another the Emperor's Mausoleum, which later became the cathedral of the city. Within it there is a circular building with a cupola. The colour-symbolism of late antiquity finds expression in the Imperial red of the internal columns.

The decorative embellishment of constructions of this period is in the first place that of a strikingly mobile style which unites light relief-surfaces with dark, shadowy backgrounds by means of a full range of transitions. This modulated style was, however, gradually replaced by one in which the outer surfaces of the decoration were broken sharply, and contrasted with the dark, shadowy, hollowed-out areas.

The splendid Imperial Villa at Piazza Armerina in Sicily (see Figure 57) forms a counterpart, but at the same time also a contrast to the palace-retreat of Diocletian in Dalmatia. It lacks the rigid axiality of the palace in Split, and is nearer to the tradition of Hadrian's Villa in Tivoli.

The Villa at Piazza Armerina became famous immediately after its excavation, which was completed at the beginning of the 1950's, on account of its unique mosaic decoration. The mosaics occupy an area of approximately 11,483 sq. ft. We are in the fortunate position here of being able to see the representations, not torn up and carefully arranged in a museum, but in their original setting. We can on this account be certain that they were not chosen at random: they stand in a significant and organic relation to the room they decorate, and have an important role in the plan of the structure.

The backbone of the Villa-Palace consists of the great suite of reception-rooms, oriented roughly east-west, with a vestibule (3), a

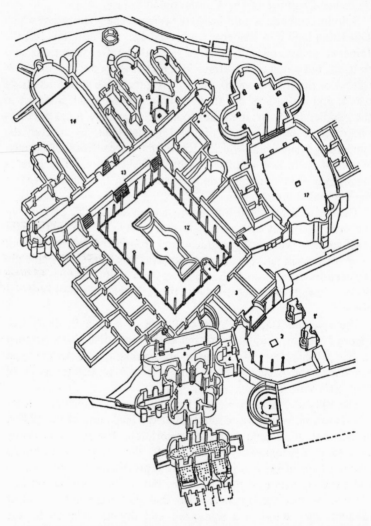

FIG. 57 Plan of the Villa Piazza Armerina. 1: Entrance. 2: Cortile. 3: Vestibulum. 4: Niche. 5–11: Bath-installations. 7: Latrine. 8: Apodyterium. 9: Frigidarium. 10: Tepidarium. 11: Caldarium. 12: Atrium (8 × 18m). 13: Large hunting-gallery with exedrae at the ends. 14: Triclinium. 15: Exedra. 16: Triclinium. 17: Courtyard

163. Hadrian.

164. Antoninus Pius.

165. Marcus Aurelius.

167. Septimius Severus.

168. Caracalla.

169. Eliogabalus.

166. Commodus as Hercules.

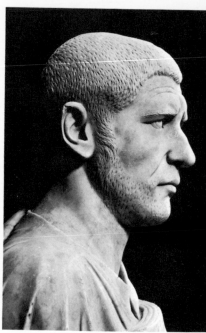

170. Gordian III.

171. Philip the Arab.

172. Decius.

173. Portrait of second half of the third
century A.D.

174. Gallienus.

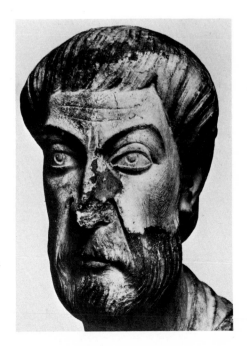

175. 'Eutropius'.

176. Roman lady of early Augustan date.

177. Livia.

178. Julia, daughter of the Emperor Titus.

180. Faustina the Elder.

179. Roman lady of the Flavian period.

181. Julia Domna.

182. Two Tetrarchs, ca. A.D. 300.

183. Maxentius (?).

184. Colossal head of Constantine the Great, from the Basilica of Maxentius, ht. 2·16m., ht. of eyes 0·3m., ca. A.D. 330.

185. Christ, marble statuette, ca. A.D. 360, ht. 0·715m. ▶

186. Mummy—portrait from Fayyum.

87. Detail from sarcophagus of Junius Bassus, ca. A.D. 359, ht. 0·59m.

188. Processus Consularis, intarsia in marble of different colours, from basilica of Junius Bassus the Elder, ca. A.D. 330.

189. Detail of silver missorium of Emperor Theodosius, ca. A.D. 388.

190 (*below*). Mosaic from a Roman villa at Piazza Armerina, Sicily.

191. Church of San Vitale, Ravenna: the Empress Theodora with attendants, ca. A.D. 547 ▶

192. Santa Sabina, Rome. Detail from wooden doors, A.D. 432.

courtyard surrounded by a colonnade (12) and a large rectangular absidal room (14). To the south-west there was a set of baths (5–11) the entrance to which was by way of the large vestibule (2), and which was also accessible from the north-western corner of the porticoed courtyard. In the southern sector there was a smaller ceremonial group of buildings with a courtyard with colonnades on two sides (17), and a hall with a threefold apse (16). So far as the plan is concerned this whole annex is dominated by semi-circles and segments of circles. A threefold complex of rooms on the southern long side of the rectangular hall, the absidal rooms of which have a semi-circular entrance-courtyard (15), forms a transition between the rectilinear main complex and the curved annexe.

The Villa Piazza Armerina, according to the interpretation of H. P. L'Orange, is a palace-retreat for Diocletian's colleague, the Emperor Maximianus, who took the surname Herculeus, after the divinity whom he represented. The plan is constructed with reference to the requirements of Imperial ceremonial. Under the influence of the oriental-Hellenistic notion of the divinity of kings the Roman Emperor had become the focal point of an apparatus of cult, which demanded its own set of ceremonial rooms inside the walls of the palace. There was thus constructed around the person of the Caesar a special sacral palace-architecture, a 'palatium sacrum', which consisted essentially of two parts: the monumental forecourt (atrium) where the court, those seeking audience and worshippers assembled, and, on the axis of the forecourt, as the crown of the whole plan, the throne-room itself.

In principle this arrangement is already to be seen in the ceremonial section of the palace of Domitian on the Palatine in Rome (cf. Figure 46). According to the investigations of E. Dyggve, the scheme is found in its complete form in Diocletian's palace in Split, dated about 300, in the Magnaura of Constantine the Great in Constantinople, dated about 330, and in the palace of the East-Gothic King Theodoric in Ravenna, built around 500.

Here we come face to face with an architectural idea which is of the greatest importance in the history of sacral architecture.

The monumental forecourt, the atrium, was designed in these palaces like a great peristyle court. The surrounding colonnades were sometimes furnished with galleries in the second storey, which were probably intended for the court ladies. At the rear of the atrium the monumental pediment of the throne-room, the triclinium, was visible. In the central opening below the pediment the divine Imperial majesty, the mystical focal point of the ceremony of audience, sat on his throne under the baldachin, the ciborium, at the back of the throne-room. This part of the audience-hall, like the eikonostaseis of Byzantine churches, was protected from the gaze of the worshippers by means of richly decorated draperies. When the Emperor took his place on the throne and the screen was removed the assembly fell on their faces.

As we have already seen there were two such ceremonial structures in the palace of Piazza Armerina, a larger and a smaller. The main entrance lay to the south-west (1). A monumental tripartite entrance-gate pierced in the surrounding wall of the palace here opened on to a cortile, or court surrounded by columns (2). Both the gate itself and the court were furnished with fountains. The floor was covered by a mosaic with a simple, un-figured pattern. From the court the visitor swung round to the right and passed by means of a flight of steps into the vestibule of the atrium (3).

We here encounter the first figured mosaics. In the centre of the monochrome mosaic floor with a geometric pattern there was a multi-coloured representation of figures, now unfortunately in a very fragmentary condition. It represents a procession of men of different ages, wearing festal attire and with crowns on their heads. They have laurel-branches in their hands or else carry candelabra with burning candles. A youth in the front is holding up a writing-tablet, from which he is evidently reciting. They are all looking towards the person entering the room; in fact, as L'Orange aptly pointed out, they are greeting the *adventus Augusti*, the arrival of the Imperial master himself.

From the entrance-porch the visitor passed to the atrium of the palace-villa (12). It was a somewhat irregular square 131 ft. long, with colonnades on all sides. The floors of the colonnades are paved with a mosaic divided into square fields: in each field was a medallion containing the head of a beast, framed in a crown of laurel. We find the whole inventory of wild animals known to the Romans from the wild-beast hunts in the arena; an elephant, a lion, a panther, a wild boar and others, including even an ostrich.

From the eastern gallery of the atrium a wide marble staircase leads up to the entrance hall of the throne-room, the 'Great Hunting Gallery' (13). It is over 196 ft. long and about 16 ft. wide, and closed at either end by a semi-circular exedra. The floor is covered with a continuous mosaic design, with a surface area of about 3,000 sq. ft.: this is the great hunting mosaic. It is a wonderfully well preserved portrayal of big-game, executed with exceptional power and intensity, in a summary but effectively rendered landscape background. The mosaics of the exedrae symbolize two eastern provinces, probably Egypt and Armenia, and thus give a clue to the scene of the hunt. The aim of the hunt is to capture the animals for their further despatch to the Roman arena. The beasts are the same as in the medallions of the mosaic of the atrium: they include rhinoceroses and hippopotami, bison, zebras and tigers.

An elderly man leaning on a staff is represented in the mosaic as spectator of this hunt. His brow is lined, his beard grey and his eyes look heavily from half-shut eyelids, without being very much involved in the dangerous proceedings around him. His dress is the typical uniform of the official of late antiquity: long trousers, a tunic with long sleeves and a cape (chlamys). He has a flat cylindrical cap on his head, which is typical of those worn by officers during the period of the Tetrarchy. It seems likely that this is a portrait of the owner of the villa, whom L'Orange has plausibly identified with Diocletian's colleague, the Emperor Maximianus. The Emperor is flanked by two shield-bearers of the Imperial bodyguard.

In the centre of the 'Great Hunting Gallery', a low wide flight of steps leads up to the throne-room, the triclinium (14). Its entrance is flanked by two columns of red granite. The hall is approximately 98 ft. long and 46 ft. wide. The walls are covered with marble incrustations, a form of mural decoration which succeeded painting for the decoration of large reception rooms. The floor is covered with intarsia of stone with a lavish use of porphyry, the lapidary counterpart of the Imperial purple. In the apse there is an opening like a triumphal arch framed by two columns. In the middle of the apse is a niche prepared for the reception of a colossal statue, in front of which the remains of the foundation of the throne were discovered. The vault of the apse was originally covered with mosaic.

The courtyard of the second (southern) ceremonial sector has an elliptical plan, with a length of about 98 ft. (17). The sidewalks are screened from the courtyard by colonnades. There are two fountains in the courtyard. The mosaic patterns of the porticos consist of a luxuriant pattern of leaves with different sorts of animals in the volutes.

A wide flight of steps leads up from the courtyard to the triclinium

(16). This consists of a square hall with three apses, separated from the hall by columns. The mosaics of the centre of the hall represent the Labours of Hercules. The central apse portrays the War of Jupiter with the Giants, with Hercules as the ally of the Olympian. The floor-mosaic in one of the side apses portrays the apotheosis of Hercules. In the corresponding apse on the other side we see Dionysus in the act of punishing Lycurgus. Lycurgus is swinging his double-axe against a Bacchant, who is changed into a vine-tendril and forms a pattern of vines with busy erotes in the tracery of the branches. The ideas behind the decoration of the palace reach their climax in this hall, dominated by the figure of Hercules.

The development which the architecture of manor-houses and villas underwent is closely associated with the social changes which gave to the large landowner an augmented importance, while the city bourgeoisie increasingly lost standing. The architecture of villas is one of those elements of antiquity with which the leading men of the new tribes, during and after the period of Migrations, borrowed ideas, when they constructed houses of a durable form.

ii Sculpture

Before the end of the Antonine period, and still more explicitly in the reign of Septimius Severus, the plastic conception of the human body inherited from the classic tradition was increasingly replaced by an incorporeal, illusionistic interpretation. One indication of this is that the old technique of the use of the chisel was more and more replaced by that of the drill; we have noticed the same change in the decoration of architecture. The original vegetable ornamentation is dematerialized and transformed into a decorative pattern of light and shade.

This technique was highly suitable for the mobile style akin to that of painting which characterizes the art of sculpture in the third century A.D. A splendid example of this is the so-called 'Ludovisi Sarcophagus' in the Museo delle Terme in Rome (Plate 149). It portrays with unparalleled intensity a struggle between Romans and Barbarians, at the moment at which the resistance of the latter is finally broken. The commander in the centre, whose head has the appearance of a portrait, confirms the victory with a triumphant gesture. In spite of the press which surrounds him he completely dominates the scene, with his outstretched arm, his frontal stance and the detailed working of the head. The calm matter-of-fact air of the latter makes it a point of rest in the general movement. In the crush of the battle we see a wealth of changing expressions and moods which are scarcely inferior even to those executed by Gothic artists.

No field of ancient art gives a clearer picture of the crisis and transformation of the ancient world than that of portraiture. The great classical tradition, which in spite of everything still dominated the conception of the human being under the Antonines, disintegrated in the third century. Through Phidias and his contemporaries Greek art had evolved a complete aesthetic synthesis of body and soul. The human body as a unit, whether it was beautiful or unathletic, was for the Greeks a bearer and interpreter of the spiritual content. It was for this reason that Greek portraits were always in the form of statues, and were not simply heads and busts as the Roman portraits frequently were.

For the Romans, as for the Etruscans, the individual personality was expressed in the features of the face. In Roman portrait-statues the body or, more precisely, its clothing, almost serves to indicate only the social status of the subject. In Imperial portraits the body with its attributes becomes the bearer of propaganda-themes as in the statue of Augustus from Prima Porta (Plate 128), or the bust of Commodus in the Palazzo dei Conservatori (Plate 166).

The art of portraiture in the third century is marked by an emphasis on impressionistic realism. The personality is captured in a momentary image which can embrace within itself the agonies of an age. This impressionism culminates in the middle of the third century in such portraits as those of the Emperors Philip the Arab (244–249: see Plate 171), and Decius (249–251: see Plate 172). These splendid portraits embody the uncertainty of Imperial power. With his nervous or crafty gaze to one side the model seems to be keeping an eye open for possible assassins.

In the following generations, however, this veristic impressionism was wholly transformed: the vibrant, irregular features are arranged in an abstract symmetry, and seem frozen into masks. This development takes place only gradually—after a classicistic interlude in the reign of Gallienus—in the second half of the century. The transformation of impressionism to expressionism is illustrated by a striking portrait-head in Naples Museum (Plate 173). It expresses in gripping and dramatic terms the destruction of the old world and the old values.

After looking at such a portrait it is almost a relief to turn to the stylized portraits of men and women of the Constantinian age, which increasingly avert their eyes from the worldly and fortuitous to a spiritual reality beyond earth's limits. In portraits of the fourth century the expression is focused on the large eyes, which frequently gaze straight in front, and which are greatly emphasized by the expressive curves surrounding them. The aim of the artist is, with the means at his disposal, to render the transcendent human ideal, according to which the body is a casket—or a prison-house for the spirit. The physical means of expression of the spirit are the gaze and the eyes. It is the ideal of the 'pneumatic' man, as expressed especially by the great philosopher of the age, Plotinus.

This ideal operates also in the creation of portraits of the Ruler, the divine crown of the Roman State, itself the earthly image of the heavenly order of things. The portrait of the emperor gives expression to the *divina majestas* of the Ruler, his divine sublimity, by its colossal size and hieratic frontality. An impressive example of this is the giant portrait of Constantine in the courtyard of the Palazzo dei Conservatori in Rome (Plate 184). It formed part of a sitting statue, originally placed in an apse in the Basilica of Maxentius in the Forum. The hair delimits the inscrutable countenance in an even curve; the eyes are unnaturally wide open and defined by regular curved lines. The face is extraordinarily impressive; we stand in front of a being raised above the human sphere.

The 'spiritual' portrait was the legacy of late antiquity to Byzantium and to medieval Europe. Step by step, through different growths of style, we can follow the stylization and abstract concentration of the human face to such a climax of ascetic idealization as the famous head from Ephesus, probably of the middle of the fifth century: see Plate 175. This is the ideal of spiritual beauty of the age reduced to a sculptural formula. The Christian artist employs the same formula for his portrayal of the saints. In a similar way Christ is portrayed with the same means used to express the majesty of the emperor, and his angels, apostles and martyrs adopt the attitudes and forms of the Imperial courtiers.

The development of relief-sculpture runs parallel with that of portraiture both technically and as regards content. It is mainly represented among surviving monuments by the reliefs on sarcophagi. After the period of picturesque impressionism in the third century, which was represented by the 'Ludovisi Sarcophagus', in the reign of Diocletian we find a reaction in favour of anti-classical

214

composition and style. On the Arch of Constantine in Rome we may observe, executed in an equally effective manner, show-pieces of the classicistic style of the Trajanic, Hadrianic and Antonine ages, associated with newly worked plaques in the anti-classical manner of the age of Diocletian. Among these recent pieces is a relief which portrays the Emperor addressing the populace (Plate 150). In earlier representations themes of this sort had been portrayed in such a way that the emperor was located near one corner of the relief, while his audience occupy the larger area before him. Here on the contrary the Emperor stands in the centre on a rostrum. Since nothing must obscure his figure the audience have been placed at the sides of the tribunal. The figures are not grouped naturally in the space, but arranged according to their inner significance, in what we may call 'value-perspective'. The Emperor dominates the frontal aspect in the centre of the picture. The audience is grouped in symmetrical rows on the sides; and their subordination to the majesty of the Emperor is indicated by their representation in profile. The size of the figures varies not according to their natural relationship but according to their importance in the general context.

During late antiquity the representation of the human body and of material things in general became increasingly representative and symbolic. The classical myths are treated in a similar manner. Human figures, like the myths, are reduced to certain fundamental elements, and become formulae for the spiritual content of the age, be it pagan or Christian. More than ever before art became a language of propaganda with a suggestive, irresistible power to impress itself.

The dominating artistic currents in the leading centres of art exercised a powerful influence in remoter provinces of the Empire also, and at various points important schools of sculptors arose. One such school is represented for example by the sculptures from Neumagen near Trier, and we find another school at Palmyra, the style of which foreshadows the Byzantine.

FROM CONSTANTINE TO JUSTINIAN (ca. 330–550)

The Christian religion was officially recognized in the reign of Constantine the Great. It has been customary to close the history of ancient art at this point, but the change in religion in fact does not carry with it so sharp a break in artistic development. Official art, and the art of the upper strata of society continued to be inspired by classical models, which still surrounded everybody on all sides.

The art of the Roman State could not avoid the classic means of expression of Imperial symbolism; at the same time it had to transform them according to the needs of the new bureaucracy and the new Imperial ideology. The figures and themes of classical mythology continued to survive in representational contexts, and they were interpreted in the Christian spirit by the Christians. In the same way the representative and utilitarian forms of architecture of the third century were adopted by the Christians to the extent that it suited their partially new and different needs; for example, the basilica and the ceremonial suites of the palaces—vestibulum, atrium and triclinium—in which the Imperial throne in the triclinium corresponded to the high altar of the Christian basilica.

In the Triumphal Arch of Constantine the relief-style of the Tetrarchy and the classicistic style had still appeared in immediate juxtaposition. But the two styles did not constitute irreconcilable opposites. There thus emerged a synthesis, such as we see exemplified on the Obelisk of Theodosius in Constantinople: see Plate 151.

The hard style in painting and sculpture of the age of Diocletian was replaced even before the end of the reign of Constantine by a softer, more luxuriant style. The human body is made less angular, and the treatment of drapery less rigid. As an example of this style, which reigns from around 325 to 360, we may mention the two statues of Constantine Augustus and Constantine Caesar, which now stand on the balustrade at the entrance to the Campidoglio in Rome. An example from the sphere of Christian art is the famous sarcophagus of Junius Bassus from the basilica of St Peter (Plate 187). Junius Bassus was Prefect of the City in Rome and died in A.D. 359. His sarcophagus is decisively classic both in choice of motives and in its refined treatment of the surface. The statuette of the sitting Christ in the Museo delle Terme in Rome belongs to the same style and date, about 350 (Plate 185).

The mosaics from a villa at Daphne near Antioch in Syria give an indication of the art of painting at this time. They include hunting-scenes, a favourite theme in contemporary art. A strong emphasis on themes involving movement is a continual element in this style. The roof-mosaics in Santa Costanza in Rome, of around 350, belong to the same style of mosaic.

The following generation exhibits a clearer, and gradually a more slender and elegant style, of which an example is provided by the famous silver missorium in Madrid, dated to 388; see Plate 189. It shows the Emperor Theodosius enthroned under a ceremonial pediment together with his Imperial colleagues. Below the main representation Tellus is to be seen surrounded by Cupids. The figures of the old religions enjoy a renaissance during this period, both on Christian and pagan monuments.

The Obelisk of Theodosuis in the Hippodrome in Constantinople belongs to the same period: it has remained in position ever since it was set up there in A.D.390 (Plate 151). From the point of view of composition it exhibits the same hieratic 'value-perspective' as the Constantinian reliefs on the Arch of Constantine in Rome. The Emperor is represented in elevated majesty in the Imperial Box in the Hippodrome, surrounded, at a lower level, by his bodyguard and the dignitaries of the court. Beneath the box genuflecting Barbarians are portrayed in the act of bringing tribute.

The arrangement of the togas worn by the officials, with the contracted shoulder-pleat folded like a fan, reappears on two portrait-statues in the Palazzo dei Conservatori in Rome. Their faces have the same tired, withdrawn features as the portrait of Theodosius on the silver missorium. Such features seem to have been characteristic of the age.

For Rome the fifth century was a period of crises and disasters, which cannot fail to have had an influence on art. Rome was conquered and plundered several times by foreign invaders. In 476 the Emperor of the West was compelled to lay down the purple and hand over the power to the Barbarian leader Odovakar.

Christianity finally conquered the old religions. As a result of the catastrophes Rome surrendered her leading position to Ravenna, which now became temporarily the capital of the western world. In spite of all this, however, works of art of great beauty were created in Rome in the first half of the fifth century. Among those which have survived the sacks of the city are the mighty wooden doors in Santa Sabina on the Aventine, which was consecrated in A.D. 423 (Plate 192). Here the predominant note is an almost classic simplicity and naturalism; the treatment of drapery emphasizes the nature of the material in a manner which, for the age, is surprisingly realistic.

The same classical influence is also to be seen in the mosaic on the triumphal arch in Santa Maria Maggiore in Rome, dated to the pontificate of Sixtus III, 432–440, and also in the mosaics in the mausoleum of Galla Placidia in Ravenna.

In about the middle of the fifth century the simple, naturalistic style was again supplanted by a transcendent expressionism. This ecstatic style may be illustrated by the above-mentioned portrait from Ephesus, now in Vienna (Plate 175). The head is unnaturally extended lengthways, the eyes and eyebrows are opened wide, as if the subject looked into a world far beyond this one. Similar portraits from Ostia show that visionary style was not restricted to the eastern half of the Empire.

After the violent tension of the fifth century and the exalted mood of retirement from the world which dominated the second half of the century, a sort of calm dawns at its end. The features of the faces are harder and more simple, the face itself petrifies into an expressionless mask. The mosaics in Sant'Apollinare Nuovo in Ravenna, dated to around 500, are typical examples of this style.

A generation later, about 525, the stiffness again vanishes, and in its place we find a weaker more picturesque style closely based on ancient models. The famous mosaics in the choir in S. Vitale in Ravenna, which was consecrated in 547, still belong to the traditional phase between the two styles. Excellent examples of the richer style

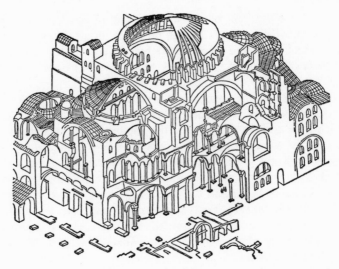

FIG. 58 Representation in perspective of the construction of Hagia Sophia (based on E. Lundberg)

218

are to be found in the great floor mosaics excavated in recent years in a hall of the Imperial palace of Justinian in Constantinople. These mosaics constitute one of the many indications that Constantinople in the time of Justinian finally became the centre of ancient culture. Architectural and other masterpieces, such as the domed structures of Hagia Sophia and Hagios Sergios and Bacchos, all richly adorned with mosaics, testify to the unparalleled vigour of ancient culture.

There is, by and large, an unbroken line from the simple majesty of the Pantheon to the daring orchestration of the church of Hagia Sophia. Without any real break the art of the ancient world still lives in the Levant and in Europe, especially where ancient culture had the opportunity of establishing firm roots. There is no gulf between the art of late antiquity and that of the Middle Ages. The tasks and conditions of artists changed with the changing state of society, but in all the wide region which had once been watered by Greek and Roman culture, both the ancient language of form and ancient ideas and symbols live on as an undying source of inspiration.

CHRONOLOGICAL TABLE
(*Approximate Dates*)

Date B.C.	Crete	Greek Mainland
—2500	Neolithic & Sub-neolithic	Neolithic & Sub-neolithic
2500–1800	Early Minoan; Seaports in East Crete	Early Helladic I–III
1800–1550	Middle Minoan I–III The older Palaces; Kamares Pottery	Middle Helladic I–III
1550–1380	Late Minoan I–IIIA The later Palaces	Late Helladic I–IIIA, 1
1475	New fresco-decoration in Palace of Knossos; Achaean Rulers	
1380	Catastrophe of Palace of Knossos (late Minoan IIIA, 1)	
1380–950	Late Minoan IIIA–Sub-Minoan	1380–1200: Late Helladic IIIA–IIIB
		1300: Construction of great Megaron-type palaces in Pylos, Mycenae and Tiryns.
		1200: Destruction of palaces; 'Return of the Heraclidae'.
		1200–950: Late Helladic IIIC–Sub-Mycenaean.
		950–675: Protogeometric–Late Geometric pottery
		950–800: Ionian colonization in the islands and on W. coast of Asia Minor.

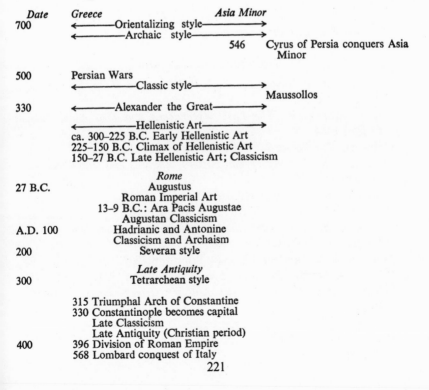

Date	Greece	Asia Minor

700 ←————Orientalizing style————→
←————Archaic style————→

546 Cyrus of Persia conquers Asia Minor

500 Persian Wars
←————Classic style————→
Maussollos

330 ←————Alexander the Great————→

←————Hellenistic Art————→
ca. 300–225 B.C. Early Hellenistic Art
225–150 B.C. Climax of Hellenistic Art
150–27 B.C. Late Hellenistic Art; Classicism

Rome
27 B.C. Augustus
Roman Imperial Art
13–9 B.C.: Ara Pacis Augustae
Augustan Classicism
A.D. 100 Hadrianic and Antonine
Classicism and Archaism
200 Severan style

Late Antiquity
300 Tetrarchean style

315 Triumphal Arch of Constantine
330 Constantinople becomes capital
Late Classicism
Late Antiquity (Christian period)
400 396 Division of Roman Empire
568 Lombard conquest of Italy

221

Select Bibliography

GENERAL SURVEYS

Hanfmann, G. M., *Hellenistic Art*, Washington D.C. 1963.

Robertson, D. S., *A Handbook of Greek and Roman Architecture*, Cambridge (2nd edn.) 1940.

Rumpf, A., *Malerei und Zeichnung* (Handbuch der Archäologie IV), Munich 1953.

Schefold, K., *Orient, Hellas und Rom*, Bern 1949.

Winter, F., *Kunstgeschichte in Bildern*, Altertum, Heft 3–13, Leipzig 1912.

Zschietzschmann, W., *Kleine Kunstgeschichte der Griechen und Römer*, Stuttgart 1955.

THE AEGEAN BRONZE AGE

A Companion to Homer, ed. A. J. B. Wace and F. H. Stubbings, London 1963.

Desborough, V. R., *The Last Mycenaeans and their Successors*, Oxford 1964.

Evans, A., *The Palace of Minos*, London 1921–26.

Furumark, A., *The Mycenaean Pottery, Analysis and Classification* Stockholm 1941.

Marinatos, S., *Crete and Mycenae*, London 1960.

Matz., F., *Crete and Early Greece*, London 1962.

—*Torsion: eine formenkundliche Untersuchung zur aigaiischen Vorgeschichte*, Wiesbaden 1952.

Mylonas, G. E., *Ancient Mycenae*, Princeton 1957.

Persson, A. W., *The Royal Tomb at Dendra*, Lund 1931.

Schachermeyr, F., *Die aeltesten Kulturen Griechenlands*, Stuttgart 1955.

Vermeule, E., *Greece in the Bronze Age*, Chicago 1964.

Wace, A. J. B., *Mycenae. An archaeological History and Guide*, Princeton 1949.

Bibliography

HELLAS

a. *General Surveys:*

Boardman, J., *Greek Art*, London 1964.

Beazley, J. D., and Ashmole, B., *Greek Sculpture and Painting*, Cambridge 1932. [2nd (revised) edn., 1966.]

Clark, K., *The Nude*, London 1957.

Curtius, L., *Die klassische Kunst Griechenlands*, Potsdam 1938.

Lippold, G., *Die griechische Plastik*. (Handbuch der Archäologie V.) Munich 1950.

Richter, G. M. A., *A Handbook of Greek Art*, London (2nd edn.) 1963.

b. *Architecture:*

Berve and Gruben, *Greek Temples, Theatres and Shrines*, London 1963.

Dinsmoore, W. B., *The Architecture of Ancient Greece*, London and New York 1950.

Fyfe, T., *Hellenistic Architecture. An introductory Study*. Cambridge 1936.

Gerkan, A. von, *Griechische Städteanlagen*, Berlin-Leipzig 1926.

Kjellberg, L., *Larisa am Hermos. Die architektonischen Terrakotten*. Stockholm 1940.

Kraus, F., *Griechische Tempel in Paestum, I*, Berlin 1959.

Lawrence, A. W., *Greek Architecture*, London 1957.

Martin, R., *L'urbanisme dans la Grèce antique*, Paris 1956.

Shoe, L., *Profiles of Greek Mouldings*, Cambridge (Mass.) 1936.

Stevens, P. G., *Restorations of Classical Buildings*, Princeton 1958.

Weickert, C., *Typen der archaischen Architektur in Griechenland und Kleinasien*, Augsburg 1929.

Wycherley, R. E., *How the Greeks Built Cities*, London 1962.

c. *Sculpture:*

Bianchi Bandinelli, R., *Policleto*. (Quaderni per lo studio dell'archeologia I) Florence 1938.

Bieber, M., *The Sculpture of the Hellenistic Age*, New York 1961.

Blümel, C., *Greek Sculptors at Work*, London 1955.

— *Der Hermes eines Praxiteles*, Baden-Baden 1948.

Brommer, F., *Die Skulpturen der Parthenongiebel*, Mainz 1963.

Brunnsåker, S., *The Tyrant-Slayers of Kritios and Nesiotes*, Lund 1955.

Bibliography

Buschor, E., *Das hellenistische Bildnis*, Munich 1949.

— *Altsamische Standbilder*, I-IV, Berlin 1934–61.

Buschor-Hamann, *Die Skulpturen des Zeustempels zu Olympia*, Marburg 1924.

Carpenter, R., *Greek Sculpture*, Chicago 1960.

Casson, S., *The Technique of Early Greek Sculpture*, Oxford 1933.

Charbonneaux, J., *Greek Bronzes*, London 1961.

Corbett, P. E., *The Sculpture of the Parthenon*, Harmondsworth 1959.

Diepolder, H., *Die attischen Grabreliefs*, Berlin 1931.

Friis Johansen, K., *The Attic Grave-Reliefs of the Classical Period*, Copenhagen 1951.

Higgins, R. A., *British Museum, Catalogue of Terracottas*, London 1954.

Homann-Wedeking, E., *Die Anfänge der griechischen Grossplastik*, Berlin 1950.

Kähler, H., *Der grosse Fries von Pergamon*, Berlin 1948.

Kjellberg, E., *Studien zu den attischen Reliefs des V.Jh. v. Chr.*, Uppsala 1926.

Krahmer, G., *Stilphasen der hellenistischen Plastik*. (Mitteilungen des deutschen archäologischen Instituts. Roemische Abteilung 1923–1924, pp. 138–84.)

Lawrence, A. W., *Later Greek Sculpture*, London 1927.

Lullies, R., *Greek Sculpture*, London 1960.

Payne, H. and Young, G., *Archaic Marble Sculpture from the Acropolis*, London 1936.

Picard, Ch., *Manuel d'archéologie classique. La sculpture*. I-IV, Paris 1948–63.

Poulsen, V., *Der strenge Stil*, Copenhagen 1948.

Richter, G. M. A., *The Sculpture and Sculptors of the Greeks*, New Haven 1957.

— *Kouroi: Archaic Greek Youths*, London 1960.

— *The Archaic Gravestones of Attica*, London 1961.

— *The Portraits of the Greeks*, London 1965.

Säflund, G., *Aphrodite Kallipygos* (Stockholm Studies in Classical Archaeology, III. 1963).

— *Sulla ricostruzione dei gruppi di Polifemo e di Scilla a Sperlonga* (Skr. utg. av Sv. Inst. i Rom, Opuscula Romana, VII, 1967).

Simon, E., *Die Geburt der Aphrodite*, Berlin 1959.

Sjöqvist, E., *The Early Style of Lysippus*. (Skr. utg. av Sv. Inst. i Athen II, Opuscula Atheniensia I. 1953.)

Bibliography

Thompson, D. B., *Troy; Terracotta Figurines of the Hellenistic Period*, Princeton 1963.

d. *Painting and Pottery:*

Arias, P. E., and Hirmer, M., *A History of Greek Vase Painting*, London 1962.

Beazley, J. D., *The Development of Attic Black Figure*, Berkeley 1951.

— *Attic Black Figure Vase Painters*, Oxford 1956.

— *Attic Red Figure Vase Painters*, Oxford 1963.

Brunnsåker, S., *The Pithecusan Shipwreck*, (Skr. utg. av Sv. Inst. i Rom XXII, Opuscula Romana IV. 1962).

Cook, R. M., *Greek Painted Pottery*, London 1960.

Devambez, P., *Greek Painting*, Amsterdam 1962.

Friis Johansen, K., *Les vases Sicyoniens*, Paris-Copenhagen 1923.

Lane, A., *Greek Pottery*, London 1948.

Payne, H., *Necrocorinthia*, Oxford 1931.

Pfuhl, E., *Malerei und Zeichnung der Griechen*, Munich 1923.

Richter, G. M. A., *Attic Red-Figured Vases*, New Haven 1946.

Robertson, M., *Greek Painting*, Geneva 1959.

Rumpf, A., *Chalkidische Vasen*, Berlin 1927.

— *Malerei und Zeichnung*, Munich (Handbuch der Archäologie, IV) 1953.

ROME

a. *Surveys:*

Koch, H., *Römische Kunst*, Weimar 1949.

Riegl, A., *Spätrömische Kunstindustrie*, Vienna 1927.

Toynbee, J. M. C., *Some notes on Artists in the Roman World* (Collection Latomus, vol. VI). Brussels 1951.

Wickhoff, F., *Die römische Kunst*, Berlin 1912.

b. *Architecture:*

Aurigemma, S., *Villa Adriana*, Rome 1962.

Boëthius, A., *The Golden House of Nero*, Ann Arbor 1960.

Blake, M. E., *Ancient Roman Construction in Italy from the Prehistoric Period to Augustus*, Washington 1947.

— *Roman Construction in Italy from Tiberius through the Flavians*, Washington 1959.

Brown, F. E., *Roman Architecture*, New York 1961.

Crema, L., *Significato della architettura romana*, Rome 1960.

Bibliography

Dyggve, E., *Ravennatum Palatium Sacrum—La basilica ipetrale per ceremonie. Studi sull'architettura dei palazzi della tarda antichità.* (Det. Kgl. Danske Vidensk. Selskab, Arch.-Kunsthist. Meddel. III: 2, Copenhagen 1941.)

Fasolo, F., and Gullini, G., *Il santuario della Fortuna Primigenia a Palestrina*, Rome 1953.

Gjerstad, E., *Die Ursprungsgeschichte der römischen Kaiserfora.* (Skr. utg. av Sv. Inst. i Rom I. Opuscula archaeol, III. 1941).

Grimal, P., *Les jardins romains à la fin de la république et aux deux premières siècles de l'empire*, Paris 1943.

Kähler, H., *Hadrian und seine Villa bei Tivoli*, Berlin 1941.

MacDonald, W., *The Architecture of the Roman Empire*, New Haven and London 1965.

Swoboda, K., *Römische und romanische Paläste*, Vienna 1924.

Säflund, G., *Le mura di Roma repubblicana.* (Skr. utg. av Sv. Inst. i Rom I.) Uppsala 1932.

Tamm, B., *Auditorium and Palatium* (Stockholm Studies in Classical Archaeology II. 1963).

c. *Sculpture:*

Blanckenhagen, P. H., *Die Flavische Architektur und ihre Dekoration*, Berlin 1940.

Charbonneaux, J., *L'art au siècle d'Auguste*, Paris 1948.

Delbrueck, R., *Denkmäler spätantiker Kunst* (Antike Denkmäler IV), Berlin 1931.

Hamberg, P. G., *Studies in Roman Imperial Art*, Uppsala 1945.

Hanfmann, G. M. A., *Roman Art*, London 1964.

Kähler, H., *Die Augustusstatue von Prima Porta*, Cologne 1959.

— *Rome and her Empire*, London 1963.

Kollwitz, J., *Oströmische Plastik*, Berlin 1941.

L'Orange, H. P., *Studien zur Geschichte des spätantike Porträts*, Oslo 1933.

L'Orange, H. P., and Gerkan, A., *Der spätantike Bildschmuck des Konstantinsbogen*, Berlin 1933.

Richmond, I. A., *The City Wall of Imperial Rome*, Oxford 1930.

Rumpf, A., *Stilphasen der spätantiken Kunst, Ein Versuch*, Cologne 1957.

Schweitzer, B., *Die Bildniskunst der römischen Republik*, Leipzig-Weimar 1948.

Strong, D. E., *Roman Imperial Sculpture*, London 1961.

Bibliography

Strong, E., *Scultura Romana*, Florence 1923–26.

Wegner, M., *Die Herrscherbildnisse in antoninischer Zeit*, Berlin 1939.

Vessberg, O., *Studien zur Kunstgeschichte der römischen Republik.* (Skr. utg. av Sv. Inst. i Rom VIII.) Lund 1941.

Wheeler, M., *Roman Art and Architecture*, London and New York 1964.

d. *Painting and Pottery:*

Beyen, H. G., *Die Pompejanische Wanddekoration*, The Hague 1938.

Borda, M., *La pittura romana*, Milan 1958.

Charleston, R. J., *Roman Pottery*, London 1950.

Curtius, L., *Die Wandmalerei Pompejis*, Leipzig 1929 (repr. Hildesheim 1960).

Dragendorff, H., *Arretinische Reliefkeramik* (herausgegeben von C. Watzinger), Tübingen 1948.

Hanfmann, G. M., *The Seasons Sarcophagus in Dumbarton Oaks*, Cambridge (Mass.) 1951.

L'Orange, H. P., and Nordhagen, P. J., *Mosaik*, Munich 1960.

Lehmann, Ph.L., *Roman Wall Paintings from Boscoreale in the Metropolitan Museum of Art*, Cambridge (Mass.) 1953.

Maiuri, A., *La Peinture Romaine*, Geneva 1953.

Nordenfalk, C., *Die spätantiken Kanontafeln*, Göteborg 1938.

Nordström, C. O., *Ravennastudien*, Uppsala 1953.

Pace, B., *I mosaici di Piazza Armerina*, Rome 1955.

Schefold, K., *Pompejanische Malerei*, Basel 1952.

Wirth, F., *Römische Wandmalerei*, Berlin 1934.

ETRURIA

Andrén, A., *Architectural Terracottas from Etrusco-Italic temples.* (Skr. utg. av Sv. Inst. i Rom VI.) Lund 1940.

Beazley, J. D., *Etruscan Vase-Painting*, Oxford 1947.

Boëthius, A., Gjerstad, E. and others, *Etruscan Culture, Land and People*, New York and Malmö 1962.

Brown, W. L., *The Etruscan Lion*, Oxford 1960.

Herbig, R., *Die jüngeretruskischen Steinsarkophage*, Berlin 1952.

Lawrence, D. H., *Etruscan Places*, London 1932.

Pallottino, M., *Etruscan Painting*, Geneva 1952.

Riis, P. J., *Introduction to Etruscan Art*, Copenhagen 1953.

Weege, F., *Etruskische Malerei*, Halle 1921.

Bibliography

Åkerström, Å., *Studien über die etruskischen Gräber.* (Skr. utg. av Sv. Inst. i Rom III.) Lund 1934.

NUMISMATICS, GEMS ETC.

a. *Survey:*

Furtwängler, A., *Die antiken Gemmen*, Leipzig-Berlin 1900.

Head, B. V., *Historia numorum*, Oxford 1911.

Regling, K., *Die antike Münze als Kunstwerk*, Berlin 1924.

Sutherland, C. H. V., *Art in Coinage*, London 1955.

b. *Greece:*

Becatti, G., *Orificerie antiche*, Rome 1955.

Boardman, J., *Island Gems*, London 1963.

Higgins, R. A., *Greek and Roman Jewelry*, London 1961.

Kraay, *Greek Coins*, London 1966.

Schwabacher, W., *Das Demareteion* (Opus Nobile: Heft 7), Bremen 1958.

Seltman, Ch., *Greek Coins*, London 1955.

— *Masterpieces of Greek Coinage*, Oxford 1949.

Westermark, U., *Das Bildnis des Philetairos von Pergamon. Corpus der Münzprägung* (Stockholm Studies in Classical Archaeology I. 1961.)

c. *Rome:*

Delbrueck, R., *Die Consulardiptychen*, Berlin 1929.

Hirmer, M., *Römische Kaisermünzen.* (Insel-Bücherei Nr. 270.) Leipzig 1941.

Mattingly, H., *Roman Coins*, London 1960.

Sutherland, C. H. V., *Coinage in Roman Imperial Policy, 31 B.C.– A.D. 68.*, London 1951.

228

Glossary

abacus
: Square block between capital and entablature of an ancient temple.

adorant
: A figure praying with raised hands.

adyton
: Literally 'What must not be trodden on'; the holiest part of a temple.

aegis
: 'Goat-Skin', the breast-plate worn by Zeus and Athena, decorated in the centre with the head of Medusa.

aetos
: The pediment of a temple.

agon
: General word for a competition, especially in the ancient Greek games at Olympia, Delphi, Athens, Nemea and at the Isthmus of Corinth. There were gymnastic (athletic) and musical (music and poetry) competitions.

agora
: The market-place in an ancient Greek city, corresponding to the Roman forum.

acanthus
: *Acanthus mollis:* a tall plant found in Mediterranean lands with prickly, deeply lobate leaves. In a stylized form the leaves are an important ornamental motive in the classic and classicizing styles. In the fourth century B.C. and later it is the chief component of the Corinthian capital.

acroterion
: Sculptured decoration on the central and side angles of the pediment of a temple, consisting of terracotta or marble ornamentation or figures; also occurs on grave-monuments (stelae).

alabastron
: See *Vase-Shapes.*

à la grecque
: See *meander.*

amphora
: Ancient clay vessel with narrow neck and two handles: see also *Vase-Shapes.*

229

Glossary

anta	Pilaster projecting lightly from lateral walls of a cella (cf. *templum in antis:* see *temple*).
apoptygma	See *peplos*
apse	Curved recess in a temple, in which the cult-statue was often placed. It is rarely encountered in Greek architecture, but is common in the Roman period: in late antiquity the curved recess is also evident on the outside of the building, and is frequently covered with a semi-cupola.
architrave	In classical architecture the lowest element of the entablature which rests on the capitals of the columns.
arched vault	Curved span between two columns or other supporting features.
arris	The sharp edge between the flutings of the Doric column.
aryballos	See *Vase-Shapes.*
astragal	An important ornamental detail in Greek, particularly Ionic architecture, consisting of a 'bead-and-reel' moulding: i.e. a horizontal, frequently oval element and one or two vertical elements.
atlantes	Male figures used as architectural supports for projecting architectural features.
atrium	Central hall in the ancient Roman house, where the images of the family's ancestors were preserved.
attic(a)	A storey above the main cornice of a building or a triumphal arch.
barrel-vault	Semi-cylindrical vault
base	Foot of a column or pillar: base of a statue, statuette, etc., frequently in the form of steps.
basilica	Rectangular room divided into three or five naves by rows of columns. In late Antiquity the central nave was higher than the others, and its walls had windows.
bead-and-reel	Moulding decorated with round or oval beads; astragal.

bee-hive tomb	Monumental tomb usually with a circular ground-plan, covered by a vault formed by the corbelling of the walls. The most famous example is the so-called 'Treasury of Atreus' at Mycenae.
black-figure vase-style	The style in which figures are painted like silhouettes on the red or yellow ground of the clay.
caldarium	Hot-air bath and warm water pool, forming parts of the Roman thermae.
canon	Measuring-rod, rule: the rules of proportion to be observed in representations of the human body, laid down by Polyclitus (see *Doryphoros*).
capital	The uppermost part of a column, pillar or pilaster, usually richly ornamented and shaped differently in the different orders, Aeolic, Doric, Ionic, Composite and Corinthian.
caryatid	Female statue supporting an entablature or other architectural feature.
cavea	Auditorium of a theatre.
cavetto	A concave moulding, the concave part of the base of an Ionic column.
cella	The central chamber of a Greek and Roman temple, containing the cult-statue of the god.
centaur	In Greek mythology a being whose body consisted of the upper part of a man and the trunk of a horse.
ceramic	Pertaining to objects made of clay (pottery); cf. the Kerameikos, the potters' quarter of Athens.
chamber-tomb	Tomb excavated from rock or hard limestone.
chiton	Ancient Greek garment, sometimes provided with arms, which was pulled on over the head and fastened on the shoulders.
chryselephantine	Of gold and ivory
cire-perdue	Conventional French term for the method of casting sculpture by means of melting wax. The advantage of this over other forms of casting is that it permits a final refinement of the wax copy. A figure roughly corresponding to the sculpture in preparation is modelled in a fire-

Glossary

proof substance and is used as a core in the casting. This is covered with a layer of wax which is smoothed externally and subsequently covered with a jacket of the same volume as the core, with channels for the wax. Metal pins are fixed in the core so as to fix the position in relation to the jacket. The wax melts with the heat and runs out and the fluid bronze is held in the vacuum thus created.

cithara
Stringed instrument, the attribute of Apollo and the Muses: cf. Kitharodos.

coffer
Sunk, square, rectangular or polygonal field used especially in antiquity and during the Renaissance as a decoration of inner roof (coffered-roof) and vault.

column-orders
There are three orders of columns in Greek architecture, Doric, Ionic and Corinthian. The *Doric* column has no base, tapers slightly upwards and is furnished with 16-20 vertical flutes separated by sharp angles (v. arris). The capital consists of the echinus, a spreading round plaque, which carries a rectangular block, the abacus. On the capital rests the entablature which consists of the architrave (the lower part), undecorated stone blocks and the frieze (the upper part) with alternating grooved plaques, the triglyphs, and blocks carrying reliefs, the metopes, and the cornice. The *Ionic* column is taller and thinner, and stands on a round base consisting in its lower part of two narrow cavetto-mouldings (scotiae) between three pairs of convex pipings, and in its upper part a convex moulding (torus) fluted horizontally. (The Attic variant was composed of a torus above, a single concave moulding, and an additional torus below.) The shaft has 20-24 flutes with fillets between them. The lower part of the capital resembles an echinus, above which is the typical bolster, the ends of which are rolled up into spirals and volutes. The

architrave consists of the horizontal layers, **and** the frieze forms a continuous strip, frequently decorated with reliefs. The *Corinthian* column differs from the Ionian only in its capital. The basic form of the capital is a calyx decorated with two crowns of acanthus-leaves of different height, from which spirals rise forming volutes in the four corners. On the capital rests a richly profiled abacus.

composite — A late type of capital formed by superimposing Ionic volutes on a Corinthian bell.

concrete — A composition of lime, cement ('pozzolana') and small stones employed for the construction of walls and vaults in Roman architecture.

console — Projecting stone which forms base or support for arches, cornices, balconies, etc.

cornice — The upper member of the entablature.

corona — The projecting vertical member of the cornice.

corbelling-out — A method of covering a room or an opening in a wall employed before the introduction of the Arch. The layers of stone project like steps above each other until they meet in the middle (cf. bee-hive tombs).

daedalic — Belonging to the 'School of Daidalos'.

deinos — A Corinthian drinking-bowl.

dentil — Ornament used in Ionic and Corinthian orders of columns, consisting of rectangular notches with equal spaces between.

diadem — Originally a fillet which was fastened round the Persian King's head-dress, adopted by Alexander and his successors as an emblem of royal power, also by Emperors of the late Empire.

Diadochi — The generals of Alexander the Great who fought for supreme power after his death.

diadoumenos — Youth portrayed in the act of binding the victor's wreath on his brow, a frequent theme in both sculpture and painting. One of Polyclitus' best known works was a Diadoumenos.

dipteros — See *Temple*.

Dipylon — The 'Double Gate', the north-western city-gate

of ancient Athens. It was the starting-point of the 'Holy Way' to Eleusis, and the site of a renowned cemetery where a large number of vases of the Geometric period, the 'Dipylon-Vases' have been discovered.

Doric order   One of the three types of columns in Greek architecture; see *column-orders*.

doryphorus   The 'Spear-Bearer', the name of Polyclitus' best-known sculpture, also called the 'Canon' because Polyclitus is said to have worked out his system of proportions for the human body on this figure.

echinus   The round spreading moulding which forms the transition between the shaft of the column and the abacus in a Doric temple (see *column-orders*).

ephebe   A youth aged eighteen in ancient Greece.

engaged column   A column semi-detached from a wall.

entablature   The part of a temple between the capital and the roof. The *Doric* entablature consists of the architrave, which is plain, and the triglyph-frieze consisting of metopes and triglyphs (q.vv.); a triglyph is placed above the centre of each capital. In the *Ionic* entablature the architrave is divided into three horizontal bands or fasciae, each of which is more or less richly profiled, and the frieze is either plain or decorated with reliefs and terminates above with a geison (q.v.) decorated with dentils (q.v.) The *Corinthian* entablature in general resembles the Ionic, but it is often crowned by a row of consoles.

entasis   The slight convex curvature of a column.

Erechtheion   The most famous temple on the Athenian Acropolis except for the Parthenon.

Esquiline   One of the Seven Hills of Rome, near the Colosseum. It was the site of Maecenas' villa and park and of Nero's Golden House and many well-known works of art have been discovered there.

234

exedra	Semi-circular or rectangular projecting structure (cf. apse) with seat, incorporated in ancient garden and domestic architecture, in baths and temple-structures.
fascia	The step-like horizontal division of an Ionian or Corinthian architrave.
festoon	A common ornamental motive, a curved runner of flowers, leaves or fruit.
fibula	Clasp with a sprung or unsprung pin of about the same form as a safety-pin.
fillet	A narrow flat moulding; the flattened arris (q.v.) between the flutes of Ionic columns.
flute	Semi-circular, vertical groove in pillar.
forum	The central market-place in a Roman city, corresponding to the agora of a Greek city.
fresco	Wall-painting executed on still damp plaster, with colours mixed with water or hydrate of lime.
frigidarium	Cold bath, part of a Roman bathing establishment.
frieze	A horizontal band running round an external or internal wall, usually below the roof, often decorated with ornamental motives or descriptive pictures.
geison	The Greek term for the cornice or corona (q.v.)
gorgons	Three female monsters in Greek mythology. Medusa, the best known, often represented with hair formed of snakes, had a petrifying gaze, but she was overcome by Perseus who cut off her head, by looking at her in a mirror.
granulation	Method of fixing small grains of metal in a pattern on a surface.
grave-stele	See *Stele*
herm	A pedestal or rectangular pillar tapering downwards, and terminating above in a male head, set up in antiquity on the sides of highways and streets; originally dedicated to Hermes the protector of communications, whence its name.
hieron	The general Greek word for a sanctuary.

Glossary

Horai	In Greek mythology the Goddesses who presided over the established order of things in nature.
hydria	See *Vase-Shapes*
incrustation	A method of decoration, by which a pattern is inlaid in a ground of another colour or another material. Incrustation with pieces of marble of different colour is the characteristic decoration of walls and floors in Imperial palaces.
intarsia	Insertion of sawn-out pieces of differently-coloured pieces of wood (or ivory, mother-of-pearl, etc.) so that when coloured they form a decoration, figures, etc.
intercolumnium	Distance between the central axis of columns.
isodomic structure	Masonry of rectangular blocks of uniform height.
kamares vase	A vase-type of the Cretan Middle Minoan period.
kantharos	See *Vase-Shapes*
kitharodos	Singer who accompanies himself on the cithara (q.v.), the attribute of Apollo.
kolpos	See *Peplos*.
kore, pl. korai, girl	The name given to Archaic Greek statues of young women.
kouros, pl. kouroi	Youth. Frequent subject of Archaic sculptors.
krater	Mixing bowl for wine: see also *Vase-Shapes*.
kylix	Bowl-shaped drinking-vessel with foot.
kymation	A wave-like moulding: a distinction is made between the Doric, Ionic (egg-and-tongue) and Lesbian Kymation. Bead-and-Reel (astragal) Egg-and-tongue (Ionic Kymation) Lesbian Kymation (leaf-and-dart) Rising Cornice Torus Doric Kymation
lekythos	Oil-flask. Ancient earthenware vessel often used as perfume-flask: a tall pot on a foot, with a narrow neck with enlarged mouth. Frequently found in graves of the Archaic and Classic period: see *Vase-Shapes*.

236

lower city	The normal unfortified area of private houses, etc., at the foot of an acropolis.
meander	(So called from the winding course of the river Maeander in Asia Minor) also termed *à la grecque:* winding ornament of continuous spiral or rectangular bands or lines.
Mausoleum	Originally the monument over the tomb of the Satrap Maussollos in Halicarnassus (ca. 350 B.C.), subsequently used of all large sepulchral buildings.
megaron	The name either of the central room in a Mycenaean palace, or a special type of house consisting of a large room with the grate in the middle beneath an opening for smoke in the roof, entered at one gable-end by means of an open porch.
metope	Rectangular plaque between the triglyphs of a Doric frieze, frequently decorated with paintings or reliefs. *V. entablature.*
monolith	Sculpture or architectural feature usually a column, made from a single block of stone. Greek columns were usually not monoliths, but Roman and early Christian ones frequently were.
narthex	Transverse portico in an early Christian church, Basilica or cruciform church.
neck-amphora	See *Vase-Shapes.*
niello	A style of decoration of silver-work, in which a dark alloy of silver, copper, lead and sulphur is infused into an engraved pattern.
nymphalum	Shrine sacred to the Goddesses of water, usually encircling a fountain.
oinochoe	See *Vase-Shapes.*
omphalos	The sacred navel of the world, a conical block of marble preserved in the sanctuary of Apollo at Delphi.
opisthodomos	Rear porch of a temple.
orchestra	The part of the theatre where the chorus danced, originally circular, later semi-circular.
ornament	See *astragal, kymation, meander, palmette, bead-and-reel.*

orthostates	Building-block set on end.
palace-style	Style of decoration on vases from Palace at Knossos in the Late Minoan II period.
palaestra	Arena for exercise or gymnastics.
palmette	Ornament consisting mainly of outspread fan-shaped leaves.
pillar	Architectural supporting element, which, in contrast to the column, has a rectangular base and is of masonry.
pediment	The part of a building above the horizontal cornice, decorated with a gable.
pelike	See *Vase-Shapes*.
peplos	Woollen garment worn by women, open at the sides, consisting of a lower part, the kolpos, and an upper part, the apoptygma.
peripteros	See *Temple*.
peristyle	Enclosed court surrounded by covered colonnades.
pilaster	A semi-detached pier, analogous to the anta, with base and capital.
polos	Cylindrical headdress, characteristic of some Greek goddesses.
poros sculpture	Work executed in poros, a soft tufa-like limestone. The archaic pedimental sculpture on the Athenian Acropolis are of poros.
portico	Hall of columns; cf. *Stoa*.
pronaos	The front porch of a temple; cf. opisthodomos.
propylaea	Monumental entrance to a sanctuary or similar construction, usually adorned with columns.
prostylos	See *Temple*.
pseudodipteros	See *Temple*.
pseudoperipteros	See *Temple*.
psykter	Wine-cooler: see *Vase-Shapes*.
pylon	Entrance-porch, especially in Egyptian architecture, with a monumental gateway flanked by rectangular towers with slightly sloping sides.
pyxis	Box with lid: see *Vase-Shapes*.

Glossary

replica	Normally a copy made by the artist himself of his own work.
rhyton	Drinking-vessel in the form of a horn, head or beast.
red-figure vase-style	The style in which figures are outlined in the black glaze of the vase.
sarcophagus	Monumental coffin usually of marble. The sculpture on sarcophagi are an important part of Etruscan, Roman and early Christian art.
shaft-grave	Rectangular grave sunk in the earth without superstructure. The shaft-graves of the early Mycenaean period found by Schliemann at Mycenae in 1876, which contained numerous gold objects, are especially famous.
sphinx	According to the ancients a being with the head of a human and the body of a lion. In Egyptian art it usually has a King's head, while in Greek and Roman art it has the head and breasts of a woman, and is frequently winged.
sima	Gutter, often moulded and, if on the flanks of a building, provided with outlet for rain-water.
skyphos	See *Vase-Shapes*.
stamnos	See *Vase-Shapes*.
stele	A standing stone slab often used for a gravestone, and frequently carrying a relief or inscription.
stereobate	The foundation below ground-level of a temple or other building either cut in the living-rock or of masonry.
stoa	Roofed portico, with a colonnade in front.
stylobate	The uppermost portion of the pedestal on which the columns of a temple stand.
sub-Mycenaean	The term given to the offshoot the Mycenaean style of vase which was produced in the transitional period between ca. 1100 B.C. and the emergence of the earliest Geometric vases.
symposium	The drinking party of the Greek male, corresponding to the Roman convivium: a frequent theme in Archaic and Classic vase-painting.
tablinum	Part of a Roman house, originally the room where the marriage-bed stood.

Glossary

Tanagra-figures	Female statues of baked and painted terracotta manufactured in the city of Tanagra in the third century B.C.
tectonic	Used of a system of decoration which associates itself with the organic construction of the object by emphasizing its most important parts, e.g. the lip and neck of a vase. The opposite decorative method which follows the curving surface of the vessel and emphasizes its complete form instead of its structural divisions, is sometimes called 'unified decoration'.
temple	Normally a building used for cult-purposes. A *Templum in antis* consists of the cella, an enclosed room where the statue of the god stood, and an entrance-hall with two columns. *Prostylos:* the columns of the entrance-hall form a portico occupying the whole width of the short side. The *Amphiprostylos* has a portico of this kind on either short side. In the *Peripteros*, the cella is surrounded on all sides by a simple colonnade. The *Pseudoperipteros* consists of a cella-temple which has half columns on the outside and is thus an imitation of a Peripteros. The *Dipteros* has double rows of columns, usually of the Ionic order. In the *Pseudodipteros* the distance from the wall of the cella to the outer colonnade is the same as in the *Dipteros*, but the inner colonnade is missing. The building gives an impression of airiness. A *Tholos* is a round temple surrounded by columns.
templum in Antis	See *Temple.*
tepidarium	Warm bath, part of Roman bath-installations (thermae).
terracotta	Baked, unglazed clay, with colours ranging from pale buff to reddish brown.
thermae	Strictly, warm baths and springs. Used generally of ancient bath-installations which evolved in the Roman period into large leisure-resorts.
tholos-tomb	Bee-hive tomb (q.v.)

240

Glossary

thyrsus	A wand of ferula-reed, crowned by a pine-cone, the attribute of Dionysus.
toga	Roman woollen garment, worn draped over the tunic(a)
torso	A sculptured figure without head, arms and legs.
torus	Large convex moulding, horizontally fluted.
treasury	Small buildings usually in the form of temples in which such objects as precious votive-offerings were preserved.
trident	The attribute of Poseidon.
triglyph	'Three-cut', a slightly projecting plaque with two runnels which divide it into three sections; together with the metopes it constitutes the Doric frieze. *V. entablature.*
tripod	Three-footed object; bronze bowl resting on three legs; Apollo's attribute, often formed as a votive-offering.
tritons	The divinities of the sea, with human body and tail of a fish.
triumphal arch	Roman honorific monument erected in honour

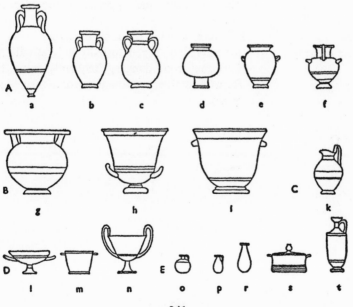

of a victorious general. It consists of 1-3 arches constructed architecturally, and is decorated with columns or pilasters, and is surmounted by an attica (q.v.).

tunic(a) Roman garment like a shirt with arms, worn under the toga.

tympanon The triangular wall enclosed by the raking cornice of the pediment and the horizontal cornice of the entablature.

vase-shapes See diagram on page 241. A. Transport and preserving vessels: a. transport amphora; b. neck-handled amphora; c. pelike; d. psykter; e. stamnos; f. hydria. B. Mixing vessels: g. column-krater; h. chalice-shaped amphora; i. bell-amphora. C. Jugs: k. oinochoe; D. Drinking Vessels: l. kylix; m. skyphos; n. kantharos. E. Perfume-Flasks and Caskets: o. aryballos; p. and r. alabastron; s. pyxis; t. lekythos.

verism Style of portraiture which faithfully reproduces the features of the subject, including the unpleasant ones: the opposite is the idealized portrait.

volute The spiral scroll of the Ionic capital.

votive-offering Gift offered to a god, usually in gratitude for salvation from danger; frequently takes the form of a statue or statuette or some other work of art.

Index

(figures in italics refer to plate numbers)

243

Index

Index

Index

Index

Index

Index

Pindar 91
Piraeus 117
Pisistratus 74, 75, 76, 78, 84, 93
Plataea 103, 120
Plato 141, 157
Pliny the Elder 92, 103, 106, 137, 140, 159, 166, 175
Pliny the Younger 181
Plotinus 214
Ploutos 132
Po Valley 164
Polyclitus 114, 118ff, 122, 126, 128, 132, 140–141, 188, 231, 233, 234, *52*
Polycrates 74
Polyclitus the Younger 148
Polydoros 156
Polyeuctus 150–151
Polygnotos 99, 103, 104, 130, 159
Polymedes 77, 81, *29*
Polyneices 171
Pompeii 132, 159, 160, 161, 167, 189, 191ff, 199, *132, 133, 134, 136, 137, 138, 158*
Pompey 174, 178
'Portland Vase' 130
Poseidon 81, 96, 108, 123, 155, 187, 241, *44*
Praeneste 176, 177, 178
Praxiteles 132ff, 136, 137, 149, 150, 172, *89*
Priene 117, 143, 145, 147, 148, 149
Propylaea 114, 116, 127, 143
Prosymna 52
Protogenes 158
Pseira 26
Pylos 49
Pythagoras 76
Pytheos 137, 145, 146
Pythia 84

Quintilian 120

Ravenna 209, 217, 218, *191*
Regolini-Galassi tomb 109
Renaissance 132, 177, 232
Rhamnus 127
Rhodes 55, 60, 68, 142, 156

Rhoecus 77, 81, 92
Rome 67, 99, 100, 132, 136, 153, 154, 156, 158, 160, 172ff
Rome, Ara Pacis 123, 125, 126
Rome, Museo Capitolino *169, 172, 179*
Rome, Museo delle Terme *37, 47, 51, 79, 122, 124, 149, 157, 159, 164, 165, 170, 174, 178, 181, 185*
Rome, Palazzo dei Conservatori *115, 117, 166*

Sallust 100, 179
Samians 92
Samos 66, 67, 71, 77, 78, 81, 108, 115, *20*
San Giovenale 166
San Vitale *191*
Santa Sabina *192*
Sappho 60, 158
Satricum 171, *114*
Schliemann 51, 239
Scopas 136ff, 149, 150, *86, 88*
Seler 101
Selene 155, *75*
Selinus 75, 101
Severus, Septimus 184, 198, 202, 212, *148, 167*
Sicily 73, 101, 110, 135, 162, 207
Sicyon 77, 78, 92, 118, 137, 143
Sicyonian Treasury 84–86, *33*
Sidon 128, 135, 159, *92*
Silanion 157, 158
Silaros 87, *34*
Siphnians 86
Siphnian Treasury 86, 87, 116, *32*
Skyllis 76
Skyros *140*
Smyrna 116
Smyrna Museum *see* Izmir
Solon 74, 87
Sophocles 103, 106
Sosicles 119
Sotades 105
Sovana 167
Sparta 33, 62, 65, 74, 75, 77, 78, 84, 99, 105
Sperlonga 149, 156, *98*

249

Index